Mystical Consciousness

Mystical Consciousness

WESTERN PERSPECTIVES
AND DIALOGUE
WITH JAPANESE THINKERS

Louis Roy, O.P.

STATE UNIVERSITY OF NEW YORK PRESS

Published by
State University of New York Press, Albany

© 2003 State University of New York

All rights reserved

Printed in the United States of America

No part of this book may be used or reproduced
in any manner whatsoever without written permission.
No part of this book may be stored in a retrieval system
or transmitted in any form or by any means including
electronic, electrostatic, magnetic tape, mechanical,
photocopying, recording, or otherwise without the prior
permission in writing of the publisher.

For information, address State University of New York Press,
90 State Street, Suite 700, Albany, N.Y., 12207

Production by Diane Ganeles
Marketing by Fran Keneston

Library of Congress Cataloging in Publication Data

Roy, Louis, 1942–
    Mystical consciousness : western perspectives and dialogue with Japanese thinkers / Louis Roy.
    p. cm.
    ISBN 0-7914-5643-9 (alk. paper.) — ISBN 0-7914-5644-7 (pbk.: alk. paper)
    1. Religion—Philosophy. 2. Philosophy, European—20th century.
3. Philosophy, Japanese—20th century. 4. Zen Buddhism—Philosophy.
I. Title.

BL51.R5996 2003
218—dc21   2002066783

10 9 8 7 6 5 4 3 2 1

Contents

Preface ix
Acknowledgments xiii
Introduction xv

Part I
Western Philosophies of Consciousness

Chapter 1. Major Contributions 3
   Brentano 4
   Husserl 7
   Sartre 10
   Lonergan 16
   Concluding Remarks 20

Chapter 2. Complementary Contributions 21
   From Intentionality to Consciousness: Searle 21
   Degrees of Consciousness: Crosby 24
   Further Clarifications: Helminiak 26
   The Affective Side: Morelli 30
   Concluding Remarks 32

Chapter 3. Accounts of Mystical Consciousness 37
   Forman on Pure Consciousness Events 37
   The Realm of Transcendence According to Lonergan 41
   Moore on the "How" of Consciousness 44
   Price on Bare Consciousness 46
   Granfield on the Mystical Difference 49
   Concluding Remarks 50

Part II
Three Classics

Chapter 4. Plotinus: Consciousness beyond Consciousness — 55
   A Grand Worldview — 56
   Intellect's Share in the Good — 58
   Ordinary Consciousness — 61
   What Happens beyond Consciousness? — 63
   No Blackout and Yet No Self-Consciousness — 65
   Ecstasy, or Enstasy? — 66
   Concluding Remarks — 69

Chapter 5. Eckhart: When Human Consciousness Becomes Divine Consciousness — 71
   The Emptiness of the Human Intellect — 72
   No Awareness — 75
   Nothingness — 79
   A Detached Love without a Why — 81
   Is the Soul Equated with God? — 85
   The Soul's Breakthrough to the Godhead — 88
   Concluding Remarks — 93

Chapter 6. Schleiermacher: Consciousness as Feeling — 95
   Feeling — 95
   Prereflective and Reflective Consciousness — 98
   Absolute Dependence — 103
   Three Kinds of Consciousness — 106
   Concluding Remarks — 109

Part III
A Dialogue with Zen Philosophy

Chapter 7. Western Views of the Self — 115
   Arguing against the Self — 116
   Arguing for the Self — 119
   Transcending the Self — 124
   Concluding Remarks — 127

Chapter 8. Japanese Views of the Self — 129
   Suzuki — 129
   Nishitani — 139
   Concluding Remarks — 142

Chapter 9. Western Views of Nothingness	145
Plotinus and Eckhart	145
Heidegger	146
Nishitani of Interpreter of Plotinus, Eckhart, and Heidegger	158
Concluding Remarks	163
Chapter 10. Japanese Views of Nothingness	165
Nishitani's Approach to Nihilism	165
Nishitani's Characterization of "Absolute Nothingness"	167
Hisamatsu's Characterization of "Oriental Nothingness"	177
Concluding Remarks	185
Conclusion	187
Notes	193
Glossary	221
Bibliography	223
Index	227

Preface

Over the last 150 years, with thinkers such as Marx, Nietzsche, Freud, Heidegger, Wittgenstein and Skinner, consciousness has been suspect in the West.[1] But in the East, by and large it has been viewed negatively for at least two and a half millennia. Nevertheless, this book will praise consciousness! A reckless endeavor? Perhaps not if we are willing to distinguish lower sorts of consciousness from the kind of consciousness involved in spiritual enlightenment—pace those who deny its presence in the highest mystical states. Accordingly, this study will aim at philosophically clarifying certain aspects of mystical consciousness which are cross-culturally reported and discussed. More particularly, it wants to join in the mutually enriching dialogue that has taken place, during the twentieth century, between Japanese and Western philosophers.

At the outset, the readers are urged to note that this undertaking presupposes a living interaction between meditation and rational thinking. All the major authors introduced here philosophized in a religious ambience, although at times they adopted a critical stance vis-à-vis the constructs of either institutional or sectarian religion. They drew upon the resources of centering prayer, Zen, or other forms of mental concentration as they grappled with issues regarding fundamental meaning and utter emptiness.

As early in his career as 1903, the great Japanese philosopher Nishida Kitaro published a short, programmatic essay in which he pointed to the lack of meaning in modern existence. He stated:

> However, the doubt of the human heart which I'm talking about is not a mere philosophical problem based on an intellectual demand. It arises from the actual demands of our will

and emotions, the basis of our relation with the world. This doubt is rooted in the facts of our sorrow and happiness, wants and desires, and is *the* problem of life which must be answered with blood, sweat, and tears.[2]

Later in this book, we shall see that his disciples Nishitani Keiji and Hisamatsu Shin'ichi also approached philosophy from a painful, personal experience of the Great Doubt. We shall also observe that this intense quest, which owes much to the eighteenth-century Rinzai Master Hakuin,[3] has much in common with European existentialism.

As Graham Parkes—a Heideggerian scholar acquainted with Japanese thought—puts it, there are seekers who practice philosophy "as a matter of life and death."[4] And the Buddhologist Paul Griffiths writes, "It is upon meditative practice that the religious life of the Buddhist virtuoso is based and from such practice that systematic Buddhist philosophical and soteriological theory begins."[5] Pierre Hadot has shown that the philosophical mainstream in the West from Socrates to Meister Eckhart was a quest for wisdom inseparable from the discipline of *exercices spirituels*.[6] From this point of view, the late medieval partition between thought and religion, which Descartes and most European philosophers have endorsed to this day, amounts to a mental compartmentalization that breeds rationalism or logicism and that rules out any influence of mysticism upon human thinking.

Over against this deplorable tendency in the modern West, and in keeping with the very fact—ancient as well as resurging in the contemporary world—of mutual fertilization between mysticism and philosophy, my purpose in these pages is to develop an understanding of consciousness, mostly rooted in Bernard Lonergan's works and applied to the mystical life. The understanding I will pursue will be philosophical, rather than a collection of psychological and spiritual observations or pieces of advice—a highly commendable enterprise, but not the kind of contribution the readers should expect from these pages.[7]

As partners for this essay in comparative thinking, I have chosen three Japanese authors: Suzuki, Nishitani, and Hisamatsu. Other candidates might have been Nishida (quoted earlier here), Tanabe, Abe, or Ueda.[8] I have selected the former, not because they are more profound than the latter, but simply because I believe that their input is likely to dovetail better with the Western perspectives I want to delineate. Accordingly, this book is not an introduction to the Kyoto School as such, let alone a presentation of Japanese philosophy in its several strands.

Although I shall present some Eastern views, my enterprise will be confined to furthering a *Western* philosophy of religion which is friendly to the insights of meditators. If some originality can be anticipated in this inquiry, it will consist not so much in my interpretation of a few Japanese authors as in the way we shall observe them in dialogue and bring them into an interaction with Western thinkers whose broad scope is close to the East. I hope that this conversation will catalyze the experiment in thinking on which we are about to embark, through which I will set out to establish a basically Western and yet interreligiously open standpoint on mystical consciousness.

Acknowledgments

The "prehistory" of this book must be traced back to guided reading of Hindu and Buddhist texts with my competent colleagues at Boston College, Francis X. Clooney, S.J., and John J. Makransky, whose stimulating presence and advice I am still enjoying on a regular basis. My heartfelt gratitude also goes to Jan Van Bragt, Nishitani's translator, who shared valuable insights with me about *Religion and Nothingness* and who offered remarks on the first draft of my chapter on Eckhart. For their comments on the content and style of various chapters, I thank Henry Gallagher, O.P., Cathleen Going, O.P., Gary Gurtler, S.J., Christopher Ives, Elizabeth Murray Morelli, Maurice Schepers, O.P., and the anonymous copyeditor and readers of SUNY Press.

I am grateful to James W. Heisig, of the Nanzan Institute for Religion and Culture in Nagoya, and to the Dominicans both in Oakland, California, and in Tokyo, for their wonderful hospitality when I was doing research. In addition to those contacts, I am greatly indebted to all the Zen practitioners with whom I meditated, participated in the tea ceremony, and/or exchanged thoughts in Japan.

Furthermore, I want to express my amazement at the efficiency of the Interlibrary Loan Department at O'Neill Library, Boston College, whose assistance was considerable. I acknowledge the dedicated work of Mary Weicher in the construction and compiling of the bibliography and the index. Finally, John Boyd Turner and Beth Beshear were most helpful with reordering of endnotes and proofreading. At SUNY Press, it has been a pleasure to collaborate with the very professional and considerate Nancy Ellegate and Diane Ganeles.

The publisher and I thank the editors and publishers of the following periodicals for permission to borrow materials from my articles.

Chapters 5, 9, and 10 contain each one section of "Some Japanese Interpretations of Meister Eckhart," *Studies in Interreligious Dialogue* 11 (2001): 182–198; chapter 6 reproduces the major portion of "Consciousness according to Schleiermacher," *Journal of Religion* 77 (1997): 217–232 (© 1977 by The University of Chicago Press. All rights reserved.); and the concluding section of Chapter 6 incorporates some paragraphs from "Schleiermacher's Epistemology," *Method: Journal of Lonergan Studies* 16 (1998): 25–46 (published by The Lonergan Institute at Boston College).

Unless otherwise indicated, italicized words or phrases are by the authors quoted.

Introduction

This inquiry explores three forms of consciousness. First, the consciousness that we have *of* things and people (= consciousness C). Second, the consciousness that we experience *in* our everyday activities: a consciousness that permeates all our acts and states (= consciousness B). Third, the consciousness that obtains when we reach a stage beyond our customary acts and states (= consciousness A). The first two kinds can be called ordinary consciousness; the third one, mystical consciousness. The three kinds are continuous with each other and they occur prior to any reflexive formulation. Whenever any kind of consciousness is adverted to, it automatically transforms itself into awareness or reflexiveness (= consciousness C when reflecting upon consciousness B or A). Insofar as we *talk* about consciousness, we have awareness of consciousness, which is an attention to consciousness. We shall have ample opportunity to explain these concepts further on in this Introduction, in part 1, in the Conclusion, and in the Glossary.

In order to explicate these various forms of consciousness and to situate the role of reflexiveness, we need an epistemology that, far from being inimical to them, can, on the contrary, help clarify them. To attain this goal, we are going to employ, not the methods of the natural or even the social sciences, but a philosophical approach which, according to a representation that goes back to Socrates, begins with self-knowledge. In chapter 1, much light will be shed, I hope, on philosophy as self-consciousness, as we study the thought of Brentano, Husserl, Sartre, and Lonergan.

Of course I appreciate the studies of consciousness done by neurologists, cognitive scientists, proponents of artificial intelligence theories, or advocates of picturing the mind as a sophisticated information processor.

They rightly assume a physiological substratum to the psychological phenomena and try to relate these two levels. Nevertheless, I do not think that examining this substratum enables us to elucidate the psychological experience itself. The direct self-acquaintance that we have amounts to a degree of human existence which is higher than its neural basis.[1]

Charles Tart relates remarkably well those two levels, respectively called the brain and the mind. "Brain" refers to the physical organs of the neurosystem; "mind" designates the "sum of all mental processes, actual or potential, of which the individual is capable."[2] The first, which is biologically determined, is comparable to the hardware, while the second, which is molded by culture, performs the function of the software. In a sense, then, the psychological structures of human consciousness correspond to the various ways in which the capacities of the brain are used.[3] In another sense, consciousness as characteristically human goes beyond what the concept of brain can explain. In other words, the states of consciousness are more complex than the changes that occur in the brain. The meanings attached to our feelings and intentions are much more numerous than our recurrent physiological operations.

In addition to my methodological decision not to attempt to correlate human consciousness and the physiology of the brain, my opting against another approach must be explained. No reference will be made to a spate of books which purport to examine mystical consciousness while assuming that consciousness is to be equated exclusively with consciousness *of something*. Misled by this object-oriented model, which is current in the social sciences, numerous students of religious experience take it for granted that mysticism amounts to a special category of phenomena perceivable thanks to an expanded consciousness. It is alleged that in paranormal events a more perceptive consciousness accesses new objects coming from outside, or receives particular revelations taking place inside. But a little familiarity with the great doctors of the spiritual life suffices to make us realize that although true mysticism may be associated with such phenomena, its essentials belong elsewhere.

In Hinduism, for example, paranormal and supranormal phenomena are regarded with circumspection.

> Their religious significance is seen as ambiguous. According to the most authoritative masters, they are not intrinsic to mystical life and may even hinder it, especially if they are sought after for their own sake. Thus the Yoga Sutras approve of the practitioners' interest in them only temporarily, because such pursuit is an impediment to the full liberation of the mind.[4]

Introduction

The same cautiousness is typical of many Christian writers. Notable in this regard is the fact that John of the Cross associates rapture and ecstasy with the limited endurance of the human body. Far from simply delighting in rapture and ecstasy, the soul suffers so much that it hankers after a state in which it would be separated from the body. As he explains, the intake of the soul at its sensory level is so restricted that it is prevented from receiving an abundant spiritual communication. True, John of the Cross does not disparage rapture and ecstasy; yet he puts no stock in them. He also remarks that such phenomena cease when the meditators have reached perfection.[5]

This position is echoed by William Johnston, who sums up the views of an authority on mysticism:

> The French Jesuit, Joseph de Guibert (1877–1942), for example, maintained that ecstasy was by no means an integral part of the mystical ascent. It was, he claimed, simply a consequence arising from the weakness of the human organism unable to stand such a powerful inflow of spirit without losing the use of its physical and psychological faculties.[6]

And with respect to Zen, Johnston notes:

> It is significant, too, that in Zen, even in the deepest spiritual experiences, physical ecstasy is virtually unknown. If anything like this does rear its head, it is promptly crushed. Indeed, the whole Zen training is calculated to counteract anything like ecstasy.

The author then proceeds to highlight a more profound sense of the word "ecstasy":

> It is an experience that is undoubtedly present also in the deepest stages of Zen: an extraordinarily powerful uprising of spirit in the human mind and heart and the transition to a new level of consciousness. It is this that I call ecstasy. . . . For the medieval mystics, ecstasy (the Greek *ekstasis* or *standing out*) was a going out from, or a relinquishing of, the self. This is the root meaning of the term.[7]

I wish to adopt this meaning of ecstasy as "a new level of consciousness." We shall find it not only in Zen but also in Plotinus and Eckhart.

Furthermore, behind the excessive interest in paranormal phenomena in the wake of William James, lurks the mistake of acceding to the commonsense view of consciousness as only "objectal," that is, as object-directed. Yet, as I shall demonstrate at length, consciousness also possesses an inner dimension: our conscious living subjectivity. Besides the "consciousness-of," everybody has a "consciousness-in." Alongside the consciousness *of* objects, there is a consciousness *in* our own acts and states.[8] Our consciousness-in allows us to realize that we know or feel, and remember having known or felt, specific objects (consciousness-of). If consciousness-in were not a matter of experience, we could never become aware of it.

Usually, in this book, "consciousness" will mean consciousness-in. I shall also speak of "awareness." This term will be understood as less broad than "consciousness." It will designate, not consciousness as still unadverted-to, but adverted-to consciousness. The former is "nonpositional" consciousness, in Jean-Paul Sartre's sense (to be presented in chapter 1); in this kind of consciousness, we are not conscious *of*, rather we are just *consciously* sensing, feeling, thinking, and so forth. The latter is "positional" consciousness, namely, that same consciousness at the moment one notices it for the first time. In other words, there is consciousness before we are aware of it. It becomes awareness whenever people pay attention to their bodily or mental states and acts (in which they are conscious). At this stage, consciousness-in begins to transmute itself into an embryonic form of consciousness-of. Thus awareness is the first stage of consciousness-of, susceptible of being more fully objectified at later stages.

In a study of Zen, a Western monk explains the difference.

> We can distinguish ourselves as the subject thinking and the object thought, or, more simply, as "I" and "me." Whenever we act or think, it is I who act or think; but whenever we think of ourselves acting or thinking, the subject of our thought is "me"—even though, be it noted, we may speak of ourselves and often (without sufficient analysis) think of ourselves as "I." The "I" and "me" are substantially identical, but cognitively, at the normal level of knowledge, they are distinct. This might be expressed by adopting a term from Buddhist psychology, the I and me exist in "nonduality." Put another way: whenever I think or act unself-consciously, it is *I*; whenever I think or act self-consciously, it is *me*.[9]

Tart, the advocate of transpersonal psychology whom I cited earlier, offers a parallel distinction:

On purely psychological grounds, it is useful to distinguish between consciousness and basic awareness. *Consciousness* is a complex, content-filled thing that fills the great bulk of our experience, whereas *basic awareness* is that something behind consciousness, that pure kind of knowing that simply knows that something is happening, rather than knowing that at this very moment I am sitting in my study looking out a glass window at rain falling after a long dry season.[10]

In Tart's terminology, "consciousness" amounts to my "consciousness-of," while "basic awareness" amounts to my "consciousness-in." Unfortunately, in the rest of his book, out of interest in altered states of consciousness triggered by dreams, telepathy, hypnosis, drugs or meditation, he confuses them with basic awareness. Those states carry contents, whereas consciousness-in as such is content-free, even though it is usually coupled with content-directed activities.

Authors of a lesser caliber than Tart who focus on consciousness as loaded with contents envision the evolution of consciousness as the acquisition of a frame of mind characterized by a greater openness to peculiar phenomena such as extrasensory perceptions. In my opinion, their mistake consists in equating higher consciousness with a greater openness to special *contents*, be they psychic, cosmic, or religious. In so doing, they ignore the subjective consciousness that traverses the whole activity by which we reach the contents. Consequently, I have made the methodological decision to turn my back on such misleading contributions. Instead, I will take the more arduous route of scrutinizing, not consciousness as having objects, but the fundamental aspect of human consciousness, which lies at the root of human subjectivity. That road will eventually direct us towards a much better appreciation of mysticism.

I do not want, however, to deny the possibility, indeed the fact of content-bearing revelations. They are very well documented. They correspond to what Thomas Aquinas analyzes as the prophetic way of being granted divine words, images, meanings, and judgments. As prophetic, they belong to the graces given for the spiritual enhancement of a religious group and they differ from the personal graces, among which Thomas places the phenomenon called rapture (*raptus*).[11]

Friedrich Heiler's distinction between the prophetic and the mystical is pertinent here, even though he (and Söderblom who has influenced him) has hardened it and even though his understanding of mysticism must be entirely revamped.[12] To my way of thinking, the prophetic mode, which is for the sake of instructing others and assisting them in relating their religious experience to finite realities, consists in receiving insightful contents; whereas the mystical mode, which is for the sake of being united to God as absolutely surpassing the human intellect, is per se without object, or without specifiable content, albeit not without content, as we shall see Rahner and Lonergan declare at the end of chapter 3.

Teresa of Avila is aware of having been accorded the grace of operating according to both modes, which seem to have been at times successive and at times conjoined.[13] When she speaks of her visions and auditions, she is engaged in the prophetic mode; when she describes the various mansions which point to the sundry degrees of her union with God, she is involved in mysticism, understood in the classic sense that goes back to Dionysius.[14]

Robert Forman, to whom I am indebted for this reference to Teresa (although he does not use Heiler's categories), reports that Roland Fisher has situated conscious states along a spectrum comprised of three categories: ergotropic, normal (at the center), and trophotropic. At one end of the chart, ergotropic states are characterized by intense physiological and cognitive arousal or "work" (*ergon* in Greek). They include such events as hallucinations, visions, auditions. At the other end, trophotropic states are marked by low levels of physiological and cognitive activity or "nourishing" (*trophon*). They include restful states mentioned by Eckhart and *The Cloud of Unknowing*.[15] Following Forman, to whom I shall return in this book, I have opted to concentrate on the type of consciousness manifested in trophotropic states.[16]

In conformity with that option, this book will tackle solely consciousness defined as consciousness-in (both ordinary and mystical). By not including consciousness-of, I am perfectly aware of leaving aside aspects of mysticism (understood in a broad sense) that are very important, to wit: not only visions, auditions, and revelations, but also holy thoughts, insights, feelings, decisions which are part and parcel of a person's relationship with God. In chapter 3, we shall notice that James Price felicitously distinguishes between "mystical consciousness" (beyond what I have called consciousness-of) and "religious consciousness" (having to do with thoughts and feelings). My aim is not to present the complex whole of Christian mysticism[17] (which, in its broad sense, includes "religious consciousness") but, as intimated in my Preface, only the facet that can more easily be brought into dialogue with the Japanese philosophy of Zen experience. In my Conclusion, based on the discoveries made in our quest, I will situate with more precision this restricted definition of mystical consciousness.

Two years ago a work of mine, entitled *Transcendent Experiences*, was published.[18] The readers who are interested in issues such as typologies, the sense of the infinite, feeling and thought, experience and interpretation, immediacy and mediation, may want to peruse that book. It offers a phenomenology and a critique of transitory experiences of the infinite. *Mystical Consciousness* treats of a quite different spiritual state. Whereas transcendent experiences are episodes that many people have (as documented in a good number of social surveys), relatively few people enjoy mystical consciousness, which is not *an* experience in the sense of an event during which we would entertain specific thoughts and emotions. (Nonetheless, for instance in the previous quotation by Johnston, mystical consciousness can be called an experience in a broad sense, namely, as a state that is conscious at particular times.[19] Then transcendent experiences and the mystical state may coincide.) Mystical consciousness is a rather permanent state, a basic disposition, a stable mood, as we shall find out in the chapters to come. Transcendent experiences occur more frequently at the beginning of the spiritual life, whereas mystical consciousness requires cultivation, that is, moral asceticism as well as the practice of meditation, and consequently is typical of advanced practitioners.

The present book consists of three parts. The first details twentieth-century Western accounts of consciousness, both ordinary and mystical. The second part aims at deepening our understanding of mystical consciousness, by introducing the thought of three classics, namely, Plotinus, Eckhart, and Schleiermacher. The third part contrasts Western and Japanese views of the self and nothingness. It approaches the human self from the viewpoint of consciousness and asks whether we can arrive at a representation that is different from an inauthentic self. It discusses the contributions of Heidegger, Suzuki, Nishitani, and Hisamatsu on nothingness and emptiness.

PART I

Western Philosophies of Consciousness

CHAPTER 1

Major Contributions

This part of the book introduces modern Western views of consciousness. Chapters 1 and 2 unfold philosophical accounts of *ordinary* consciousness, that is, of consciousness as present and hence discernible in commonsense, artistic, scientific, or scholarly activities. Chapter 3 presents philosophical accounts of *mystical* consciousness.

We begin our quest for a model of consciousness by having recourse to four thinkers: Brentano, Husserl, Sartre, and Lonergan, later to be supplemented with more recent contributions (in chapter 2). Franz Brentano (1838–1917), who influenced Husserl, ushered in a new era for philosophical psychology. Edmund Husserl (1859–1938) founded phenomenology and endeavored to establish it as a rigorous science. Jean-Paul Sartre (1905–1980) laid out fine distinctions regarding consciousness. Bernard Lonergan (1904–1984) adopted a version of the transcendental method that resembles Husserl's.

Common to both Brentano and Lonergan is their intimate acquaintance with the works of Aristotle and Thomas Aquinas. In particular Brentano's and Lonergan's ideas on intentionality and consciousness are a direct result of their reading of those two classical authors. Common to Husserl and Lonergan is their appraisal of the transcendental, or cross-cultural dimension of conscious intentionality, albeit in a manner that differs from Kant's.

What stands out as most helpful for our purposes is the fact that Brentano, Husserl, Sartre, and Lonergan all distinguish, while uniting, intentionality and consciousness. These are two sides of the same coin: intentionality is the object-directedness of our mind; consciousness is the lived experience that we have of our intentionality. However, the first two philosophers emphatically lay stress on intentionality, whereas Sartre and Lonergan are equally interested in both themes and have more to offer regarding consciousness.

BRENTANO

According to Heidegger, Brentano's contribution must be situated in the following historical context. Under the influence of British empiricism (mostly of John Stuart Mill), Wilhelm Wundt and other German thinkers, in the second half of the nineteenth century, modeled psychology on the positivistic paradigm of the natural sciences. Psychology became experimental in the sense of a physiological science of consciousness. In reaction against the reduction of psychology to its biological substratum, Brentano attempted to specify its subject matter by acknowledging the actual elements of psychic life, so as to highlight the distinctness of a genuine science of consciousness. In his major work, *Psychology from an Empirical Standpoint* (1874), he clarified what is given in psychic, lived experiences.

For Brentano, the psychic phenomena are not the same as the physical. The difference lies in the fact that in the former, something objective indwells, for example the represented in representing, the judged in judging, the willed in willing. Through its operations the mind orients itself towards something objective which comes to be present in the mind. Brentano calls this phenomenon "intentional in-existence" (existence in) and he uses the scholastic word "intention" to characterize the object-directed nature of intentionality.[1]

In the lectures that have just been referred to, Heidegger concentrates on Brentano's concept of intentionality and does not speak of his concept of consciousness. But by perusing a few passages of Brentano's principal work, we can find out how he construes the relation of consciousness to intentionality.

As Heidegger notes, Brentano distinguishes "physical" and "mental" phenomena. The former are the objects of our sensations, what is sensed, what is directly given in perception, for instance what is seen (color, figure), what is heard (sound), what is felt (warmth, cold, odor), what is imagined (image). The latter are the act of presentation, the presenting of the object, for instance seeing, hearing, feeling, imagining, remembering, expecting, thinking, doubting, judging, willing, and all emotions.[2]

A mental phenomenon is a mental act or process by means of which we are conscious of something. In this first sense, "consciousness" overlaps with intentionality. Alluding to the grammar of the German word *Bewußtsein*, which strictly speaking means "to be conscious," Brentano writes that "it refers to an object which consciousness is conscious of" and it has "the property of the intentional in-existence of an object" (102).

For anything to exist in the knower and thus to be known, an object and a mental act are required at the same time. The first is called "the primary object" and the second, the "secondary object." For example, the sound and the act of hearing. At this point, Brentano tells us something important concerning the mental act: "the secondary object of an act can undoubtedly be an object of consciousness in this act, but cannot be an object of observation in it" (128). In other words, whereas the primary object can be observed, the secondary object cannot (see 29). The mental act that becomes the secondary object cannot be observed (*beobachtet*), because it is not a second act, different from the one through which we observe the primary object (see 127).

One cannot be aware of the secondary object except in the mental act. Thus "the hearing itself is only apprehended concomitantly in the hearing of sounds" (129). Our mental activity is so naturally orientated towards objects (for instance, sounds) that we are but indirectly aware of it. "It is only while our attention is turned toward a different object that we are able to perceive, incidentally, the mental processes which are directed toward that object" (30). "There are undoubtedly occasions when we are conscious of a mental phenomenon while it is present in us; for example, while we have the presentation of a sound, we are conscious of having it" (126).

Here we hit upon Brentano's second sense for consciousness. It is no longer intentionality as consciousness of an object, but rather the consciousness that traverses our entire mental activity.

> The consciousness of the presentation of the sound clearly occurs together with the consciousness of this consciousness, for the consciousness which accompanies the presentation of the sound is a consciousness not so much of this presentation as of the whole mental act in which the sound is presented, and in which the consciousness itself exists concomitantly (129).

The first consciousness is the "consciousness of" or "presentation of," while the second is the "consciousness of this consciousness," elsewhere called "inner presentation" (127). "Consciousness *of* this consciousness," however, is not a felicitous phrasing. As Dan Zahavi perceptively remarks about Husserl's project, "Despite his criticism of the reflection theory, he continues to speak of consciousness taking itself as its own object, and thus of self-awareness as a (secondary) *object*-awareness."[3] This is the reason why, in my Introduction, I have named the accompanying consciousness, not a second kind of consciousness-of, but consciousness-in, since it is detectable in our mental activity. Such consciousness permeates our mental phenomena.

Brentano subdivides this accompanying consciousness into two layers:

> Just as we call the perception of a mental activity which is actually present in us "inner perception," we here call the consciousness which is directed upon it "inner consciousness" (101, note).

The subdivision seems to be between nonreflexive and reflexive consciousness. Thanks to reflexive knowledge, our conscious acts become secondary objects. Commenting on Brentano, David Bell writes: "In addition to its possessing a primary object, a mental act may also possess a secondary object, namely, itself, which is intended along with (*nebenbei*) the primary object."[4]

However, Brentano leaves unexplained the transition from the former to the latter. Lonergan will have more to say about this transition. He will concur with Brentano, who states that reflexive consciousness culminates in judgments: "we only have knowledge when we make judgments" (138). To unreflexive and reflexive consciousness Brentano adds a third, affective dimension: "Consciousness of this secondary object [the mental phenomenon] is threefold: it involves a presentation of it, a cognition of it and a feeling toward it" (154). As we shall note later in this chapter, Sartre more fully thematizes this affective dimension of consciousness.

Lonergan will agree with Brentano's contention that, in contrast to external perception, which is not in itself reliable, inner perception possesses an immediate evidence and infallibility due to the directness of its presentation in our consciousness: "We are absolutely certain of the veracity of inner perception" (139). Thus, in contrast to the hypothetical character of scientific assertions, the judgments that express inner perception are invulnerable. Yet we shall see presently that Husserl helps us qualify this invulnerability.

Finally, Brentano discusses the unity of consciousness. Our mental activity is complex in that it brings together many acts (for instance, we can see and hear at the same time) and therefore many objects. He points out that the totality of our mental activities constitutes a real unity. They "all belong to one unitary reality only if they are inwardly perceived as existing together" (164; see 155–165). Interestingly, William James, to whose views on the self we shall give attention in chapter 7, writes, "Altogether this chapter of Brentano's on the Unity of Consciousness is as good as anything with which I am acquainted."[5] There is always in us a tendency to relate acts and objects, by differentiating or identifying them with one another. Further on in the current study, this remark regarding the unity of an individual's consciousness will be the starting point of our reflections on the self.

HUSSERL

Husserl discusses three concepts of consciousness:

1. Consciousness as the entire, real (*reelle*) phenomenological being of the empirical ego, as the interweaving of psychic experiences in the unified stream of consciousness.
2. Consciousness as the inner awareness of one's own psychic experiences.
3. Consciousness as a comprehensive designation for "mental acts", or "intentional experiences", of all sorts.[6]

The first sense corresponds with William James's "stream of thought," about which I shall have something to say in chapter 7. The second sense is also called "inner consciousness." Using Brentano's phrase, "inner perception," Husserl explains: "This is that 'inner perception' thought to accompany actually present experiences" (Investigation V, §5, 542). He adds: "Undeniably the second concept of consciousness is the more 'primitive': it has an 'intrinsic priority'" (§6, 543). The third sense is intentionality. Husserl is much more interested in this third sense, to which he dedicates his whole chapter 2, than in the first two senses, on which he briefly comments in his chapter 1.

These three senses of consciousness closely match three of Brentano's tenets. The first of these is that human psychic life includes "*any mental process whatever of consciousness* in an extraordinary broad sense." Husserl's list is almost as long as Brentano's. The stream of mental operations comprises mental acts, called *cogitationes,* such as "'I perceive, I remember, I phantasy, I judge, I feel, I desire, I will,' and thus all egoical mental processes which are at all similar to them, with their countless flowing particular formations."[7]

The second tenet common to both thinkers is consciousness as the "object" of inner perception. However, Husserl disagrees with Brentano's contention that "inner perception distinguishes itself from outer perception: 1. by its evidence and its incorrigibility, and 2. by essential differences in phenomena." On the contrary, "not every perception of the ego, nor every perception of a psychic state referred to the ego, is certainly evident." In both cases, inner and outer perception, one can be misled in one's judgments about them. Inner perception does not have an edge on outer perception, for they are "of an entirely similar epistemological *character*" (Appendix, 859). Yet in Investigation V itself, Husserl concedes (rightly, in my opinion) that there is something "self-evidently certain" in empirical judgments such as "I am" and other "judgments of inner (i.e., adequate) perception."

> Not only is it self-evident that I am: self-evidence also attaches to countless judgments of the form *I perceive this or that*, where I not merely think, but am also self-evidently assured, that what I perceive is given as I think of it, that I apprehend the thing itself, and for what it is—this pleasure, e.g., that fills me, this phantasm of the mind that float [sic] before me etc. All these judgements share the lot of the judgement "I am", they elude complete conceptualization and expression, they are evident only in their living intention, which cannot be adequately imparted in words (§6, 544).

The third sense of consciousness that both Brentano and Husserl highlight is intentionality, namely, meaning (*meinen*) as the pointing at something, or intending directedness (*intendierende Gerichtetheit*) towards objects. "The essence of consciousness, in which I live as my own self, is the so-called intentionality. Consciousness is always consciousness of something."[8]

Husserl asserts that "intentionality is a fundamental characteristic of psychic life which is given quite immediately and evidently prior to all theories."[9] By declaring intentionality to be "prior to all theories," Husserl surpasses Brentano. Not that the latter has not recognized the basic character of intentionality. But what is going to be more and more underlined by Husserl is the unique status of intentionality as prior to all theories and indeed to all scientific or commonsense enterprises. According to him, "Brentano had not gone beyond an externally classificatory-descriptive consideration of intentional lived experiences or, what amounts to the same, of species of consciousness."[10]

To Husserl's mind, Brentano's descriptive psychology still is typical of the natural attitude that his emancipated disciple wants to overcome. The mathematician Husserl contends:

> Whenever something like numbers, mathematical multiplicities, propositions, theories, etc., are to become subjectively

given, become objects of consciousness in subjective lived experiences, the lived experiences which are needed for that to happen must have their essentially necessary and everywhere identical structure.[11]

The latter part of this sentence has a Kantian ring which we do not hear in Brentano. Although Brentano had already maintained, as we saw, that mental processes (here: "the lived experiences") are more basic than the objects, it is only with Husserl that they are seen, in a clearly transcendental fashion, as the conditions of possibility of any objectification.

Brentano's brilliant follower becomes a philosopher in his own right as he moves from the natural to the transcendental or, more exactly, phenomenological attitude. Since it is not free from commonsense or scientific prejudices, the natural attitude entails belief in pseudo-objective entities, whereas the phenomenological attitude critically grounds the movement "to the things themselves." For phenomenology to be the foundation of all sciences, it must go beyond the contingent life and uncover the formal structure of conscious intentionality.

One of the characteristics of this underlying structure is the unity it confers both on the succession of mental processes and on the objects that are thus related. Whereas Brentano, as we saw, contents himself with registering and describing the fact of such unification, Husserl posits a transcendental ego to account for this unifying dynamism in us: "intentional consciousness owes its specific form of unity to the ego."[12] He is not interested in the empirical self, that is, in an individual having acquired a definite self-image and a worldview through idiosyncratic experiences. He is interested in "the general essence,"[13] in what is grasped as the universal human structure, namely, the transcendental ego, the pure consciousness which gives organization to all the intentional processes. To attain this, a bracketing of the merely factual or concrete characteristics is required.

Husserl applies his phenomenological method, with its transcendental and eidetic reduction, to how intentionality as a whole is constituted. But since we are pursuing an account not so much of intentionality as of consciousness, we shall not enter into the details of Husserl's intricate phenomenology, especially in its effort at providing a rigorous and secure foundation to all sciences. Let us simply focus on his procedure insofar as it touches upon consciousness.

In contrast to a descriptive psychology, Husserl proposes a transcendental phenomenology characterized by reflection. "Only in reflection do we 'direct' ourselves to the perceiving itself" (for example the perceiving of a house), "an experiencing experiencing of the house-perception with all its moments."[14] In fact, as was said above, Brentano had already discovered this key to consciousness: a double awareness (*of* objects and *in* our intentional processes) in a single activity. As Sokolowski explains, "experience of acts takes place in the *same* stream of consciousness in which the acts are formed." The fact of "experiencing experiencing" is not the result of a second mental act, which would amount to some observation or introspection. "The difficulty we must overcome is a tendency to forget the distinction between inner experience and perception, and to talk as though we did 'perceive' or 'see' our own acts."[15]

Apart from those oblique allusions, Husserl offers less than Brentano on consciousness itself, probably because his interests resided in intentionality and in the founding of an apodictic science called phenomenology.[16]

SARTRE

Sartre began where Husserl left off.[17] Still, being a Frenchman, he could not escape the influence of Henri Bergson (1859–1941). In 1889, Bergson publishes *Essai sur les données immédiates de la conscience*.[18] By "states of consciousness," he means the "psychic states" of which we are conscious. As in Brentano and Husserl, the gamut is broad: sensations, feelings, passions, efforts (1), as well as the acts of pondering and deciding" (125). In a manner similar to theirs, he distinguishes "immediate" consciousness (128) and "reflective" consciousness (90). His main thesis runs as follows. On the one hand, in the former kind of consciousness, time is experienced as a qualitative multiplicity, since its elements are not homogeneous. On the other hand, the latter kind of consciousness projects our psychic states into space and represents them as a discrete and quantitative multiplicity, since the terms of a succession can be posited as identical while remaining outside of one another along a continuum (90, 124, 129). Although Bergson overwhelmingly prefers the former, called "pure duration" or "inner duration," and unfairly considers the latter (reflective consciousness) to be a mere distortion of the former (91, 226–227), he has the merit of having uncovered our tendency to confuse the two and to speak of the former with images that befit only the latter (129).[19] This is a problem that Sartre inherits from Bergson.

In a book entitled *The Psychology of Imagination*, originally published in 1940, Sartre mentions the fact of self-consciousness, called "an immanent and natural consciousness of itself." He goes on to say that we must find out:

How the non-reflective consciousness posits its object. How this consciousness appears to itself in the non-thetic consciousness which accompanies the position of the object.[20]

The best answers to these questions can be found in *The Transcendence of the Ego*, an essay first published a few years before, that is, in 1936.[21] Sartre differentiates three levels of awareness. First, *nonpositional* consciousness, which does not posit itself as its own object. It stands in contrast to the awareness of objects, which does posit those objects. Nonetheless, such consciousness is necessarily twined to the awareness of some object: "consciousness is purely and simply consciousness of being consciousness of that object" (40). Nonpositional consciousness is "consciousness in the first degree, or *unreflected* (*irréfléchie*) consciousness" (41).

Second, *reflected* (*réfléchie*) consciousness, obtained as the result of "a reflective (*réflexive*) operation, that is to say, as an operation of the second degree." Nonpositional consciousness is now reflected thanks to "reflecting (*réfléchissante*) consciousness" (44). "It becomes positional only by directing itself upon the reflected consciousness" (45). Reflecting consciousness is the reflective operation that takes consciousness as its object and makes it reflected consciousness. Thus reflected consciousness dawns in a reflecting-reflective act and attains its completion when it becomes objectified. Sartre must be credited with the distinction nonpositional/positional consciousness. He must also be praised for having noticed the transition from nonpositional to positional consciousness—a transition indicated by his use of the adjective *réfléchissante*, "reflecting."

Third, the *Cogito*, or the "I" that thinks, which posits not only the reflected consciousness, but itself as reflecting consciousness. "All reflecting consciousness is, indeed, in itself unreflected, and a new act of the third degree is necessary in order to posit it" (45).

We find the same doctrine in Sartre's mature work, *Being and Nothingness*.[22] First, in the prereflective phase, he begins by emphasizing consciousness-of. "All consciousness, as Husserl has shown, is consciousness *of* something. This means that there is no consciousness which is not a *positing* (*position*) of a transcendent object" (liii). Consciousness (conscious intentionality would have been a better term) posits objects that transcend purely immanent mental operations. Then he introduces what I have called consciousness-in as the condition of consciousness-of:

> However, the necessary and sufficient condition for a knowing consciousness to be knowledge of its object, is that it be consciousness of itself as being that knowledge. This is a necessary

condition, for if my consciousness were not consciousness of being consciousness of the table, it would then be consciousness of that table without consciousness of being so. In other words, it would be a consciousness ignorant of itself, an unconscious—which is absurd (liv).

Later in the same book, Sartre affirms that "the consciousness which we have of ourselves" is no addition to the consciousness that we simply are. He writes, "This consciousness, as we know, can be only non-positional; it is we-as-consciousness since it is not distinct from our being" (462). A few years after *Being and Nothingness* appeared, Sartre summarized it and reiterated that consciousness is "a mode of being." The very title of his lecture announces his fine distinction between consciousness and knowledge. Of the former he says, "everyone *is* it at each instant." There also, he insists that consciousness is not "immediately reflective" and therefore neither "a knowledge of knowledge" nor even a "knowledge" (*connaissance*)."[23]

In a second, reflexive phase, the person acquires "*reflection* or positional consciousness of consciousness, or better yet *knowledge of* consciousness" (liv). There is an echo here of Brentano's distinction between inner perception (= Sartre's nonpositional consciousness) and the knowledge posited in judgment: "the reflecting consciousness posits the consciousness reflected-on, as its object. In the act of reflecting I pass judgment on the consciousness reflected-on" (lv).

Further on in *Being and Nothingness*, Sartre indicates that since "consciousness was *there* before it was known," "the being of self-consciousness could not be defined in terms of knowledge." Hence his distinction between "selfness" (*ipséité*) and "the Ego" (*l'Ego*), the former being prereflective and the latter being the outcome of reflection (239). Moreover, he plays with two senses of the French word *réflexion*, which can mean either mirroring or thinking:

> consciousness is a reflection (*reflet*), but *qua* reflection it is exactly the one reflecting (*réfléchissant*), and if we attempt to grasp it as reflecting, it vanishes and we fall back on the reflection. This structure of the reflection-reflecting (*reflet-reflétant*) has disconcerted philosophers (75–76).

He grammatically conveys the enigma of the self's presence to itself by placing the "of" in parenthesis in the phrase *conscience (de) soi*—a consciousness he once more characterizes as "non-positional" (lvi). This practice of Sartre's illustrates the problem of whether the self can successfully objectify its consciousness. This issue will periodically recur in our enquiry.

Based on *The Transcendence of the Ego*, Phyllis Sutton Morris clearly sorts out the dual structure of nonpositional/positional consciousness:

> In ordinary prereflective experience Sartre said there is (a) positional consciousness of an object and (b) nonpositional awareness (of) the act of consciousness, but no consciousness of an ego. Sartre claimed that an ego was encountered only in acts of reflection. Reflective consciousness has the same dual structure as does prereflective consciousness; there is (a) positional consciousness of an object and (b) nonpositional consciousness (of) the act of reflecting.[24]

We can realize that the pair nonpositional/positional does not always overlap with the pair prereflective/reflective. In another article, commenting on the first pair, Morris states,

> In distinguishing between the thetic (positional) and the nonthetic (non-positional) dimensions of consciousness, Sartre reminds us that each directed act of consciousness exhibits both focused and unfocused awareness.[25]

By focusing on an object (positional consciousness), we leave other objects and our self-consciousness in the background (nonpositional).

What is the precise difference, then, between the two pairs? Morris states,

> Whereas for Sartre, the distinction between positional and nonpositional consciousness is the difference in degrees of focus and clarity, the distinction between prereflective and reflective consciousness is the type of positional object toward which each is directed.... It is only when someone takes his own conscious activities as the object of his attention that he has begun to reflect in Sartre's sense.[26]

For him, then, reflection means self-reflection. Accordingly, the transition from the non-reflective to the reflective amounts to a transition from the nonpositional to the positional self-consciousness.

Lest this analysis by Sartre sound overly intellectualistic, let us heed a remark he inserts in *Being and Nothingness*: "Not all consciousness is knowledge (there are states of affective consciousness, for example)" (liv). In another study, *The Emotions*,[27] Sartre tries to situate emotions in regard to consciousness. He asks, "Can types of consciousness be conceived which would not include emotion among their possibilities, or must we see in it an indispensable structure of consciousness?" He opts for the latter: "An emotion is precisely a consciousness" (15). He explains, "Emotion is the human reality which assumes itself and which, 'aroused,' 'directs' itself toward the world" (14). "Emotion is a certain way of apprehending the world" (52). Conscious emotion is primarily intentionality.

At this prereflective stage, again we have the two sides of consciousness, that is, nonpositional in regard to itself and positional in regard to the world that it necessarily intends:

> Emotional consciousness is, at first, unreflective, and on this plane it can be conscious of itself only on the non-positional mode. Emotional consciousness is, at first, consciousness *of* the world (51).

In this brilliant passage, Sartre makes us realize that unreflective emotion is neither "unconscious" nor "conscious *of* itself" (54). Having finely situated consciousness halfway between the unconscious and the reflexively conscious, he sums up his thesis as follows:

> The thing that matters here is to show that action as spontaneous unreflective consciousness constitutes a certain existential level in the world, and that in order to act it is not necessary to be conscious of the self as acting—quite the contrary. In short, unreflective behavior is not unconscious behavior; it is conscious of itself non-thetically, and its way of being thetically conscious of itself is to transcend itself and to seize upon the world as a quality of things (56–57).

The thetical or positional consciousness is first operative as the intentionality which transcends itself towards the world. At the same time a non-thetical or nonpositional self-consciousness is also present.

Interestingly, earlier in the same book, after affirming that, in contrast to the psychologist, who attends to psychic states as accidental facts, the phenomenologist must study the *signification* of emotion (see 15-16), he states:

> The emotion signifies, *in its own way*, the whole of consciousness or, if we put ourselves on the existential level, of human reality. It is not an accident because human reality is not an accumulation of facts. It expresses from a definite point of view the human synthetic totality in its entirety (17).

He suggests that at the existential level "the whole of consciousness" or "the human synthetic totality in its entirety" is at stake. This Kierkegaardian accent on the existential level of consciousness, where the future of the human self is in question, has deeply marked Lonergan's thinking.

However, before introducing the thought of Lonergan on consciousness, let us pay attention, at least briefly, to Sartre's views about nothingness in *Being and Nothingness*. As distinct from the "in-itself" (*en-soi*), the "for-itself" (*pour-soi*) "is already a non-thetic self-consciousness" (150). The human person is at one and the same time a thing ("in-itself") and a subject ("for-itself"). Thus it has to both affirm and negate itself (118). In the process of reflection "the reflected-on . . . makes himself an object for—" that is, for oneself or for whatever other subject, and thus discovers that it has "an outside," and that it has established "a distance from itself" (152). "To know is to *make oneself other*" (155). Because of consciousness, reflexiveness, and self-questioning, the "for-itself" experiences a *néant* ("nothingness"), a gap, a radical difference vis-à-vis its factual, unconscious being.

Sartre seems to construe the emergence of this nothingness in the context of an inadequate philosophy of perception. For him, an individual's own "being," as observed from within, is an "outside," namely, the "in-itself" (158). The human subject realizes that it is non-being, in contradiction to its "in-itself" perceived as a compact, self-contained bulk of being, opaque to itself, solid (*massif*), full positivity (*pleine positivité*), perfectly identical with itself, and absolutely unrelated to anything other than itself (lxv–lxvi). So, because it is "not coincidence with itself,"[28] the "for-itself" is "a nihilated in-itself" (154). Sartre misconceives of self-objectification, interpreted in terms of such physical and spatial metaphors, which cannot but strongly suggest a dualism within self-presence.[29] Accordingly his analysis ends up in the paradox of a self-reflection that must remain a "failure" (154). Yet it is unsuccessful only in the measure that he wants judgment to resemble perception. We shall observe that problem in Plotinus's representation of Intellect's self-consciousness.

Elizabeth Morelli rightly discerns "a vacillation between experience and knowledge in his discussion of reflection." She explains:

> Sartre is presupposing here, as he does in his account of conscious intentionality in general, a notion of object which is fundamentally empiricist. It is the notion of object as over against the act, as standing before the act. This notion of object presupposes what Lonergan terms an "ocular model" of knowing. The empiricist assumes that all knowing must be modeled on what takes place in the act of looking."[30]

This epistemological inadequacy, in Sartre's account, is regrettable, given that his sense of the nonpositional is correct, which is no mean achievement. The end-result is that the transition from consciousness to adequate reflection is not correctly expounded.

To sum up: Sartre has made a remarkable contribution to the understanding of consciousness. However, his thoughts on reflection and nothingness suffer from two shortcomings. First, they are distorted by his empiricist epistemology, and second, they remain within the compass of an anthropological subjectivity. We shall have opportunity to mention them again, when we examine the views of Heidegger and Nishitani on nothingness.

LONERGAN

Like Brentano and Husserl, Lonergan pays a great deal of attention to human intentionality. However, he differs from them by the fact that he accentuates and analyzes consciousness more than they do. His account of consciousness owes much to Sartre's, which he held in high esteem.[31]

Inspired by Husserl, who called his own approach "intentional analysis,"[32] Lonergan's "intentionality analysis" distinguishes the data of a twofold awareness: the contents of one's operations, and the operations themselves. The inquiring subject is aware both of the objects that he or she intends and of the several acts that constitute the intending. Such intending is the ongoing effort to come to know and respect what is other than oneself. Elusive though it is, the intending is no less conscious than the intended, since people are at least vaguely aware of their cognitive and volitional operations.

> Man's sensitive, intellectual, rational, and moral operations have two distinct but related characteristics. They are both

intentional and conscious. Insofar as they are intentional, they make objects present to us. Insofar as they are conscious, they make us present to ourselves. However, if I have used the same word, present, twice, I also have used it in two different senses. Intentionality effects the presence of an object to the subject, of a spectacle to the spectator. Consciousness is a far subtler matter: it makes the spectator present to himself, not by putting him into the spectacle, not by making him an object, but while he is spectator and as subject.[33]

Intentionality analysis brings to expression the second kind of presence, namely, the conscious intending. It does so, first by adverting to, and thus heightening the usually dim consciousness that accompanies all human activities; secondly by seeking to understand the relations between these activities; thirdly by checking the adequacy of that understanding. In addition to this three-step procedure, one can, in a fourth step, make a commitment in favor of the value of human intentionality. Such are the four basic levels of human intentionality, uncovered in Lonergan's magnum opus, *Insight*: attentiveness to the data, insights into them, judgments that insights are correct or not, and decisions to act in conformity with right understanding.[34]

Lonergan proposes an intentionality analysis that explores the data of consciousness, namely, the several degrees of consciousness that pervade our waking activities. Such inner data belong to the entire range of our cognitional and volitional acts, and of our affective states. The common denominator is that they are conscious events in a person's life, prior to the intentional act of paying attention to them.

By the conscious act is not meant an act to which one attends; consciousness can be heightened by shifting attention from the content to the act, but consciousness is not constituted by that shift of attention, for it is a quality immanent in acts of certain kinds, and without it the acts would be as unconscious as the growth of one's beard.[35]

In Lonergan's list, acts are as numerous as in Brentano's and Husserl's lists.

Operations in the pattern are seeing, hearing, touching, smelling, tasting, inquiring, imagining, understanding, conceiving, formulating, reflecting, marshalling and weighing the evidence, judging, deliberating, evaluating, deciding, speaking, writing.[36]

In addition to conscious operations, feelings or states also are conscious. As contradistinguished from non-intentional feelings, intentional feelings respond to values.[37] Intentional feelings that are relatively permanent, and thus called states, play a leading role in the mystical life, as we shall find out, beginning with our next chapter.

Is it unwarranted pretension to stake out the bold claim that this structure is universal? Lonergan considers it an invariant pattern. And he explains why: any attempt to question it must implement the very structure it questions, by engaging in such activities as attending, understanding, verifying, and assessing the functioning of human intentionality. Thus those who reject what they are as intentional agents simply disqualify themselves. Denying the invariant pattern amounts to "the admission that one is a nonresponsible, nonreasonable, nonintelligent somnambulist."[38] In a humorous vein, Lonergan states:

> Not even behaviorists claim that they are unaware whether or not they see or hear, taste or touch. Not even positivists preface their lectures and their books with the frank avowal that never in their lives did they have the experience of understanding anything whatever. Not even relativists claim that never in their lives did they have the experience of making a rational judgment. Not even determinists claim that never in their lives did they have the experience of making a responsible choice.[39]

Following Brentano and Husserl, Lonergan maintains that the inner data of consciousness, that is, our operations as consciously performed, cannot be observed. They cannot be established as a result of some inner perception or introspection: there is no inward look or peering directed to the self's mental activities.[40] These just happen consciously; they are simply conscious. However, the consciousness of our activities can be explicated as inner data if we take notice of them and ask questions about their interworkings. Hence Lonergan's distinction between "consciousness as given," which is "neither formulated nor affirmed," and "an account of consciousness."[41] Lonergan clearly delineates the transition from mere consciousness in our operations to its objectification, unlike Brentano and Husserl, who leave that transition in the dark, while Sartre tackles it but ends in a paradox, as we saw, because of his inadequate epistemology.

Furthermore, like Brentano, Lonergan contends that knowledge resides neither in sensory perception nor in consciousness, but in judgments. Hence the distinction that both of them accept between experience (which Brentano calls inner perception) and judgment of fact. While consciousness is simply given, knowledge of consciousness is obtained at the end of a process of thematization, namely, in judgments. For both of them, such objectification is an exercise of intentionality, which consists in more than naming or attaching a label to objects.

The fact that Lonergan is not a conceptualist distinguishes him from authors who envision human knowledge as *primarily* a matter of objectification in the sense of conceptualization. For him, an adequate account of consciousness never amounts to a mere turning back of the self upon itself (a first looking at its inner life), which would be followed by a conceptualization extrinsic to the subject matter (a second looking, this time at concepts). In total contrast to this imaginary representation, his view is that the reflexive acts that formulate consciousness consist of questions, insights, and judgments. Because it is not extrinsic, such thematizing does not betray the nature of consciousness.[42] It does not duplicate consciousness as pure consciousness (that would inevitably distort it), but rather stems from an understanding of its elements. In other words, the benefit and truth of thematization do not derive from its capacity to relive consciousness as experienced, but from the correct insights into it that it offers. At the end of this intelligent process, the correct insights (as correct, or verified, they are also called judgments) present realities (also called objects) that are defined thanks to interrelated concepts.

To bring home the difference between the two stages in self-awareness, Lonergan has recourse to the metaphor of infrastructure and suprastructure: "that consciousness [of our operations] is not knowledge but only the infrastructure in a potential knowledge that few get around to actuating by adding its appropriate suprastructure."[43] Or again:

> As inner experience it is consciousness as distinct from self-knowledge, consciousness as distinct from any introspective process in which one inquires about inquiring, and seeks to understand what happens when one understands, and endeavors to formulate what goes on when one is formulating, and so on for all the inner activities of which all of us are *conscious* and so few of us have any exact *knowledge*.[44]

Introspection, which Lonergan had outright rejected in earlier works, is here called "introspective process" and is given a new meaning as the rise and development of self-awareness. After an initial stage, in which we simply have consciousness in all our acts and states, a second stage begins which eventually comprises the entire series of acts by which we pay attention to consciousness and reflect on it. These intentional acts are triggered by some wondering about our conscious acts and states. How is it that besides relating to external realities, I am aware of such relating taking place in me? At this initial phase characterized by the desire to elucidate what happens in us, consciousness becomes awareness, which is advertence to one's own consciousness. Such questioning allows for the transition from mere consciousness to gaining some understanding of it.

Mark, however, that I am distinguishing consciousness (= consciousness-in) and self-awareness (= consciousness of consciousness) in a way a bit more precise than Lonergan's. In fact, he uses the two terms equivalently, although his preferred one is "consciousness." But he would entirely agree, I think, with my usage of "self-awareness" as indicating a stage beyond mere consciousness, namely, the stage wherein consciousness of mere consciousness begins to emerge.

In sum, as we undertake to philosophize about consciousness, we engage in a double-decker enterprise, so to speak: the fourfold consciousness that traverses our activities becomes adverted to, understood, judged to be true, appreciated. In other words, the thematization that parallels the fourfold consciousness is also fourfold. Whenever successful, such a duplication is neither a direct uncovering of consciousness (a first look at it) nor a distorting interpretation (a second look at it), but a sound account based on verified understanding of it.

CONCLUDING REMARKS

This chapter has explored how four twentieth-century thinkers depict human consciousness, its inseparability from intentionality, its reflective thematization, which then becomes self-knowledge, and its affective side. There is little to conclude at the moment, since our inquiry will go on in the following chapter. In chapter 2 our account will be enriched by the more recent thoughts of four other scholars.

CHAPTER 2

Complementary Contributions

Let us complete our description of ordinary consciousness by drawing from a few recent authors. Some repetitions are unavoidable, but in such a notoriously murky topic they will help us consolidate a philosophical account of consciousness that, at the end of this chapter, should be sufficiently rounded out.

FROM INTENTIONALITY TO CONSCIOUSNESS: SEARLE

Let us now turn to the Berkeley philosopher John Searle, who confesses:

> It is possible to describe the logical structure of intentional phenomena without discussing consciousness—indeed, for the most part, I did so in *Intentionality*,[1] but there is a conceptual connection between consciousness and intentionality that has the consequence that a complete theory of intentionality requires an account of consciousness.[2]

Consequently, in a more recent work, from which this quotation is taken, he highlights the connection between consciousness and intentionality: "Only a being that could have conscious intentional states could have intentional states at all" (132).

Husserl would strongly approve of Searle's following statement:

> The reason for emphasizing consciousness in an account of the mind is that it is the central mental notion. In one way or another, all other mental notions—such as intentionality, subjectivity, mental causation, intelligence, etc.—can only be fully

understood as *mental* by way of their relations to consciousness (84).

Moreover, he clarifies the sense in which consciousness is subjective. We may speak of "objective" and "subjective" as having to do with judgment, whose character can be pronounced "objective" or "subjective" depending on whether it is independent or not of a person's attitude or feelings about the reality in question. But in contradistinction to this *epistemic* mode, "subjective" may refer to an *ontological* category.

> Consider, for example, the statement, "I now have a pain in my lower back." That statement is completely objective in the sense that it is made true by the existence of an actual fact and is not dependent on any stance, attitudes, or opinions of observers. However, the phenomenon itself, the actual pain itself, has a subjective mode of existence, and it is in that sense which I am saying that consciousness is subjective (94).

He sums it up as follows: "Every conscious state is always *someone's* conscious state" (94–95). And: "the ontology of the mental is an irreducibly first-person ontology" (95).

This distinction between ontological subjectivity and epistemic status enables us to qualify the previously mentioned Brentano's statement concerning the immediate evidence and infallibility of inner perception. Along with Husserl, Searle does not accept the Cartesian doctrine that "first-person reports of mental states are somehow *incorrigible*. According to this view, we have a certain kind of *first-person authority* in reports of our mental states" (145). He comments:

> Perhaps the answer has to do with confusing the subjective ontology of the mental with epistemic certainty. It is indeed the case that conscious mental states have a subjective ontology, as I have said repeatedly in the course of this book. But from the fact of subjective ontology it does not follow that one cannot be mistaken about one's mental states (145).

What is true in Descartes's and Brentano's position is the incontrovertible fact of human conscious subjectivity. What must be rejected is the suggestion that accounts of that subjectivity are inevitably correct.

How can we validly talk about mental states? Searle points out that "the standard model of observation simply doesn't work for conscious subjectivity" (97). He asserts that we cannot observe our own inner goings-on.

Why? Because where conscious subjectivity is concerned, there is no distinction between the observation and the thing observed, between the perception and the object perceived. The model of vision works on the presupposition that there is a distinction between the thing seen and the seeing of it. But for "introspection" there is simply no way to make this separation (97).

Like Brentano, Searle objects to the word "observation." As the former remarked, we can observe the primary object of any intentional act, but not its secondary object, namely the observing itself. As we saw, Lonergan concurs with Searle in this warning about the misleading model of vision. Nevertheless, unlike Lonergan, Searle does not find the term "introspection" irredeemably flawed (although, as we saw at the end of chapter 1, Lonergan reconciled himself with the phrase, "introspective process"). Yet Searle cautions his fellow philosophers:

> The problem, I believe, is not with the ordinary use of the notion of introspection, but with our urge as philosophers to take the metaphor literally. The metaphor suggests that we have a capacity to examine our own conscious states, a capacity modeled on vision. But that model or analogy is surely wrong. In the case of vision, we have a clear distinction between the object seen and the visual experience that the perceiver has when he perceives the object. But we can't make that distinction for the act of introspection of one's own conscious mental states (144).

Introspection is warranted provided we construe it as a consciousness that pertains to any intentional act. Introspection begins with a consciousness that belongs to "one's own conscious mental states," as Searle puts it. To keep close to his phrases: "the thing seen and the seeing of it" are the same; "the object seen and the visual experience" are the same. As we shall discover, Helminiak and Forman call this sameness a presence or knowledge by identity.

Lonergan stressed the possibility of our becoming attentive to our inner experience. Similarly Searle writes:

> We can always shift our attention from the *object* of the conscious experience to the *experience* itself. We can always, for example, make the move made by the impressionist painters. Impressionist painters produced a revolution in painting by shifting their attention from the object to the actual visual expe-

rience they had when they looked at the object. This is a case of self-consciousness about the character of experiences (143).

DEGREES OF CONSCIOUSNESS: CROSBY

Like Searle, another contemporary philosopher, John Crosby, sees no opposition between consciousness and attentiveness to the other:

> the stronger my self-presence, the more I can enter into the object outside of me; my self-presence does not compete with my transcendence towards the object but rather renders this transcendence possible and perfects it (85).[3]

He stresses the relation of intentionality to consciousness:

> The *outward thrust* of the intentional act is anchored in the *interiority* of my personal being. I who turn to the object am present to myself in the turning. However far I go in losing myself in the object of my act, I can never lose my self-presence entirely; my consciousness-of can never completely repress my conscious self-presence. This relation of me to myself as subject, which constitutes the interiority of my existence and of my acting, is what I mean by subjectivity.

This carefully worded statement is exact in regard to the kind of consciousness associated with intentionality. In mystical experiences, however, it may be not always true that "I can never lose my self-presence entirely." That issue will be tackled later in this book. But to the extent that ordinary consciousness is discussed, Crosby's remarks are worth pondering.

For instance, self-presence is irreducible to "a subject-object relation to myself" (86). Yet Crosby in no way denies the fact of the subject-object relation to oneself: "There undoubtedly are intentional acts in which I bend back over myself as object, as when I describe my inner life to someone" (84). He pictures self-presence as "a certain dwelling of the person with himself that is not an intentional act" (85). One finds in it a "sense of *inwardness* and *interiority*" which is comparable to "an experience of my body from within" (87), in contrast to an intentional characterization of my sensory activities.

This experience of one's interiority he illustrates as follows:

> Whether we speak of persons as having confidence in themselves, or lacking self-confidence, or pitying themselves, or being ashamed of themselves, or having self-irony, or self-hatred, or despairing over themselves, or accepting themselves—in all such cases we speak of a more than cognitive relation of the person to himself, and in most of these cases of a certain stance that the person takes towards himself. And it seems that in all these self-relations persons have to do with themselves subjectively and not only objectively. It is, for example, as subject and not only as object that I accept myself and will to be the self that I am (90).

The author is aware that such self-relations are partly subjective and partly objectified ("subjectively and not only objectively"), since the feelings he mentions could not be identified without language.

Another important point he makes is that the higher we climb on the ladder of intentionality, the more quality our consciousness has. This phenomenon is particularly noticeable on the fourth level of conscious intentionality, where the individual relates more intensely both to oneself and to other people. On that level of decision, the subjective relation to oneself has not only a cognitive but also a volitional character (see 88). In reflecting acts regarding what is to be done, the free will deliberates at once about the good to be pursued and about what one is going to become as the result of the decision taken. Hence the heightened interiority of deliberation: "The determination of myself in conscience is a determination of myself *from within*" (89; see 91).

Not everyone attains such a high degree of self-consciousness. "It seems to take a loving or at least a love-like relation of me to myself in order to exercise fully my subjectivity in a volitional way" (90). This inward relation to myself must be cultivated: "The more recollected I am, dwelling with myself, the more I experience myself from within myself." But the prize is invaluable: "In recollecting ourselves we recover ourselves as persons, and achieve, or move towards achieving, the fullness of personal life" (105).

Yet the gift may be too great to be accepted. Adding to what Pascal says about *divertissement* as the flight from our misery, Crosby perceptively writes:

> Pascal says that we cannot endure the sight of our misery and mortality, and that this is what we are fleeing from when we distract ourselves. But my idea is that it is *not just the misery but the greatness* of the human person that makes us flee from

ourselves. . . . and yet this [our selfhood] too can be a burden for us, a too heavy "weight of glory," and then we want nothing more than to blunt our sense of selfhood by immersing ourselves and losing ourselves in many things (105).

As for the expression of subjectivity, Crosby offers a caveat: "We can seriously interfere with the authenticity of our inner life by carrying self-observation too far; we have to live in our acts and not outside of them as observers of them." And he proceeds to balance his statement:

But this important fact about our inner lives is far from implying a general unknowability of personal subjectivity. It implies only that certain elements of *my own* subjective experiencing are unavailable to my objectifying act, it implies nothing about my apprehension of the experiencing *of others*; and it implies that these elements are unavailable to me only *as long as* I have the experience, but not *before or after* having the experience. And it in no way tells against the possibility of understanding subjectivity in principle, that is, understanding philosophically what it essentially is (97).

The intrinsic value of both the experiencing and the understanding are wisely asserted here. There are times when the experiencing should prevail, without the intruding of introspection; and there are times when the desire to know should prevail and prompt a more explicit self-awareness that eventually culminates in objectification:

We understand subjectivity in an objectifying, intentional way, yet not so as to understand it to be itself an objectifying, intentional form of consciousness; we can put subjectivity in front of us as object, yet understand it precisely as subjectivity (96).

FURTHER CLARIFICATIONS: HELMINIAK

Daniel Helminiak has felicitously expressed Lonergan's views on consciousness and has compared them with those of contemporary psychologists. We shall glean from him several useful observations concerning this whole business of grasping the elusive fact of our living consciousness.[4]

First of all, he stresses the dual nature of human consciousness. In it we notice a "double awareness." Besides the awareness that we have of the intended object, we find a simultaneous, concomitant "awareness of the subject's awareness of the object" (45). Perhaps Helminiak's vocabulary should have been a bit different, by employing the following three terms: in *attending* to objects, we find a *consciousness* which, when adverted to, becomes an *awareness*. Accordingly, whereas consciousness ought to be restricted to our being present to ourselves as subjects, the attending that is usually directed to external objects may also be directed to consciousness and turn it into awareness by beginning to represent it.

Still, Helminiak has a point when he cautions against uncritical usage. Having noted that language juxtaposes subjects of sentences and objects—he should have mentioned verbs as well—while being geared to reporting about objects, he adds:

> How could such language express nonreflecting consciousness, which does not involve subject and object but regards subject as subject? We may speak of "self-awareness," but the most likely understanding of this term implies a self which becomes an object to oneself. We may speak of "presence to oneself," but the preposition *to* takes an object and suggests again a self become an object to oneself. There is no way around this problem as far as linguistic structure is concerned (47).

This problem constitutes a wonderful challenge to those who want to treat meaningfully self-knowledge and mysticism. It is important to appreciate the indispensable role of metaphorical language, which facilitates understanding, and at the same time to acknowledge its capacity to mislead us if we fall captive to imaginary representations. Thus Lonergan, Crosby, and Helminiak talk about "self-presence," which is helpful as a first approximation, and yet they explain both what it is not and how it relates to further stages of self-appropriation. For his part, Zahavi equates "self-presence" with "self-acquaintance," although cautioning that "we are acquainted with our own subjectivity in a way that is radically different from the way in which we are acquainted with objects."[5] My presentation of Lonergan in chapter 1 omits the phrase "presence to oneself," which he indeed uses,[6] but which I think is fraught with difficulties. In this respect, let us heed Patrick Byrne's wise remark:

> Given post-modern critiques of the "privilege of presence," I believe it is important to stress that Lonergan's use of the term "presence" is merely metaphorical. . . . Lonergan's notion of consciousness . . . is in no way intrinsically dependent upon a

privilege of presence, and indeed offers a solution to the conundrums of post-modern construals of subjectivity and agency.[7]

As Brentano has taught us, the kind of philosophy that engages in self-knowledge, while being empirical, differs from experimental psychology, based on evidence which comes from outside. Helminiak indicates that it is empirical if "empirical" is defined as what "refers to evidence of whatever kind." Thus, in addition to the data of sense, we come across the data of consciousness. "Whatever is experienced is valid evidence, so the experience of subjects who are conscious 'of' themselves is evidence. Consciousness provides data on itself" (58; see 55).

Talking about the human spirit, Helminiak brings extra precision to describing the unique character of consciousness:

> Its self-possession is not its grasping itself as an object. Its self-possession is simply its being itself. Being itself, it is fully aware "of" itself, unmediatedly present "to" itself, nonreflectingly conscious. It is present "to" itself not by confrontation but by identity. It is present "to" itself by being itself, for to do so is precisely its peculiar nature (57)

In contrast to the evidence of the sciences, which is obtained indirectly through the senses ("by confrontation"), the evidence of the inner data is directly available ("by identity"). While the scientist examines external objects, he himself is by identity the examiner. As Helminiak writes elsewhere, "I am present to myself not as a specific object of concern but as the agent in the act, as the seer in the seeing, as the thinker in the thinking, as the 'understander' in the understanding." And again: "To know not only the object that I saw but also the fact that I was seeing the object, I must have in some way been aware not only of the object but also simultaneously of myself as seeing it."[8] Because of the identity between themselves as conscious and their conscious acts, all knowers are ever free to pay attention to their conscious subjectivity at work in any field.

Helminiak makes a point similar to Sartre's as he asserts that "nonreflecting consciousness is the condition for the possibility of knowing any object. Consciousness as conscious is logically—but not chronologically—prior to consciousness as intentional" (63). At the same time, I would mention that consciousness and intentionality mutually condition one another, or, better, that what we observe here is a conscious intentionality, or an intentional consciousness. Without consciousness, intentionality would be caught in the immediacy of the present and would not be capable of relating past and present observations.

If you were not aware of your experiencing, you would have no experience to reflect back on. Were you aware only in one mode—reflectingly—and only of one thing at a time—only of objects—you would have no experience on the basis of which to say *you* ever experienced anything. You would indeed have experienced a series of objects, all passing by as some stream of stimuli, and a human observer could report on your string of "experiences." But you yourself could not report having experienced those objects; you would not be conscious of your experiencing (63).

A final remark by Helminiak will help us clarify the reflective process. Lonergan's consciousness as intentional, he calls "reflecting awareness"; and Lonergan's consciousness as conscious, he calls "nonreflecting awareness" (45). He explains that this word pair is the same as "reflexive" and "nonreflexive," but that the participial forms are preferable to the simple adjectival forms because they dynamically "highlight the fact that consciousness always is an act; it is always a doing, and it is experienced in the doing" (45, n. 1). I beg to disagree here, at least insofar as *nonreflecting* awareness is concerned. It seems to me that consciousness as such is not an act but a continuing process that accompanies our operations and makes them events for us. Such events are experienced not only "in the doing," but also in our affective states. Hence, the conscious process is both cognitive and affective. However, what is true in Helminiak's understanding is the fact that *reflecting* is an act and is best expressed by the participial form.

While "nonreflecting" and "nonreflexive" overlap, it is important to distinguish "reflecting" (or "reflective") and "reflexive." Unfortunately, as some readers may have noticed, Sartre's translators have rendered "conscience réflexive" by "reflecting consciousness." This reinforces an ambiguity, which can be unraveled as follows. On the one hand, human thinking in general can be *reflecting* in regard to both the data of sense and the data of consciousness. The reflective activity can exert itself with respect to both intentionality and consciousness. In both cases it consists in an inquiry that leads to judging, as the knowing subject reflects upon the connection between one's understanding of something and its actuality.

On the other hand, not all reflecting activity is *reflexive*. In reflexiveness the subject takes itself as an object of inquiry. As stated earlier, the reflexive process begins with wonder directed at one's own subjectivity and transforms mere consciousness into awareness. In other words, the reflexive process is a species in the genus of reflectiveness. And in philosophical accounts of mysticism it is the very legitimacy, or even the possibility, of this reflexive process that is often questioned and that we will have to discuss later.

THE AFFECTIVE SIDE: MORELLI

Let us recall and expand our account of the affective side of consciousness, mentioned by Brentano and underlined by Sartre. In chapter 1, I talked not only about consciousness in our operations, but also about consciousness in our states. This was a minor departure from Lonergan's usage. At the time of *Insight*, Lonergan had not paid a great deal of attention to the affective side of human intentionality. Accordingly he began writing about consciousness in our operations (also called acts) and he continued to do so, without mentioning consciousness in our states, even after he had clarified the role of intentional feelings, thanks to Dietrich von Hildebrand's highlighting of them. Now introducing Elizabeth Morelli's reflections on feelings is going to help us speak more accurately about the consciousness that we have in our affective states.

Morelli establishes a linkage between states and acts by showing that far from being contradictory attributes, they are two sides of the same experience. She writes, "I think the phenomenon of affective states underlying and giving rise to intentional acts is so common as to be ineluctable."[9] In her book on anxiety, she explains that we are in "a mental or an emotional condition" (namely, in a state) while being involved in a "process of doing, operating, performing" (a series of acts). Ours is an "active state," for example what Lonergan calls "the dynamic state of being in love." Hence Morelli's statement: "Different kinds of states qualify different kinds of acts."[10]

In what kind of state are we when we pursue a goal on each of the four levels of intentionality spelled out by Lonergan? There is definitely a feel to such consciousness, and indeed a feel proper to each of the four levels. To my knowledge Lonergan does not advert to the specificity of this feel on each level. Fortunately Morelli spells out that specificity.

Surprisingly, however, she does not characterize the specificity of the first level. This omission might be accounted for by the fact that there is no common denominator here, since the moods that mark the multifarious sorts of perception do take myriad forms, for example, vitality, fatigue, comfort, irritability, and so on. On the other levels, however, we find a principal mood for each.

In an interesting article published three years after the book from which I have quoted so far, Morelli notes that "any state must itself qualify an underlying act or intention." Such a basic intention operates on each level of intentionality. Thus the state of anxiety characterizes the chief intention of the fourth level: "Anxiety is the mood or disposition, the state-like affect, of the level of freedom and real self-transcendence, that qualifies the notion of value." And she proceeds to specify two other levels, both in terms of intentionality and affect:

> As qualifying such a fundamental intentionality, anxiety is analogous to wonder, which qualifies the intentionality of the second level of conscious intentionality, the intention of intelligibility; and, to doubt, which qualifies the intention of the third level, the intention of truth and being.[11]

In a more recent piece, Morelli brings useful precision to the topic of the uneven quality of consciousness, which Crosby noticed. With respect to Lonergan's four levels, she comments:

> Moral consciousness is more aware than rational, intelligent, and empirical consciousness, but I think it would be incorrect to say that moral consciousness is more self-conscious. . . . The way in which we are self-conscious in moral consciousness is qualitatively different from the way in which we are self-conscious on the preceding levels, but it would be misleading to speak of a quantitative change in self-consciousness.[12]

Inspired by the phenomenologist Stephan Strasser, Morelli introduces a further distinction, that is, between affects (or feelings) that are act-like and affects that are state-like. The act-like affects include von Hildebrand's intentional responses, which are the active feelings found on the fourth level of intentionality. Of the state-like affects, she writes, "A state, disposition, mood, *Befindlichkeit*, is a pervasive condition of indefinite duration that underlies all conscious operations and contents—it colors one's conscious flow."[13] Fear (of a specific object) is an instance of the former, whereas anxiety is an instance of the latter, as we shall see when we examine, in chapter 9, Heidegger's thought on this topic. As instances of such a basic disposition, Strasser also lists liveliness, depression, emptiness, cheerfulness, vigor, anger, and happiness.[14]

Wondering about what kind of basic disposition characterizes religious experience, Morelli points out that on the fourth level the quality of consciousness can undergo a radical intensification:

> Moral consciousness is a heightened consciousness in relation to the preceding levels, but it also has the inherent potential for

even greater intensification. As we learn in Chapter 20 in *Insight* and in Chapter 4 in *Method,* the introduction of the habits of charity, hope, and faith transforms our knowing, deciding, and feeling. "Being in love with God is the basic fulfilment of our conscious intentionality" (*Method in Theology,* 105). The intensity of this transformed consciousness is suggested by Lonergan's references to the experience of deep-set joy, radical peace, and the mysterium fascinans et tremendum.[15]

In our next chapter, we shall ask about the basic feel pertaining to this transformed consciousness that Lonergan equates with mysticism.

CONCLUDING REMARKS

Let us recapitulate. Of our two kinds of consciousness, intentionality (consciousness-of) is the more obvious. Fundamentally outward, its impulse consists in intending the world and relating its parts. The other kind of consciousness (consciousness-in) is usually found in the former. Ordinary consciousness-in is part and parcel of intentionality. But, as our next chapter will demonstrate, there is an exception: mystical consciousness.

Our flow of consciousness is essentially dual. On the one hand, we intend objects; on the other hand, we consciously intend them. Through our operations we develop consciousness. We are conscious in our acts. Concomitant with our activities is consciousness; the two are co-given. Consciousness is not an additional phenomenon apart from our activities. Therefore, with Andrew Beards, we can express the two sides of the same reality by speaking of a "conscious experience." Having given the example of looking at a tree, he writes,

> There is an awareness or consciousness of the tree which I do experience. For if there were not, how could I advert to my prior conscious experience of looking at the tree in order to answer the question put to me "What were you doing just then?"[16]

In itself consciousness is preverbal, that is, unobjectified. But as soon as we advert to it, consciousness becomes awareness. In addition to Lonergan and the other thinkers introduced so far, another author, D. C. Dennett very clearly articulates the distinction between these two words. He begins by noting the Intentional (curiously spelled with a capital I) and non-Intentional uses that are made of the adjectives "conscious" and "aware":

On the Intentional side, we speak of being conscious *of* this or that, aware *of* this or that, aware *that* such and such is the case, and—less naturally—conscious *that* such and such is the case. On the non-Intentional side, we speak of being just plain conscious or unconscious, and of being a conscious form of life, and, in rather artificial speech, of someone's simply being aware, in the sense of being "on the *qui vive*" or sensitive to the current situation.[17]

He then proposes "to group all and only the Intentional senses of our two words under 'aware', and all and only the non-Intentional senses under 'conscious'."[18] As early as in my Introduction, I have followed this recommendation, albeit in a more particular case, that is, for the sake of marking the transition between being conscious and being aware of that consciousness.

Dennett does not envision the possibility that the non-intentional consciousness could become a special form of intentional awareness. Yet, as we found out with Lonergan, once pure consciousness has become aware of itself, the next spontaneous step is to wonder about this awareness, to identify and name the acts and states permeated with consciousness. As Hans-Georg Gadamer puts it, "there is an act of reflecting that, in the fulfillment of an 'intention,' bends back, as it were, on the process itself."[19] Out of a desire to understand, we endeavor to catch on to what we are doing when we consciously live, namely, to catch on to our various modes of consciousness. Therefore we reflect upon our conscious activities and succeed in situating them in meaningful sequences. Since we want to grasp our own consciousness, this process is called "reflexive." In regard to one's consciousness, one is reflexive before becoming fully reflective. Reflexivity emerges halfway between pure consciousness and reflection. Only at the end of the inquiry does reflection culminate in a judgment about the structure of human consciousness.

Thus, as was pointed out earlier, reflexivity is a kind of reflection. The latter characterizes any intentional process. But whenever one applies one's intentional capacity to awareness and asks questions about the data of awareness, such a reflective dynamism happens to be also reflexive. Intentional consciousness bends back on pure consciousness. It is reflexive in the sense of self-understanding and self-affirmation; it is reflective as part of the general effort to understand and affirm reality.

All the thinkers who have wondered whether human consciousness can be somehow brought to expression have stumbled upon a paradox. How can subjectivity be made objective? Doesn't objectifying amount to betraying the essentially subjective? Jacques Maritain affirms:

> Subjectivity *as subjectivity* is inconceptualisable; is an unknowable abyss. It is unknowable by the mode of notion, concept, or representation, or by any mode of any science whatsoever—introspection, psychology, or philosophy. How could it be otherwise, seeing that every reality known through a concept, a notion, or a representation is known as object and not as subject?[20]

Because he construes knowledge as conceptualization, Jacques Maritain exaggerates the unknowability of human subjectivity, of which one has only "a virtual and ineffable knowledge, a vital and existential knowledge of the totality immanent in each of its parts" (70). I want to take exception to his twofold assertion that subjectivity consists in an ineffable knowledge. On the contrary, it is a consciousness (not a knowledge, since knowledge is obtained only in judgment) and it can be expressed (hence it is not ineffable). In my opinion Maritain's conceptualism makes him unduly oppose subjective awareness and objectification.[21]

He is less wide of the mark, however, when he distinguishes individual and universal self-knowledge. "It is in relation to the individuality itself of the subject . . . that objectisation [sic] is false to the subject" (80). I noted this point in a previous book, when I stated that the very individuality of personal experience cannot be conceptually reproduced, although it can be evoked through literary or artistic devices.[22] Therefore, thematizing should not vainly try to duplicate consciousness as lived. In other words, consciousness as individually experienced is not captured by objectification. Maritain adds, "On the other hand, in relation to its essential structures, the subject is in no wise betrayed when it is made object" (80). By essential structures he means the scholastic account of the soul, its potencies, its properties, and so forth. As we saw, Lonergan has rephrased this account in the contemporary terms of intentionality analysis.

Most of the authors we have studied so far think that, at least to a degree, consciousness can be brought to expression. And yet the aforementioned paradox remains. As noted by Helminiak, our language, which has been fashioned by intentionality, is an awkward tool when we apply it to consciousness. Since its data are different from the data of sense, consciousness, as well as the "I" behind it, cannot be observed.

The psychiatrist Arthur Deikman insists on the uniqueness of what he calls "the observing self." He stresses "the fact that the observing self is an anomaly, not an object, like everything else." It is "not part of the object world," "of a different order from everything else." Therefore "the observing self can be known but not located, not 'seen.'"[23] And the

Swiss phenomenologist Pierre Thévenaz pronounces, "Consciousness of self is not the appearance of a new *object* to consciousness, nor the sudden looming up of a pure or transcendental ego, but a becoming aware of self."[24]

Prior though it is to any self-concept, this "becoming aware of self" does not rule out self-imaging and self-objectification. At the philosophical stage of what Sartre calls "reflecting consciousness," the concept of the transcendental ego is validly obtained as a condition of possibility of consciousness and of the continuity of the conscious self. More will be said on this topic in our chapter on the self.

Finally, we can say, with Illtyd Trethowan, "It is awareness, then, in the first place, that makes us human persons. And it is always a self-awareness."[25] Consciousness is a person's being present to the world and to oneself. As Lonergan and Crosby insist, consciousness has various psychic and ontological degrees. At best, it permeates interpersonal knowing and loving. This is the apex of what I have termed ordinary consciousness. But we cannot rest here. Too many impressive human beings have underlined the significance of another form of consciousness, to which we now turn.

CHAPTER 3

Accounts of Mystical Consciousness

This chapter begins with useful clarifications by Robert Forman concerning both ordinary consciousness and the field of pure consciousness events. Then we examine how Lonergan extends his views on consciousness into the realm of transcendence. Finally the contribution of three interesting thinkers are introduced: Sebastian Moore, James Price, and David Granfield, who develop Lonergan's ideas on mysticism.

FORMAN ON PURE CONSCIOUSNESS EVENTS

Forman has edited two remarkable books on mysticism, to which a third, entirely his own, has been added more recently.[1] He and the other contributors attempt to rebut the "constructivist" approach taken by Stephen Katz and others. Since elsewhere I have expressed my sympathy with Forman's position and offered my own discussion of the constructivist stance, I shall not repeat what I wrote there. The readers can find in a previous book of mine both a recognition of good points in Katz's thesis, and arguments against the constructivist contention that everything in religious experience is mediated by cultural forms.[2] In this section I will rather pay attention to two valuable items offered by Forman: the well-documented fact of pure consciousness events and the less underscored but nevertheless paramount fact of knowledge by identity.

In his Introduction to *The Problem of Pure Consciousness*, Forman points out that there are countless reports of "pure consciousness events" (PCE), which he defines as "wakeful contentless consciousness" (21). In fact many reports could be added to the ones his volumes contain. But the three narratives that are cited in his first book suffice to characterize PCE. The first report states: "I experienced a silent inner state of no thoughts; just pure awareness and nothing else" (27). The second report records "a sort of complete silence void of content. The whole awareness would turn in, and there would be no thought, no activity, and no perception, yet it was somehow comforting." And further on: "this inner space was not an emptiness but simply silent consciousness without content or activity, and I began to recognize in it the essence of my own self as pure consciousness" (27). The third report is even more phenomenologically instructive than the first two:

> I had been meditating alone in my room all morning when someone knocked on my door. I heard the knock perfectly clearly, and upon hearing it I knew that, although there was no "waking up" before hearing the knock, for some indeterminate length of time prior to the knocking I had not been aware of anything in particular. I had been awake but with no content for my consciousness. Had no one knocked I doubt that I would ever have become aware that I had not been thinking or perceiving (28).

The second narrative, which mentions the realization that the thoughtless awareness is "somehow comforting," confirms the significance of the affective side of pure consciousness, underlined in our previous chapters. And the third narrative, which affirms a state of being awake without being aware of anything in particular, concurs with an insistence of Sebastian Moore's, as we shall see presently.

Given that at the end of my Introduction I have affirmed that mystical consciousness is not essentially *an* experience, readers may want to ask if Forman is well inspired when he speaks of pure consciousness *events*. In my opinion they are events or experiences inasmuch as they occupy a definite stretch of time: the experiencer remembers having had, for a while, a state of consciousness remarkably different from ordinary consciousness. However, as we shall find out with virtually all the thinkers introduced in this inquiry, mystical consciousness is more than an event or an experience. It is an empty and yet dynamic state which takes over the mystic's soul independently of her or his will and remains there permanently, whether or not accompanied by specific thoughts, affects, or actions.

In his Introduction to *The Innate Capacity*, Forman makes a persuading case for the existence in human beings of an innate capacity for PCE (8–12 and 31). He solidly bases his thesis upon claims of innateness found in mystical texts. The capacity in question is "not something acquired from outside, learned, or even thought," but "something inherent or prelinguistic within us" (11). What Forman uncovers corresponds with what Husserl and Lonergan call the transcendental structure of consciousness.

Forman offers very helpful observations on consciousness as awareness per se, which may or may not be aware of anything at all (13, 16, 17). He warns us that it is a mistake to construe such consciousness after the model of intentional consciousness (14–15). He finds that mystical texts testify to "the subject's sheerest awareness itself . . . , unalloyed with the usual intentional content" (13).

Forman comes very close to Lonergan and Helminiak in his section entitled "Of Knowledge by Identity" (18–24), completed by "Remembering Pure Consciousness Events" (24–27). His perceptive remarks on knowledge by identity constitute, in my opinion, a brilliant contribution to the understanding of mysticism. His thesis is that "we know what it means to be conscious *by virtue of being conscious.*" Consciousness is a fundamental datum, the experience of which amounts to "a firsthand familiarity with it" (19). Anything we can say about it constitutes a knowledge that must be assessed in reference to that basic datum. "The final arbiter of any theory or so-called fact of consciousness is my own intimate acquaintance with what it is to be conscious" (20).

In addition to William James's *knowledge-by-acquaintance* and *knowledge-about*, which are intentional, "our knowledge of our own consciousness represents a third major form of knowledge. I call it *knowledge-by-identity*. In knowledge-by-identity the subject knows something by virtue of being it" (21). Consciousness is essential to being a subject. Therefore one cannot physically point to it, like in an ostensive definition. "I cannot hand you your own consciousness and say, 'Here this is what I mean.' I must count on the fact that you know what it is to be conscious in the same direct and reflexive way that I do" (21–22).

Very well explained though all this is, Forman nevertheless lacks Lonergan's precision regarding the passage from consciousness to awareness in the process of objectification. Pace Forman, consciousness itself is not reflexive. Reflexivity and objectification come later, when one adverts to one's consciousness. Forman does not clearly enough distinguish consciousness from reflexive awareness. As soon as consciousness is detected, it becomes awareness, namely, my experience of being conscious.

Forman asserts, "Other than the knowledge I have of my own awareness, I know of no other cases of knowledge-by-identity" (22). This is surprising, given the age-old tradition initiated by Aristotle on this topic. According to Aristotle, followed by Plotinus, Thomas Aquinas, and Lonergan, knowledge-by-identity consists in the intentional phenomenon of the known being identical with the knower in the latter's mind. This identity goes along with the ontic difference between the object and the knowing subject. But Forman's single case has to do with another aspect of human activity: the fact that consciousness is endemic to the subject's very life.

Without referring to Brentano and Husserl, Forman conveys important tenets that are theirs also. For instance, Brentano's assertion that inner perception is indubitable: "Although I cannot be absolutely certain exactly what I was thinking or perceiving half a minute ago, I am absolutely certain that I was conscious" (23). Another instance is, as pointed out in chapter 1, Husserl's conviction that conscious intentionality is logically, or transcendentally, prior to the reaching of any content and any naming: "For a child to learn any language at all, he or she must be conscious. Being aware, or having a consciousness, is presupposed by language acquisition, not the other way around" (23). Finally, as also noted by Husserl, the unity in a person's stream of consciousness: "awareness per se simply ties past and present together as one single continuous awareness" (24).

In contrast to Hume and James, whose views will be discussed in chapter 7, Forman shares with Lonergan the thesis that there is a single conscious self: "If we were to tie ourselves together over time and not at some unspoken level know that what is being tied together is a single thing, a single me, then we would not be able to hold the present perception as being encountered by the same awareness as was the past one" (24). Nonetheless, he differs with Lonergan in his contention that we are totally ignorant about "the mechanics of how a consciousness knows itself or ties itself together continuously through time" (24; see 23). He seems to have noticed only the "consciousness-of" in intentionality and ignored the other side of the coin, namely the "consciousness-in." With this too rudimentary account of intentionality, he concentrates solely on the pure consciousness of non-intentional events; he rightly observes that the latter is different from the former; but the contrast he draws is excessive.

At variance with Forman on this point is Lonergan who, by beginning with intentional consciousness, is able to spell out our various conscious acts and states, along the spectrum of a fourfold intentionality, as described in chapter 1 and as will be explained in some detail in the following section. Only after having developed this systematic understanding of ordinary consciousness does Lonergan present mystical consciousness. By detecting consciousness first in intentionality itself, he can philosophically differentiate its various aspects and, in a second stage, relate this account of ordinary consciousness to the special kind of consciousness found in mysticism.

In concluding this section, we must credit Forman for recognizing, in Eckhart and in others (including himself) a more complex form of religious consciousness, which he adumbrates in *The Problem of Pure Consciousness* (8–9) and examines more at length in *Mysticism, Mind, Consciousness*. There, he calls it "the dualistic mystical state" (DMS) and he defines it as "an unchanging interior silence that is maintained concurrently with intentional experience in a long-term or permanent way" (151; see 131–167). Perhaps "dual" or "twofold" would characterize this mystical state better than the adjective "dualistic," which connotes separation between pure and intentional consciousness. At any rate, we may want to keep this duality in mind later in this chapter, especially when we come across Price's intimate relating of the mystical and the religious.

THE REALM OF TRANSCENDENCE ACCORDING TO LONERGAN

Lonergan's epistemology carries momentous implications for the philosophy of mysticism. An assumption often mars the contemporary discussion of whether mystical experiences are immediate or mediated. They are valid, one supposes, if they are immediate in the sense of sensory or suprasensory perceptions. This perceptual character seems to accord with the directness that the word "experience" suggests. But Lonergan's account of consciousness helps us to move away from our natural fascination with the perceptual and the widespread perceptualist model.[3]

In contradistinction with sensory immediacy, the immediacy that grounds self-knowledge derives not from the data of sense, but from the data of consciousness—two different kinds of "experience," according to Lonergan. Thus consciousness accompanies all our operations. It is mediated in the measure that, as soon as it begins to be accounted for, it is already shaped by language; at the same time it is also immediate, because it is directly given to us in the awareness we have of our own acts and states. Likewise, as Lonergan explains in *Method in Theology*, the prayerfulness of the mystic is mediated inasmuch as it takes on its significance from previously established beliefs, insights, and decisions, while it is immediate as constituting a withdrawal from the objectified world in order to move into a "cloud of unknowing" (77, 112, 266, 342).

Reflection on the consciousness attendant upon our human operations is the key to the exploration of this inner-directed kind of mediated immediacy. What we find here are two dimensions of interiority. Lonergan calls the first one, "interiority" or "other interiority" (266), to distinguish it from "religious interiority" (290), to which he more frequently refers as "transcendence" or "religion." Religious interiority is a furtherance of the "other interiority" (the consciousness that accompanies all our acts and states).

For Lonergan, the unmediated immediacy experienced by infants does not provide an adequate model of knowledge and reality, since it is sensory. What humans encounter directly is not the fully real, because it has not yet been questioned and verified. Sense data are only one step in the process leading to objectivity. Reality can be accessed solely through sets of operations comprised of experiences, memories, questions, insights, and judgments. Such operations are the constituents of mediated immediacy. When objectified, they offer us an adequate model of the way we reach out to reality. Then it becomes clear that the world mediated by meaning is not the "already out there now." It is easy to commit the blunder of imagining the religious realm as an object experienced in another kind of contact or perception, as an "already in here now."[4] To escape from this error, one must extirpate the tenacious myth that infantile presence to the environment is our best link to reality. Nothing less than an intellectual conversion is required if one is to uncover that illusion and proceed to another account of human knowledge (238–240 and 262–263).

Although Lonergan does not explicitly say so, all he writes about mediated immediacy suggests an enormous difference between the union that takes shape among humans and the one that characterizes the mystic and the divine. The first kind of union—the fellow-feeling found in sex, sports, music, and other sorts of unitive activities—is embodied in sensory perception and movement. Therefore, it is a return to the first immediacy, typical of children. And because this kind of union is also experienced by adults, it is mediated by meaning and value. In contradistinction, the mystical union, though prepared by perception, meaning and value, nevertheless transcends these activities by negating their limits and by heading towards what is infinite in meaning and value. In other words, interhuman union is mediation going *back* to the first immediacy, whereas mystical union is mediation going *beyond* itself and entering a second immediacy.[5]

This second form of mediated immediacy is inward. It consists in the consciousness that traverses all our acts and affective states. As previously noted, Lonergan calls it "interiority." This interiority is not necessarily religious. Although it can become religious as soon as it acknowledges a relationship with the transcendent, human interiority is in itself secular, since its interactions begin with finite realities. Human interiority encompasses both the consciousness that accompanies all our acts and states, and the consciousness that accompanies our openness to the infinite. Lonergan sees the latter, mystical consciousness, as the prolongation of the former, which is consciousness in the world.

Again it is easy to collapse the inward immediacy into the outward one. How do they differ from each other? Whereas the outward immediacy is perceptual, the inward immediacy characterizes our whole intentionality, including its openness to the transcendent. We are immediately conscious throughout the four levels of our intentionality.

According to Lonergan, on the fourth level of intentionality we find values, both secular and transcendent. As contradistinguished from meaning and truth, attained on the second and the third levels, values trigger affective responses. Among such responses are feelings that are not transient, but relatively permanent. Those stable feelings are affective states or dispositions (think of Aristotle's concept of virtue, principally of friendship). The most basic of such human dispositions is the state of being in love. Such being-in-love may characterize a human relationship. It can also constitute the kind of religious disposition that is unconditional and unrestricted. Thus Lonergan writes:

> Being in love with God, as experienced, is being in love in an unrestricted fashion. All love is self-surrender, but being in love with God is being in love without limits or qualifications or conditions or reservations. Just as unrestricted questioning is our capacity for self-transcendence, so being in love in an unrestricted fashion is the proper fulfilment of that capacity (105–106).

Adding that such being-in-love is "not the product of our knowing and choosing," he distinguishes two phases in this dynamic state. In the first phase, it is conscious without being known; in the second phase, it is both conscious and known. By "being known," Lonergan means being intended through questioning and being objectified. He sums up his position as follows:

> To say that this dynamic state is conscious is not to say that it is known. For consciousness is just experience, but knowledge is a compound of experience, understanding, and judging. Because the dynamic state is conscious without being known, it is an experience of mystery (106).

MOORE ON THE "HOW" OF CONSCIOUSNESS

In an article written early in his life, the English Benedictine Sebastian Moore highlights the consciousness that the human subject possesses. This consciousness is of greater significance than the consciousness one has of objects: "The search for truth means, for me, not the attempt to understand better *what* is over there but the attempt to become more conscious."[6] The "what" of consciousness is less important than its "how."

The "how" of consciousness is comparable to the light of the mind: "We look at things in the light, not at the light." Like consciousness, light adds no new object to existing objects; what it does is to allow objects to appear. Thus usually light serves to make objects visible. However, sometimes people become interested in the light for its own sake. "Turner got to the stage of painting pretty well pure light. In the late pictures, the things are for the light, not the light for the things" (308).

In Moore's insightful piece, we find many gems like those just mentioned. They are pithy, lapidary sentences. For instance, the increase of awareness prompts the following insight: "I am not conscious of more, but more conscious" (311). And again, to characterize consciousness: "It is not something that comes to us, but something we come to. Things happen to us, but we happen on consciousness." The author adds: "This is not a playing with words, but an attempt to do justice to the witness of the mystic who knows, obscurely, in the moment of realization, 'here I have always been'" (312). Accordingly, God makes sense, not "as an object of consciousness," but "as the wholeness of consciousness" (314).

Moore ends his article with another clue:

> When St. Paul says that eye hath not seen nor ear heard nor hath it entered into the heart of man, what God has prepared for those that love him, he is saying far more than "it's better than you think". He is pointing to the vision, in which we see in God, not from ourselves (324).

In the increase of awareness that characterizes full enlightenment, we no longer see from ourselves exclusively, but in God, in the sense that our awareness partakes of the divine self-consciousness.

In one of his later books, Moore writes:

> The expression "self-awareness" suggests having myself as the *object* of my awareness. It really means the opposite of this: myself as the *subject* of awareness. Self-awareness is something

I bring, and have to bring, to every act of thought or feeling or decision.[7]

Moore here calls "self-awareness" what Lonergan usually calls "consciousness." Yet as a Lonergan scholar, Moore would not disagree with the restriction of "self-awareness" (in Lonergan's sense) to the moment in which advertence to oneself succeeds simple consciousness. Moreover, as we found out in Lonergan, self-awareness is the beginning of the process of self-objectification. In the preceding chapter I have tackled the gnoseological difficulties involved in this process. But Moore's point is worth noting: prior to reflection, consciousness is not an object, but one's own living subjectivity, experienced in "every act of thought or feeling or decision."

Moore helpfully distinguishes three kinds of "knowing" (a knowing which, in each case, is prior to knowledge). "First knowing is a simple knowing*ness* of nothing in particular." "Second knowing is always of something definite." This second knowing is what Brentano and others call intentionality. Insofar as the third kind is concerned, we are told: "Meditation techniques attempt to get us into a *third* way, of *being* in our first knowing" (10). And again:

> Through creative solitude and inner silence, meditation and centring prayer, we learn a capacity in ourselves for attending to what seems to be nothing but is really the nothing-in-particular which is God. Centring prayer is a technique for giving breathing-space to a desire in us for we know not what, which is the cause of desire (55; see 65).

The first knowing is of nothing in particular and hence pure consciousness, distinguishable, though ordinarily linked up with, the intending of specific objects (second knowing). And the third knowing takes up the first mode of knowing while adding a higher degree to it. As we shall discover shortly, Price establishes the same connections.

Moore also underscores the affective side of consciousness:

> Now if self-awareness precedes and undergirds all *thinking* about myself, if I *consciously am* before I am able to say that I am this or that, then also I *consciously want* before I am able to say that I want this or that. As all my thinking about myself and my life depends upon a prior presence of myself to myself, so all my desiring depends on a prior *affective* presence of myself to myself.

He sums it up as follows: "As my basic *awareness* of myself grounds all that I come to *know*, so my basic *love* of myself grounds all that I come to *want*" (15). Moore has the merit of having shown that consciousness is not a neutral knowing, but a knowing permeated with feeling. There is a feel to one's being conscious. In other words, being conscious is at once knowing and feeling. As Moore puts it: "The self, feeling, is the self felt" (17).

Finally, quoting from Eric Voegelin, Moore brings out the fact that far from being disincarnate and individualistic, consciousness is "bodily located" in concrete persons who share in a communion of conscious being (52). A few pages later, this time quoting from Jacob Needleman, Moore points out that consciousness becomes visible in a person's eyes, for example, in the eyes of a boy who got excited with a real question (59).

PRICE ON BARE CONSCIOUSNESS

In an article on twentieth-century typologies of mysticism, James Price argues that they all have the same defect: they construe mystical experience as an "experience of," as having an object (for instance, the self, or God). The basis for classification is the "doctrinal" language utilized in the descriptions that are examined. Price contends that this approach leads to an impasse. Those who have tried to classify them according to the way they are *interpreted* have spun out an intractably complex web. Therefore, following Lonergan, he points to another route, which starts with seeing religious events as products of human consciousness. Instead of working with the doctrinal concepts, one focuses on the operations of consciousness.[8]

Price rightly repudiates the approach he dubs "doctrinal." Perhaps he should have eschewed the connotation of a dogmatic stance and called it "themes-centered" since it concentrates on symbols and ideas. All the same, I agree with him that there is a way to avoid excessive conceptual complexity in discussing mystical experiences. This way consists in focusing on the cross-cultural consciousness that gives rise to those experiences.

Some of Moore's most important thoughts on consciousness and mysticism recur in the writings of James Price. In another article, entitled "Transcendence and Images," talking about Dionysius's "overwhelming light," Price asks: "What is disclosed in that overwhelming light? We may never know in this lifetime. But the point here isn't the *what*, it's the *how*."[9] He stands in perfect agreement with Moore.

Yet he goes a little further as he distinguishes between bare consciousness and mystical consciousness.

> Bare consciousness is the state traditionally identified with the apophatic state. It is consciousness which is devoid of both operations and objects. In the state of bare consciousness, the subject is conscious, alert, aware, but not conscious *of* anything. There are no objects because the operations of consciousness that we normally employ in knowing and acting upon objects have been stilled (198).

Bare consciousness is related to, but not identical with, mystical consciousness, which is "a state in which an explicit awareness of union with the transcendent emerges" (198). In the latter, "the operation of consciousness itself is not simply stilled; it is reconfigured" (199).

Drawing from Eckhart, Price remarks, "The mystic becomes explicitly aware of, present to, consciously one with the source or ground of consciousness itself." Shortly I will discuss the fact that the mystic is consciously one with the source. For the moment, I will just note that Eckhart would disagree with the adjective "explicitly aware"; as I shall demonstrate in the chapter on Eckhart, he insists that the perfect unity amounts to a total self-oblivion.

This oneness is the result of "a reconfiguration or transformation of the operation of the mystic's consciousness." Price explains the transformation as follows: "The mystic's consciousness becomes conformed to, or mediated by, the operation of the transcendent ground itself. In Aquinas's language, it begins to operate with the simplicity of the divine intelligence" (199). A full-grown philosophy of God and theology of grace underpins Price's rendering of Eckhart. Since it would be premature to unpack it at this stage, we shall wait until we discuss Eckhart's views.

The important thing to notice is the series of terms that Price distinguishes (200): intentional consciousness (which we found in Brentano, Husserl, and Lonergan), religious consciousness (kataphatic, that is, mediated by images and ideas), bare consciousness (apophatic, that is, without operations and without objects), mystical consciousness (bare consciousness as participative in divine life), and the ground of consciousness (namely God). Both intentional and religious consciousness (Moore's second knowing) carry contents. Bare consciousness (Moore's first knowing) is contentless. And mystical consciousness (Moore's third knowing) is bare consciousness elevated by grace. Noteworthy also is the fact that in Price's list of basic terms, God is not envisioned as the supreme Object, but as the ground of consciousness (200).[10]

I welcome those systematic terms and relations, and I hope readers will find them helpful. In an earlier article, Price tackles two of those basic terms: mystical and religious consciousness. They correspond with "two discrete moments of religious experience," namely, "the gift of God's love" and "being in love with God, that is, the human response to this gift."[11] Although we do not find this explicit distinction in Lonergan, it nonetheless matches his acceptance of Thomas Aquinas's distinction between operative and cooperative grace: the former being the gift and the latter being the human response.

For Price, Lonergan's characterization of the realm of transcendence as the experience of being unrestrictedly in love supports its differentiation into two aspects: the mystical and the religious. To explain this differentiation, Price employs consciousness as a criterion. In the mystical mode, intentionality is inoperative: there is no question, no intellectual operation, no decision, only an affective state. In the religious mode, intentionality emerges: the individual asks questions about what has happened. In particular, he or she wonders if this affective state is to be consented to; and he or she may decide to respond wholeheartedly.

Then mystical consciousness could amount to Forman's pure consciousness event, whereas religious consciousness would constitute the existential ambience in which mysticism is situated, fostered, and related to everyday life. My sole reservation concerning Price's treatment is that he ascribes object-like content to mystical consciousness. For example, he claims that it is "intersubjective" (169); it also seems to include the judgment "I am you" (171) or the realization by mystics that they are receiving "God's gift of his love" (169). But if, in the case of *mystical* consciousness, intentionality is inoperative, surely this mode of consciousness cannot provide the mystic with the knowledge that the experience is intersubjective or that the union is so intimate that the "I" becomes the "you" or the "we." All such awareness amounts to a beginning of objectification and therefore belongs to what Price rightly considers to be *religious* consciousness.

Accordingly, in "Transcendence and Images," the second article of Price's to which I have referred in this section, I find ambiguous his characterization of the mystic as "explicitly aware of, present to, consciously one with the source or ground of consciousness itself" (199). In chapter 6, section entitled "Three Kinds of Consciousness," I shall have occasion to discuss Schleiermacher's view, here picked up by Price, that the experience of utter dependence requires a "Whence." However, if with both Lonergan and Price, we endeavor to speak the language of interiority, not of theory, then all we can say about mysticism is that it consists in consciously being in love unrestrictedly. By contrast, being "explicitly aware of, present to" a source or a ground involves intentionality, thinking, thematic appreciation, and so belongs to *religious* consciousness.

GRANFIELD ON THE MYSTICAL DIFFERENCE

In a book on mystical consciousness, the Benedictine David Granfield emphatically asserts the presence of a divine consciousness in us. He also goes a long way towards accounting for it. He commences his explanation with the fact that conscious intentionality is orientated to the infinite. The unrestricted openness of the human mind "enables the subject . . . to become conscious of itself in its orientation to God."[12] I understand him to be saying that the subject is aware of its intentional quest for absolute meaning and love. This conscious thrust towards the infinite constitutes the first step of mysticism.

There is an affective side to this quest. In the face of temporal goods and created beauty, one undergoes a bittersweet reaction and one feels dissatisfied, melancholy, ever longing for more (59–60). Then there takes place in the soul what Gregory of Nyssa calls an *epectasy*, a "stretching forth," a pressing towards the mark in the spiritual race (176).

In conjunction with this affective side of our orientation to God, the apophatic denial of everything as possibly substituting for the infinite mediates what becomes divine consciousness in us. The apophatic distancing with regard to finite objects prepares the way for the reception of divine consciousness. We consciously share in divine consciousness thanks to "the gift of divine energy" (45; see 144–145).

Three components seem to be involved here: (1) the human spirit's unrestricted openness, which is at once intellectual and affective; (2) the apophatic exclusion of everything as not being God, which brings about a void in the human soul; and (3) the filling of this emptiness with the fullness of divine life. Each of these components is conscious. Throughout these stages the religious person experiences not "a mindless vacuity" (although the emptiness has to be felt), but "a loving watchfulness" (178–179; see 109).

Granfield's analysis is underpinned by the same distinction as Moore's between first and third knowing, and as Price's between bare and mystical consciousness. For all these writers, the pure, apophatic, or contentless consciousness is the receptacle, so to speak, of divine consciousness. Granfield warns us, however, that having a share in divine consciousness does not amount to identifying human nature with the divine (146).

But how does our partaking of divine nature become humanly conscious? Since the apophatic attitude performatively stresses the inadequacy of our images and concepts regarding God, bare consciousness amounts to an awareness of nothingness. Yet such emptiness is nothing other than our openness to the holy mystery. But thanks to the divine gift, our "emptied" consciousness has been heightened and as a result is at the same time a loving consciousness.

> If we remove all forms and images from our minds so that we seem to have opened ourselves to God, we have not yet fully expanded our minds; we have merely emptied them as far as knowing is concerned. An intelligent mind can arrive at the conviction that God transcends its capability for knowing, and can reject the use of created forms and images. It can even go farther by being aware of this transcending through a conscious opening of the mind—not just rejecting a concept or image but going beyond them, beyond the very notion of the created. But this is only a necessary step in the right direction; the unitive strength comes from loving. There is no true mysticism without love (177–178).

Thus, for Granfield as well as for Lonergan, mystical consciousness consists precisely in a participating in divine consciousness: "The human subject is aware, through the power of the Spirit, of being loved infinitely and of loving totally" (180).

CONCLUDING REMARKS

One of the significant gains of this chapter is the connection between pure consciousness, detached from object-directed intentionality, and mystical consciousness. Mystical experience occurs in an objectless consciousness and yet includes more. This "more" is the element of infinite lovingness.

The emptiness of pure or bare consciousness must be elucidated. Does the fact that emptiness involves no object also imply that there is no reality in it? Here is Granfield's answer: "God is positive nothingness; he is no-thing, but he is not nothing. We cannot know God's essence in itself; but we can know it to be real" (90). In chapter 5 we shall see that this position conforms with that of Eckhart. Karl Rahner is also helpful here, as he mentions that Ignatius of Loyola's consolation without a cause is an "experience of transcendence as such, . . . an experience which is 'without object' (non-conceptual), though not without content."[13] Divine reality is present, albeit as an unspecified content.

In this chapter, we have seen how Lonergan, Moore, Price, and Granfield emphasize the affective nature of mysticism. I will conclude with the beautiful formulation of Herman F. Suligoj, who concentrates on the experience of identity in the mystical life:

> When Identity is experienced in the process of awareness, an emotional deautomatization occurs; there is simply a positive general mood, without specific emotions, for there are no specific contents. In the experiences of Identity in which the process of awareness becomes identical with the contents of awareness, a strong affective quality which we described as an actively receptive neutrality seems to surface and permeate our awareness as the latter identifies with its contents. . . . With emotional neutrality come peace, harmony, a rationally inexplicable positive mood in face of life's obvious contingencies, and a gradual detachment from all those values which tend to inflate the social ego. . . .[14]

Besides conveying the affective side of mystical experience, this text also links it with the fact that there are no *specific* contents. Yet, as the author states, there is content. But in the kind of consciousness he is referring to, such content is identical with the very process of awareness. His observation confirms Forman's remarks on mysticism as being a knowledge by identity, as well as Rahner's and Lonergan's statement that Ignatius Loyola's "consolation without a cause" means "consolation with a content but without an object."[15]

PART II

Three Classics

CHAPTER 4

Plotinus: Consciousness beyond Consciousness

Neoplatonic writings hold rewards of many kinds for those who want to fathom mystical consciousness. In this part, three authors of genius who belong to that tradition have been selected: Plotinus, Eckhart, and Schleiermacher. The first lived in late Antiquity and wrote in Greek; the second lived in the Middle Ages and wrote both in Latin and in German; the third lived in the early nineteenth century and, like his contemporary Schelling, whose philosophy deeply marked him, was endowed with a Neoplatonic religious sensibility.[1] At that time, excerpts from Eckhart were circulated and enthusiastically received by the German Romantics, to whose circle Schleiermacher belonged.[2] It is probably through Schelling that Schleiermacher absorbed some of the views propounded by Plotinus and Eckhart.

Plotinus (205–270), who resided in Alexandria and in Rome, merely wanted to be a disciple of Plato and to explicate what the founder of the Academy had left implicit in his thought. In the course of this process, however, Plotinus became a very original philosopher as well. Although he remained aloof from communal worship, he was extremely religious and his vocabulary was influenced by the mystery cults of the Greco-Roman world, for instance "the ascension and descension of souls, purification, sanctuary imagery, . . . [t]he famous final phrase of VI.9, 'flight of the alone to the alone',"[3] or the vision of a great light.[4]

He proposes a threefold ascent—moral, rational and mystical—towards the One. The person who wishes to acquire wisdom has first to purify himself or herself and to grow in virtue. Second, he or she must engage in dialectical exercises and develop a new interpretation of reality. Third, the individual can open him- or herself to unification with the One.

Plotinus envisages the philosophical guidelines that he offers to his companions as a preparation for mystical union. Accordingly, before talking about his account of religious experience, we must introduce his thought structure, which displays a remarkable architectonic beauty, regardless of whether one agrees with it or not. We need at least a sketchy outline of his metaphysics of participation.

A GRAND WORLDVIEW

Plotinus's fundamental schema includes a hierarchy consisting of matter (at the lowest level) and three hypostases: Soul, Intellect, and the One. We must avoid conceiving of these three as entities which would be spatially separate. Rather, they are distinct and yet interpenetrating layers of reality. This interpenetration depends on the fact that the higher hypostases bestow being and light upon the lower. "The First, then, should be compared to light, the next, to the sun, and the third, to the celestial body of the moon, which gets its light from the sun" (V.6.4).[5] Hence the physical body receives life from the soul, while the soul partakes of the higher degree of being that Intellect enjoys, and while Intellect has a share in the more perfect unity that the One possesses.

With the exception of the One, the hypostases are not all of a kind. Instead, of both Soul and Intellect we must say that each in its own manner is a continuum of different levels of awareness. Soul, for instance, successively engages in sensory, rational, and intuitive activities.[6] Intellect, which possesses self-knowledge, can also be united with the One. For Plotinus the goal of human existence consists in reaching up to the maximum degree of life: "what is really worth aspiring to for us is our selves, bringing themselves back for themselves to the best of themselves" (VI.7.30). "But we exist more when we turn to him [the One] and our well-being is there, but being far from him is nothing else but existing less" (VI.9.9).

Salvation amounts to an ascent towards the Good, or the One, who allures all beings to himself (Plotinus uses the masculine and also occasionally calls him God, or the Father). Thus mysticism, namely union with the Good, is located at the last stage in Plotinus's grand schema. His metaphysics coherently encompasses psychology (or the doctrine of the soul), epistemology (or the theory of knowledge), and mysticism (or the personal experience of the divine that an individual can have and that Plotinus himself did have, as will become evident later in this chapter).

The individual soul imparts being, life, and movement to a body. As attached to a body it can be called the lower soul. And yet, thanks to its capacity for reasoning, the soul elicits acts that have a broader scope than the mere sensory and appetitive acts. Distinguishing between seeing or hearing on the one hand, and intellectual operations on the other, is part and parcel of a process of education which enables the soul to break loose from being confined to the function it exercises in respect of the body. The higher soul has access to the level of contemplation (*theoria*) by discovering the basic principles it receives from Intellect. It partakes of Intellect inasmuch as it contemplates the Platonic forms or basic categories such as Being, Otherness, Sameness, Motion, and Rest (V.1.4), which are all reconciled in Intellect's unitary comprehension.

The individual soul expands its cognitive ability by coming under the influence of Intellect. Not only does it derive its existence and its capacity for "discursive reasonings" from its "upper neighbour" (the Intellect), but it is also "an image of Intellect," "the expressed thought of Intellect" (V.1.3) so far as Intellect illuminates it.

> Our soul then also is a divine thing and of a nature different [from the things of sense], like the universal nature of soul; and the human soul is perfect when it has Intellect; and Intellect is of two kinds, the one which reasons and the one which makes it possible to reason (V.1.10).

Since the discursive rules that it naturally applies do not come from itself, the soul realizes that there must be "something better than itself, which does not seek, but totally possesses" (V.3.4). This "something better," namely, Intellect, has a more unitary way of working than discursive reasoning has, since it does not have to take successive steps. "Intellect and intellection are one; and it thinks as a whole with the whole of itself, not one part of itself with another" (V.3.6). In other words Intellect's coming to know is not progressive or discursive, but always unrestricted and complete. Speaking Aristotelian language, Plotinus explains that "this Intellect is not potential"; instead "it is actuality" (V.3.5).

What does Intellect grasp in a single embrace? The intelligible world of all the forms or forming principles, the pattern on which concrete individuals are shaped. These are known all at once. Plotinus sees Intellect as a knower who understands all the living and intelligent forms. There is no separation between individual forms or intellects and the whole Intellect. By knowing all the forms together in itself, it knows none other than itself. Whereas the soul, as it knows, *becomes* everything, Intellect *is* everything: "the knower, the known and the knowledge are the same and all together" (VI.6.15). Intellect's unity, however, is less perfect than the One. Intellect's self-knowledge maintains a distinction between the knowing subject and the known object. Its self-awareness implies a certain epistemological duality.

A final precision is in order. Is Plotinus's "soul" the same as our modern concept of self? Plotinus has no word for "self." Instead he uses terms such as "soul" (*psyche*), "this one" (*autos*), "we" (*hêmeis*), or the reflexive *hauton*. Still he has "clear awareness of the importance of a concept of self . . . to account for the identity of a human subject at the several levels of existence possible to man."[vii] To him the self or the soul appears as fundamentally divine, albeit not infinite. Far from being static, it ever increases or decreases in the measure that it realizes or ignores its real identity. Moreover, although the boundaries between the soul and Intellect (as well as with the One) are not watertight, Plotinus assumes an ontological difference between the soul and the One. More follows on this topic.

INTELLECT'S SHARE IN THE GOOD

As the soul partakes of Intellect, so does Intellect partake of the Good. Intellect utterly depends on him: it receives from him its being and its cognitional light. Intellect has a twofold power:

> Intellect also, then, has one power for thinking, by which it looks at the things in itself, and one by which it looks at what transcends it by a concentration of attention (*epibolê*)[8] and by reception . . . . And that first one is the contemplation of Intellect in its right mind, and the other is Intellect in love, when it goes out of its mind "drunk with the nectar"; then it falls in love, simplified into happiness by having its fill; and it is better for it to be drunk with a drunkenness like this than to be more respectably sober (VI.7.35).[9]

Intellect's twofold power entails two kinds of consciousness: first the self-understanding that we described in our previous section; and second, a mystical experience that I claim, in a purposefully paradoxical contention, is a consciousness beyond consciousness. Both manifest a connection with the One. In self-knowledge Intellect realizes that its power to understand and to transmit life to souls comes from the Good. Such an intellectual awareness lies at the basis of Plotinus's metaphysics. It allows him to raise the question, can one go beyond this intellectual peak attained by thinking?

In his positive answer to this question, Plotinus highlights the affective side to the ascent towards the One. All things are attracted to the Good. Intelligent beings, however, while reaching the intellectual stage, do not stop there: "What they desire is not Intellect in so far as it is Intellect, but in so far as it is good and from the Good and directed to the Good' (VI.7.20). It is a matter of intense "longing" (*pothos*, I.6.7, VI.7.31 & 34).

The affective character is spelled out in terms not only of desire, but also of rest: a "passionate experience (*erôtikon pathêma*) like that of a lover resting in the beloved" (VI.9.4). Further on, the interpersonal character is stressed:

> he was as if carried away or possessed by a god, in a quiet solitude and a state of calm, not turning away anywhere in his being and not busy about himself, altogether at rest and having become a kind of rest (*stasis*) . . . a being out of oneself and simplifying and giving oneself over (*epidosis autou*, VI.9.11).

Another connotation, close to rest, is fulfillment: "the soul, receiving into itself an outflow from thence, is moved and dances wildly, and, stung with longing, is filled and becomes love" (VI.7.22; Armstrong's translation slightly emended). It is the result of a gift, as if one had encountered a god, "one who did not appear visibly but filled the soul of the beholder" (VI.7.35).

Fulfillment indicates that in mystical experience one has not been deceived: "But the attainment is confirmed when a thing becomes better and has no regrets, and fulfilment (*peplêrôsthai*) comes to it and it remains with the Good and does not seek something else" (VI.7.26). After having reached out eagerly for that goal, the soul "would not exchange this for anything in the world. . . . So then it has the ability *to judge* rightly and to know that this is what it desired, and to establish that there is nothing better than it . . . so great a degree of happiness (*eupatheias*) has it reached" (VI.7.34; my italics). This final assessment consists in a judgment, as Brentano emphasized, but based on an antepredicative (or rather, for Plotinus, postpredicative) experience.

Because the beauty that is pursued is measureless, one experiences a forceful drive towards it.

> Truly, when you cannot grasp the form or shape of what is longed for, it would be most longed for and most lovable, and love (*erôs*) for it would be immeasurable. For love is not limited

here, because neither is the beloved, but the love of this would be unbounded; so his beauty is of another kind and beauty above beauty (VI.7.32).

Plotinus repeatedly underwent an experience of the Good. His disciple Porphyry witnesses that during the years he spent with his master, the latter enjoyed, in Porphyry's presence, perfect union with God: "Four times while I was with him he attained that goal, in an unspeakable actuality and not in potency only" (*The Life of Plotinus*, §23). Plotinus himself suggests that it happened not infrequently:

> Often I have woken up out of the body to my self and have entered into myself, going out from all other things; I have seen a beauty wonderfully great and felt assurance that then most of all I belonged to the better part; I have actually lived the best life and come to identity with the divine; and set firm in it I have come to that supreme actuality, setting myself above all else in the realm of Intellect (IV.8.1).

Elsewhere he alludes to such a personal "experience" (*pathêma*) and he employs the typical mystery-initiate's motto, "whoever has seen, knows what I am saying" (VI.9.9; see I.6.7 and VI.7.40).[10]

Plotinus does not seem to have entertained the idea that mystical consciousness might consist in a lasting state. He talks about what I described, in my Introduction, as a transcendent experience, which comes "suddenly" (*exaiphnês*, V.3.17; VI.7.34 & 36) and is but momentary. Interestingly he observes that one cannot bring the illumination about simply by wishing it to occur:

> It appears or does not appear. So one must not chase after it, but wait quietly till it appears, preparing oneself to contemplate it, as the eye awaits the rising of the sun; and the sun rising over the horizon ("from Ocean", the poets say) gives itself to the eyes to see (V.5.8).

The idea of gift is worth underlining. The self-gift on the part of the Good ("the sun . . . gives itself") seems to elicit, on the part of Intellect, a conversion and a self-gift: "turning and giving itself up to him." Furthermore, the experience surpasses the capacity of Intellect: "Intellect sees him, when it does see him, with that of it which is not Intellect" (V.5.8). This idea of gift dovetails with the theme of fulfillment, which we mentioned a few paragraphs ago.

Again I wish to stress that Plotinus's mystical experience perfectly fits within his grand metaphysical schema. There is a supreme degree in the hierarchy, which transcends the greatest of thinking activities, even the grasp of the whole. Therefore it makes sense to recognize a state beyond the normal range of Intellect, that is, beyond self-knowledge. This experience can be found at the apex of Intellect's life, when it turns to the One. We may add that although Plotinus, in contrast to Lonergan, Eckhart, Schleiermacher, and most Zen meditators, does not mention the possibility of a constant mystical consciousness, he nevertheless gives us a philosophy of consciousness, ordinary and metaordinary, that is worth recording.

ORDINARY CONSCIOUSNESS

Plotinus warns against two perils that beset consciousness. First, consciousness as awareness of things that are below the soul's dignity. The soul may be concerned with them and cling to them. Second, preoccupation with oneself. Andrew Louth puts it clearly:

> The passage above [V.1.1] suggests that the fallen soul has become self-centred, and yet centred on a self that is not purely its self (cf. IV.8.4). . . . What it grasps at as the centre of its being is not the true centre at all: there is then what we might call a certain ec-centricity (out-of-centredness) in the fallen soul. And this ec-centricity engenders tension in the soul, a tension that it feels as self-consciousness.[11]

In another text Plotinus first characterizes self-awareness as follows:

> It seems as if awareness (*antilêpsis*, grasping) exists and is produced when intellectual activity is reflexive (*anakamptontos*, bending) and when that in the life of the soul which is active in thinking is in a way projected back, as happens with a mirror-reflection when there is a smooth, bright, untroubled surface (I.IV.10).

He goes on to give, as evidence of somewhat crippling self-consciousness, the awareness that one is reading, or that one is being brave. And he states:

> Conscious awareness, in fact, is likely to enfeeble the very activities of which there is consciousness; only when they are alone

are they pure and more genuinely active and living; and when good men are in this state their life is increased, when it is not spilt out into perception, but gathered in one in itself (I.4.10; see IV.4.4).

Understood as "conscious awareness" (*parakoloutheseis*, literally the accompanying thoughts), self-consciousness proves distracting in that it prevents us from being totally at one with both our outward actions and our inward activities (and with their objects, with which we ought to coincide intellectually). Although he does not expressly say so, Lonergan would agree that such distraction hampers what he calls self-transcendence. So the kind of conscious awareness that Plotinus warns against is the one that bars us from ceasing to cling to our limited self and from attaining full self-transcendence.

Soon enough, however, in the same Ennead, Plotinus mentions an affective kind of self-presence that is positive:

> The good man [must have] only those pleasures which accompany the presence of goods, pleasures not consisting in movements, which are not the results of any process: for the goods are there already, and the good man is present to himself (*hautô paresti*, I.4.12).

In another passage, the author argues that since "the intellect which thinks that it thinks will be altogether the same as the intellect which did the thinking," the fact of reflexivity does not entail the need to multiply intellects. As we saw in chapter 1, Sartre offers the same argument. Plotinus explains: "Its thinking is a single application of the mind not unaware of its own activities" (II.9.1).

In the Enneads, *parakoloutheisis* (this time translated as "consciousness of its own activities") is equated with *synaisthêsis*, and the latter is introduced along with *synesis* as synonyms (III.8.4 and V.8.11).[12] Armstrong translates *synaisthêsis* by "self-awareness" but it could also be rendered by a phrase such as "perceiving-with," since it suggests the combination of a cognitive act and its reflexive apprehension (IV.3.26). This dual consciousness is useful during the intellectual ascent, wherein it allows the soul to recollect what it truly is and to realize its affinity with Intellect. Precisely the remembered contents are images of thoughts. "Therefore, even though the soul is always moved to intelligent activity, it is when it comes to be in the image-making power that we apprehend it" (IV.3.30). Plotinus maintains that the imagination reflects and expresses our thoughts. It helps us reflexively to apprehend them and subsequently to bring them back to life again. Thus he clearly identifies a self-knowledge based on his distinction between the intellectual act (*noêsis*) and our apprehension of it (*antilêpsis*). And as we have just seen, this knowledge of the empirical self is facilitated by memory.

Even beyond the imagination, that is, in the pure realm of the intelligible, when the soul "comes to Intellect and accords itself to it," it has "a concurrent awareness of itself" (*synaisthêsin hautês*, IV,4.2), a definite "self-knowledge" (*gnôsis heautou*, V.3.2). Yet this highest kind of self-awareness falls short of the perfection of the One, who is so self-sufficient that it need not think itself. In this "consciousness of the whole" which characterizes Intellect, there is "a consciousness of something which is many: even the name bears witness to this" (V.3.13). In *synaisthêsis* the *syn* indicates this plurality of elements brought *together* in self-consciousness.

Unfortunately this self-consciousness of Intellect is not differentiated from its objectification. In III.9.9, for instance, where Plotinus contends that self-consciousness is a characteristic not of the Good but of Intellect, he writes: "That which is conscious of itself and thinks itself comes second, for it is conscious of itself in order that in this actuality of consciousness it may understand itself." He equates *to de parakolouthoun heautô* (being conscious of oneself) with *to noun hauto* (thinking oneself), thus confusing the accompanying consciousness with self-understanding. We shall return to the consequences of this lack of differentiation at the end of this chapter.

Although Plotinus tends to depreciate self-consciousness in order to extol union with the One, he would not disagree, I think, with my underlining the fact that a wise person must come to know oneself by participation in Intellect's self-awareness, before being ready to experience something higher than self-awareness.

WHAT HAPPENS BEYOND CONSCIOUSNESS?

We still have to delineate Plotinus's stance with respect to a possible state beyond consciousness. In a nutshell, on the one hand he claims that one achieves a stage beyond the awareness of duality that he views as typical of self-consciousness (understood as self-awareness, hence reflexive); and on the other hand no text of his indicates that this stage could be a kind of blackout or a total loss of consciousness (consciousness being, this time, understood as postreflexive). Let us attend to the first of these assertions. We shall examine the second in our next section.

Plotinus asserts the actuality of a stage beyond consciousness. It can be found perfectly in the One, and imperfectly in intelligent beings on whom the One bestows a part of his perfection. According to Plotinus, the perfection enjoyed by the One rules out any movement, any activity, any duration, any multiplicity—not even the duplicating of Intellect which coincides with itself. Therefore, he affirms: "When it is altogether immobile, it will not think" (V.3.10).

Elsewhere, realizing the oddity of his assertion that the One does not think, Plotinus raises the obvious objection: "If it is unthinking, it will be ignorant even of itself; so what will be grand about it?" His answer is that it is greater than Intellect, being "the origin of life and the origin of intellect and all things" (III.8.9). The One is above thinking and being. He is absolute Goodness, even though our ideas of goodness cannot match the transcendent quality of the Good.

Informative also is the other question Plotinus poses in this passage: "by what sort of simple intuition (*epibolê athroa*) could one grasp this which transcends the nature of intellect?" And he states that this is possible "by the likeness in ourselves" (III.8.9). Far from being unshareable, the power beyond consciousness, typical of the One, can be approximated in the exact measure that we resemble him. And in what does such resemblance consist? "For one must come to the sight with a seeing power made akin and like to what is seen" (I.6.9). More will be said later about the pivotal role of this seeing power in mystical experience.

In the following section (III.8.10), after splendidly comparing the One to a spring from which everything flows and to the life that he gives to a huge plant, Plotinus analogically refers to what makes something *one*, to the principle of unity in beings that are not simply one, in contrast to the One. And he asks: "If we take the *one* of the beings which truly exist, their origin and spring and productive power, shall we lose faith (*apistêsomen*) and think of it as nothing?" His reply is worth quoting in full:

> It is certainly none of the things of which it is origin; it is of such a kind, though nothing can be predicated of it, not being, not substance, not life, as to be above all of these things. But if you grasp it by taking away being from it, you will be filled with wonder. And, throwing yourself upon it and coming to rest within it, understand it more and more intimately, knowing it by intuition (*tê prosbolê syneis*) and seeing its greatness by the things which exist after it and through it (III.8.10).

The author has just given us an explanation of this encounter with nothingness which might cause the loss of faith: the One is "none of the things" that exist side by side with one another, and hence limited. Elsewhere he writes of the Intellect:

> It does not know where to stay and where he [the One] stays, that is in nothing. And if it was possible for Intellect to abide in that nowhere—I do not mean that Intellect is in place: it is no more in place than he is, but [in that sense] absolutely nowhere—it would always behold him, or rather not behold him, but be one with him, not two (V.5.8).

Besides, Plotinus tells us that the soul, which participates in Intellect, must be entirely void of any act of understanding, which grasps an intelligible shape: "the soul also, when it gets an intense love of it [beauty], puts away all the shape which it has, even whatever shape of the intelligible there may be in it" (VI.7.34). The soul must "be without form" and "ignoring all things" (VI.9.7). As we shall see in our next chapter, Eckhart repeats these assertions almost word for word.

NO BLACKOUT AND YET NO SELF-CONSCIOUSNESS

Coexisting with the risk of despairing, the experience of wonder evoked by III.8.10 unequivocally demonstrates that at the summit of Intellect's ascent, what is intimately enjoyed is not an *ontological* nothingness, but a supreme simplicity, that is, something great and admirable, transcending anything we can know. At the same time, it disconcertingly appears as an *epistemological* nothingness.

That the experience of the One is no blackout becomes evident as soon as attention is paid to the vocabulary with which Plotinus depicts that experience. Plotinus uses several metaphors to point to this unique experience. To give but an incomplete list: it is a vision (*thea*, VI.7.31), the receiving of light (*phôs*, V.3.17), a touching (*thigein*, VI.9.7), a contact (*epaphê*, V.3.10), a joining (*synaphê*, VI.9.8), "embracing (*periptyssein*) him with the whole of ourselves" (VI.9.9), "a presence (*parousia*) superior to knowledge" (VI.9.4; such presence is reciprocal, see V.8.11 and VI.9.7 & 8), a "being united" (*henoun*, VI.9.9 &11), an "existence-with" (*synousia*, VI.9.7), a coinciding of our own center with the shining center of all things, respectively compared to circles joining the center of the encompassing sphere (I.7.1; IV.3.17; V.1.11; VI.8.18; VI.9.8 & 10).

In such an abundance of metaphors, it is not easy to pinpoint the nature of the experience. Yet we find a text where Plotinus offers a fascinating explanation:

> By the continuity of his contemplation he [the individual who sees the god] no longer sees a sight, but mingles his seeing (*opsin*) with what he contemplates, so that what was seen before has now become sight (*opsin*) in him, and he forgets all other objects of contemplation (VI.7.35; see V.3.8).

The authors seems to suggest that the object ("what he contemplates" or "what was seen before") vanishes and that the contemplator is left with mere "sight in him." A transition is adumbrated here between an object-directed contemplation and an objectless and pure "seeing." Moreover such seeing is said to come from within ("in him").

In the next paragraph Plotinus writes:

> The vision fills his eyes with light and does not make him see something else by it, but the light itself is what he sees. For there is not in that Good something seen and its light, nor intellect and object of intellect, but a ray which generates these afterwards (VI.7.36; see V.5.7).

One's intellectual light is received from the Good that has generated intellect. This interior reception is no object; rather it amounts to the very ability to think. Yet, as distinguished from its particular acts of reasoning, the luminous ability of such originating light is present in itself as well as flowing from its source, the Good, also called the One.

Given this epistemological context, we ought to be extremely wary of speaking of an experience *of* the One, as if the One could be contemplated like an object outside of the human self. Let us mark that Plotinus approvingly refers to his master: "Plato says the One is not outside anything" (VI.9.7). Perhaps we may say, in modern parlance, that the human subject has intentionally become the Subject. Still, being united to the One defies the capacities of human language.

ECSTASY, OR ENSTASY?

Furthermore, we may ask: During mystical experience does one become a greater human self, or an Other? Does the soul pass out of itself into its own greater self, or into an Other? All depends on whether the greater Self, which Plotinus calls Intellect, is ontologically distinct from the One.

Now there is no doubt that the One is distinct both from Intellect and from all individual souls. It is "alone," that is, solitary and apart. Accordingly Plotinus conceives of the mystical experience not as an identity, but as a union. The Greek prefix *syn* recurs (for example at III.8.10), a "with" that is in tune with the doctrine of participation. Intelligent beings are not the One, but they are united and indeed one with him, by experientially sharing in his goodness. And once again, let us remind ourselves of the interpersonal vocabulary, often very affective, Plotinus employs as he alludes to our union with the One.[13]

VI.7.34 offers us more precision on this union. It says:

> When the soul turns away from the things that are there, and has prepared by making itself as beautiful as possible and has come to likeness . . . and it sees it [formless beauty] in itself suddenly appearing (for there is nothing between, nor are there still two but both are one (*hen amphô*); nor could you still make a distinction while it is present . . .), it has been seeking it, and meets that when it is present, and looks at that instead of itself; but it has not even time to see who the soul is that looks.

In this experience two kinds of awareness are superseded: the soul's self-awareness ("it looks at that instead of itself," which indicates self-transcendence; see also VI.7.35: "It does not even think that it does not think") and the soul's awareness of a distinction between itself and formless beauty ("nor could you still make a distinction"). Of course, this passage and the rest of the Plotinian corpus make it clear that it is a union.[14] Nonetheless, "when it is present," what happens is an experience of identity. Ontological distinction is compatible with a union felt as identity.

Another text confirms the experience of identity while maintaining difference:

> The seer does not see and does not distinguish and does not imagine two, but it is as if he had become someone else and he is not himself and does not count as his own there, but has come to belong to that and so is one, having joined, as it were, centre to centre. For here too when the centres have come together they are one, but there is duality when they are separate. This also is how we now speak of "another". For this reason the vision is hard to put into words. For how could one announce that as another when he did not see, there when he had the vision, another, but one with himself? (VI.9.10)

In the next and final section of VI.9, the author first denies that the union actually consists in a vision, because the usual distinctions do not apply any longer: "the seer himself was one with the seen (for it was not really seen, but united to him). . . . He was one himself, with no distinction in himself either in relation to himself or to other things." Then, after adding a few negations (such as "no emotion, no desire . . . not even any reason or thought"), he characterizes the vision as "another kind of seeing (*idein*), a being out of oneself (*ekstasis*)" (VI.9.11). *Ekstasis* is a word used by Plotinus with a technical sense only in this passage, to characterize what nevertheless remains an "austere and quiet mysticism," as Armstrong reminds us.[15]

To return to the question raised at the beginning of this section regarding this passing out of oneself, I would contend that what is attained is both a greater self—the soul at its summit, when identifying with Intellect—and the One. In a first stage, the boundaries of the individual self are overcome:

> When he has nowhere to set himself and limit himself and determine how far he himself goes, he will stop marking himself off from all being and will come to all the All without going out anywhere, but remaining there where the All is set firm (VI.5.7).

Then the soul becomes Intellect:

> When this soul has become intellect it contemplates, when it has been, so to speak, made intellect and has come to be in the intelligible place; but when it has come to be in it and moves about it, it possesses the intelligible and thinks (VI.7.35).

Yet Plotinus, for all his esteem for Intellect's grasp of the whole, makes bold to claim that, in a second stage, "The soul is so disposed then as even to despise intelligence." And he brings in a comparison:

> It is as if someone went into a house richly decorated and so beautiful, and within it contemplated each and every one of the decorations and admired them before seeing the master of the house, but when he sees that master with delight, who is not of the nature of the images [in the house], but worthy of genuine contemplation, he dismisses those other things and thereafter looks at him alone, and then . . . he looks and does not take his eyes away (VI.7.35).

The master of the house, who is the One, remains distinct from the visitor and from everything else in the house (the universe).

Still, the *ecstasis*—being out of oneself, is also an *enstasis*—a being in oneself.[16] On the one hand, in VI.9.11 Plotinus twice mentions the word *stasis*, rest, in a passage we have already quoted in the second section of this chapter. He also clearly states that at "the end of the journey . . . it [the soul] will arrive, not at something else but at itself, and in this way since it is not in something else it will not be in nothing, but in itself." This is enstasy. On the other hand, the journey ends in the "escape in solitude to the solitary" [= the One] (VI.9.11). This is ecstasy.

CONCLUDING REMARKS

Some perceptive readers may have noticed that most of the time, for Plotinus ordinary consciousness is not prereflexive consciousness, but reflexive awareness. At its highest degree, consciousness is equated with Intellect's self-knowledge, that is, with thinking as self-awareness. Despite the experience of identity that characterizes Intellect's self-contemplation, there still is a certain duality at that penultimate level of the ascent towards the One. Plotinus does not distinguish, as Lonergan does, between the consciousness in our acts and the reflexive awareness of our acts, although he comes very close when in IV.3.30 he differentiates the intellectual act (*noêsis*) from the apprehension (*antilêpsis*) that we can have of it. In other words he fails to see that the *consciousness-in*, which is prior to its objectification in thinking, implies no duality. Only *consciousness-of* involves duality.

A good number of commentators have considered that penultimate level as mysticism. There are reasons to do so, in particular the fact that Intellect's wholistic comprehension might be legitimately regarded as a unitary consciousness, itself often dubbed mystical. I would prefer to treat it as an intellectual anticipation of mystical unity. As this chapter has tried to show, Plotinus's mysticism should be equated, not with the residual consciousness that we find in Intellect's self-apprehension, but in the stage beyond consciousness that Intellect enters when it affectively turns towards the One.

However, had he viewed consciousness (consciousness-in) as more fundamental than awareness (consciousness-of), Plotinus could have stated that union with the One carries with it no absence of consciousness, but rather another kind of consciousness-in, which I have called a consciousness beyond consciousness, that is, beyond ordinary consciousness. In fact, in VI.7,16 Plotinus associates the gift of light from the One with Intellect's "self-consciousness" (*synaisthêsis*) and with "being fulfilled" (*plêrôtheis*). Moreover, in an early text (V.4.2) he ascribes to the

One a "thinking of itself" and a certain "self-consciousness" (*synaisthêsis*) which he understands as "different from the thinking of Intellect." But the mature Plotinus is opposed to the idea of attributing anything to the One.

Another issue has to do with the "object" of mystical experience, which we might preferably call its "objective," as Lonergan suggests.[17] How are we to interpret the "escape in solitude to the solitary" of VI.9.11? Solitude is not isolation, whether physical or epistemic, but rather the freedom from all that could be fragmentary and thus alien. The One is completely solitary in the sense that it is not an "object" and that there is no object beside or besides him.

Plotinus's denial of being, in the case of the One, is also puzzling. After Plato he locates the One, here called God, "beyond being," since

> he is not a slave to substance (*ousia*), or to himself, nor is his substance his principle, but he, being principle of substance, did not make substance for himself but when he had made it left it outside himself, because he has no need of being, he who made it (VI.8.19).

Being, understood in a Greek fashion as substance, cannot but be derivative, hence limited. If Plotinus refuses to ascribe being to the One, it could be because he has no inkling that "unrestrictedly to be" (the infinite *ipsum esse subsistens* of Thomas Aquinas) can be analogically posited. The Thomist analogy, reiterated by Eckhart, as we shall see in the next chapter, includes the negation that God is *a* being while it asserts that he is the fullness of being—a fullness that we humans utterly fail to comprehend.

Be that as it may, it is imperative to remind ourselves that Plotinus was not concerned with fine ontological distinctions in the way the medieval scholastics or the modern rationalists were. We find no gaps but rather numerous transitions along the continuum from the soul (itself subdivided into a lower and a higher state) through Intellect (itself similarly subdivided) into the Good. Instead, Plotinus is more interested in charting the way of reaching up to the Good and in placing it within a metaphysical setting. Therefore it is with no surprise that we should hear him declare, from the standpoint of the One, that nothing changes: so the soul, which is divine, "having become—but rather, being—a god" (VI.9.9) has always been there, in its true home. This journey, which is no-journey, is the most important point in Plotinus. Our next chapter will show that it also subtends the whole message of Eckhart.

CHAPTER 5

Eckhart:
When Human Consciousness Becomes Divine Consciousness

The German thinker and mystic Meister Eckhart (1260–1328) was at once a *Lesemeister* and a *Lebemeister*, that is, a lecturer in theology and a spiritual master. As a master in sacred doctrine (hence his title, *Meister*), he carried on the intellectual tradition of the Dominican order, to which he belonged. As a preacher with a knack for stunning, arresting phrases, he deeply influenced the lives of those who heard him.

His cast of mind was indebted mostly to Neoplatonism, not directly by reading Plotinus, but through the latter's enormous impact on authors such as the Greek philosopher Proclus, the Catholic bishop Augustine (the thinker whom Eckhart quotes more often than any other), the Syrian monk Dionysius, the Muslim author of the Book of Causes, and the Dominican friar Albert the Great. Some of his favorite themes, for instance the *Wesenmystik* of the identity between the human soul and God, or Margaret Porete's view that true poverty consists in willing nothing, not even the divine will, overlap with texts composed by women mystics of the Middle Ages.[1]

However, in contrast to most of those women authors, for instance Mechtilde and the Beguines, Eckhart displayed scant interest in special states of religious experience such as visions, locutions, and ecstasies. Moreover, for him neither sensible consolation nor sensible desolation was a central factor in the spiritual life. "Eckhart's real appeal is to an intellectual and above all to a religious conversion, one in which our eyes are finally opened to see what has always been the case."[2] As this judgment of McGinn's suggests, his mysticism is very close to Plotinus's.

In this chapter, the readers must expect simply a study of Eckhart from the perspective of our research on consciousness. Hence I will select themes that shed light on that topic and I will say little on other themes that would distract us from the set of issues I want to explore. We shall begin with Eckhart's insistence on emptiness and nonexistence, which we notice concerning both the human intellect and God. This first section will be followed by an examination of his statement that in its identity with God the soul reaches a state beyond awareness. Third, we shall clarify the senses in which he uses the word "nothing." Fourth, his views on detachment will be presented. Fifth, we shall deal with the issue of whether the soul is equated with God. Last, we shall treat of the soul's breakthrough to the Godhead.

THE EMPTINESS OF THE HUMAN INTELLECT

In Paris, during the scholastic year 1302–03, Meister Eckhart conducted disputations that are of special interest to our inquiry.[3] Question 1 asks: "Are Existence (*esse*) and Understanding the Same in God?" After giving the standard Thomist answer that they indeed are the same in God, Eckhart proceeds to teach the unThomist thesis of the priority of intellect over being:

> It is not my present opinion that God understands because he exists, but rather that he exists because he understands. God is an intellect and understanding, and his understanding itself is the ground of his existence.

He finds support in New Testament texts stating that God is Word and Truth, which both imply a relation to an intellect. He also invokes the Book of Causes, which says, "The first of created things is existence." He adopts this Neoplatonic sense, restricted to finite beings, of 'existence' as he comments: "Hence as soon as we come to existence we come to a creature. Existence, then, has primarily the nature of something creatable."

This early stance of Eckhart, which is based on a restricted sense of being, is worth noting since it will recur often throughout the corpus of his works. But we shall also find the unrestricted sense in several of his later pronouncements, for instance in a German sermon: "if we take being (*wesen*, by which Eckhart renders the Latin *esse*) naked and pure, as it is in itself, then being is loftier than knowledge or life," or: "all that God is, is being," and: "God's characteristic is being" (Pr. 8).[4] This fact has misled some of his commentators into thinking that he had changed his views on the subject. Instead, is it not perfectly legitimate to adopt sometimes a restricted and sometimes an unrestricted sense for being, and then to deduce *apparently* contradictory propositions such as "God does not exist" (in the restricted sense) and "God does exist" (in the unrestricted sense)?

The foregoing remark of mine is meant to prepare the way for an adequate interpretation of seemingly paradoxical declarations by the Meister, which will be discussed later. Now Question 2 can also contribute to such a preparation. It asks: "Is an Angel's Understanding as Denoting an Action, the Same as his Existence?" As in Question 1, Eckhart begins by agreeing with Aquinas that they are not the same. And similarly he departs from Aquinas by announcing intriguingly: "But I have other ways of proving this."

His first argument derives from Aristotle's position that in order to be capable of knowing everything, the intellect must be unmixed with anything and have nothing in common with anything. Eckhart concludes: "If the intellect, therefore, insofar as it is an intellect, is nothing, it follows that neither is understanding some existence." This statement that both the intellect and its act of understanding are nothing will be amplified in his sermons, when no longer the intellect but the ground of the soul will be pronounced void. In the present case the emptiness is based on an epistemological requirement: to receive an intellectual representation, the intellect must be void. We shall see later that the emptiness of the soul is also based on a mystical requirement.

In addition, his seventh argument is worth noticing: "The intellect, as such, is neither here, nor now, nor a definite thing. But every being or existence is in a definite genus and species. So the intellect, as such, is not a being, nor does it have an existence." This is repeated in his tenth argument: "A being is some definite thing. This is why a genus is not a being, for it is something indeterminate. Now the intellect and the act of understanding are something indeterminate; therefore they are not a being." What Eckhart says of the intellect is very close to what Heidegger suggests about being. As a Heideggerian philosopher puts it, "There are 'things,' beings that *are*, but not being, the essence of beings. *There is* no being."[5]

For those who would misunderstand him, Eckhart cautions that his assertion does not mean that the intellect is absolutely nothing. "My reply is that the intellect is a natural power of the soul. Consequently it is something." Thus the Meister typically balances one aspect with a different one.

In several vernacular sermons, Eckhart the preacher asserts the superiority of intellect over being. For example he declares: "If we receive God in being, we receive him in his forecourt, for being is the forecourt of his dwelling. Where is he then in his temple, where he shines in holiness? Intellect is the temple of God." He goes on to affirm the superiority of intellect over the will, which elicits acts of love: "A pagan master says the soul that loves God takes hold of him under the garment of goodness. . . . Intellect draws this garment of goodness off God and takes him bare, where he is stripped of goodness and being and of all names" (Pr. 9).

In this context, both being and goodness belong in the realm of the determinate and the nameable, whereas intellect dissociates itself from being as it penetrates into the bareness of God. Yet in other sermons, the preacher associates human intellect with being, for example when he states that intellect goes further than love: "Love takes God as he is good, but intellect presses upwards and takes God as he is being" (Pr. 45). Obviously Eckhart here thinks of God as unrestricted Being. The same meaning is rendered by "essence" (*wesen*) in the following passage:

> Intellect penetrates right up into the essence without heeding goodness or power or wisdom, or whatever is accidental. It does not care what is added to God, it takes him in himself, sinks into the essence and takes God as he is pure essence (Pr. 37).

It is very important to observe that by "intellect" Eckhart does not always refer to the normal functioning of that faculty, but often entertains another meaning:

> Now comes the highest intellect, that which receives all things barely from God, and says: 'I have apprehended the highest good wherein naught can stand but unity.' Understanding says: 'I shall remain, you must let me stay with you.' Intellect says: 'Understanding and love, you must remain behind' (Pf 37 = Walshe 37).

Understanding (= intellect in its usual functioning) and love must remain behind whereas "the man in the soul" (= intellect as taken up into divine life) presses upwards until "the soul is merged in pure unity" (ibid.). In Pr. 42, the preacher explains:

> God is so lofty in himself that neither understanding nor desire can attain to him. . . . All that understanding can grasp, all that desire can desire, that is not God. Where understanding and desire end, there is darkness, and there God shines.

How can one attain to this darkness? By letting the soul's highest power (called "man") be "un-formed (*entbildet*), informed (*ingebildet*) and transformed (*überbildet*) in the divine uniformity wherein it is one with God" (Pr. 40).[6] In other words, man must be "un-formed" or de-formed in the sense of de-imaged, that is, cut off from the realm of worldly imagery, then be formed in the divine image, and finally be transfigured so as to become one with the divine.

There is a power in the soul that is *entbildet*, "void of alien images," "free of all names and void of all forms, entirely exempt (*ledic*, vacant) and free (*vrî*)" (Pr. 2). As we see, the theme of emptiness is inseparable from the theme of de-imaging.

> If I should have gone out of myself and were entirely empty, then indeed the Father would bear his only-begotten Son in my spirit. . . . Now then, to hear this Word in the Father (where all is stillness), a man must be quite quiet and wholly free from image, indeed from all forms (Pr. 42).

Accordingly, the soul is nameless. "Whoever would name the soul according to her simplicity, purity and nakedness, as she is in herself, he can find no name for her" (Pr. 17). The soul is also said to be an unknown "something" (*was*), an "I-know-not-what" (*neizwas*, Pr. 71). Being utterly indeterminate, the soul is as ineffable as God: "The soul, too, has no name. Just as no one can find a true name for God, so none can find the soul's true name" (Pr. 38). Here we begin to observe Eckhart's tendency to ascribe divine characteristics to the human intellect. Such a tendency prepares the way for a future identification of the soul with the Word of God.

NO AWARENESS

For Eckhart, God resides in a no man's land, so to speak. "Having no place" (*illocalis*), God is not "where" (*ubi*) but rather "everywhere" (*ubique*).[7] The same is said of the soul: "the location (*setzunge*) of the soul proceeds from this ground (*grunde*)," that is, from "that place which is nameless" (Pr. 36a). The divinized soul dwells in a nameless place because it is not an item in our world:

> There is something in the soul in which God is bare (*blôz*), and the masters say this is nameless, and has no name of its own. It

is, and yet has no being of its own, for it is neither this nor that (*noch diz noch daz*) nor here nor there (Pr. 24).

The divinized soul is bare or naked, that is, without distinctive attributes. It inhabits a desert (*wueste, wuestunge*), a solitude (*einoede*, a term translated by McGinn as "oneness-solitariness" because its word play is indicated by a word that immediately follows in the text, namely, *ein*, the One).[8]

In another version of Predigt 36, Eckhart details his thinking on that topic:

> The place is God and the divine essence, which gives a place, and life and being and order to all things. In that place the soul will rest, in the highest and inmost part of that place. . . . And in the same ground, where he has his own rest, we too shall have our rest and possess it with him. The place has no name, and no one can utter a word concerning it that is appropriate. Every word that we can say of it is more a denial of what God is *not* than a declaration of what he *is*. . . . Therefore it is a much greater thing to be silent about God than to speak (Pr. 36b).

Consequently one must let go of all words, all images, all likenesses. To illustrate this process, Eckhart employs the following comparison:

> The shell must be broken and what is inside must come out, for, if you want to get at the kernel you must break the shell. Accordingly, if you want to find nature unveiled, all likenesses must be shattered, and the further you penetrate, the nearer you will get to the essence. When the soul finds the One, where all is one, there she will remain in that One (Pr. 51 see Pr. 13).

And elsewhere Eckhart stresses the importance of "traversing and transcending all creatureliness, all being and getting into the ground that is groundless" (Pr. 42). Beyond finite being, one can no longer be grounded in anything created.[9]

This groundless ground justifies the fact that, as we saw, Eckhart downgrades the faculties of the soul, namely the intellect and the will. For instance, he dismisses both of them: "neither knowledge nor love unites." What he hankers after is a state in which the faculties no longer operate, which amounts to "that great union we are destined to have with God, in one being, not (just) in one act." And he endeavors to communicate his fascination with "something very secret and hidden in the soul, yet far above it, from which there burst forth the powers of intellect and will" (Pr. 7). This is the ground of the soul, which underlies the faculties.

> When the soul is separated from the body she has neither reason nor will. She is one, and would be unable to exercise the power of turning to God: she has these powers in her ground (*grunt*), as in their roots, but not as functioning (Pr. 8).

For the ground of the soul to be accessed, its powers must become idle and silent. In another sermon, the preacher seems to be alluding to an actual experience when he recommends: "If only you could suddenly be unaware (*unwissend*) of all things. . . ." He explains that the man who stops exercising his faculties must draw them in to a unity, "turn his powers inward and sink into an oblivion of all things and himself." He mentions several faculties that have become inactive: "memory no longer functioned, nor understanding, nor the senses, nor the powers that should function so as to govern and grace the body, vital warmth and body-heat were suspended." In the ground of the soul, only God can operate. Yet in answer to the question, "What does God do without images in the ground and essence," he replies that the soul does not know. She enters a state of "not-knowing" (*Nicht-wissen*) or "unknowing knowing" (*nichterkennende Erkennen*, QT 57 = Walshe 1).[10]

This sermon makes it clear that Eckhart *experientially* knows what it means to pass from awareness to unawareness. Therefore, I would qualify Denys Turner's anti-experientialism, while agreeing with his point that, since William James, students of mysticism have overrated experience in a manner of which the genuine mystics disapprove.[11] As McGinn rightly observes,

> According to Eckhart, our union with God is a continuous state, at least in some way. . . . For Eckhart, this continuous union with God is not an "experience" in any ordinary sense of the term—it is coming to realize and live out of the ground of experience, or better of consciousness.[12]

Although Eckhart does not tackle the issue of self-awareness, occasionally he declares that the inactivity of the soul's powers rules out self-awareness. For instance, in "On the Nobleman," he concedes that "as man, the soul, the spirit, contemplates God, he also knows and perceives himself perceiving; that is, he perceives that he is contemplating and perceiving God" (*sô weiz er ouch und bekennet sich bekennende, daz ist: er bekennet, daz er schouwet und bekennet got*). And yet he also indicates that perfect happiness lies beyond the activity of contemplating God which is accompanied by self-perception. He points out that "the first thing in which blessedness consists is when the soul contemplates God directly (*blôz*)" and that "she knows nothing about knowing or about love or about anything at all." He emphatically stresses that "everlasting life is to know (*bekennen*) God alone (*blôz*) as the one true God (Jn 17:3), not to know that we know God."[13]

In this passage, *bekennen* has more than one sense. Colledge has translated it successively by "perceiving" and by "knowing." Interestingly, in Pr. 40, as we shall see shortly, Walshe translates it by "awareness." To sort out the various senses, perhaps it will be helpful to return to the distinctions previously introduced between consciousness (in our acts and states) and self-awareness (paying attention to that consciousness). The text quoted in our previous paragraph does not distinguish consciousness and self-awareness. As Eckhart speaks of knowing or perceiving oneself perceiving, he combines the consciousness that permeates our knowing (either finite realities or the infinite) with the awareness that such a consciousness becomes when adverted to. His point is that mystical consciousness ("to know God alone") is direct since it is not encumbered by a concomitant awareness of our knowledge ("to know that we know God"). Elsewhere, in his *Predigte*, he states that this knowledge of God that we have is "without a medium" (*sunder mittel*, for instance in Pr. 15, 48, 69, 83). Such immediacy is epistemologically explained by the emptiness of the human intellect, which we examined earlier in this chapter.

Furthermore, Eckhart draws a parallel between immediate presence to oneself (ordinary consciousness) and knowledge of God (mystical consciousness):

> The soul knows herself without a "little bit," without image and without likeness, immediately. If I am to know God, that must occur without images and immediately. The greatest masters say that one knows God without means (Pr. 70).

The raison d'être of the utter lack of self-awareness (Pr. 67: "totally denying my awareness of self"; see also Pr. 68) seems to be that the experienced state is no longer a merely human but rather a divine-human state: "He [man] has one knowing with God's knowing, and one action with God's action, and one awareness (*bekennen*) with God's awareness" (Pr. 40). Even ordinary consciousness, which precedes self-awareness, is excluded, because the acts of knowledge and love that it normally accompanies are no longer performed: "it [something in the soul] does not itself know or love in the way the powers of the soul do." Hence Eckhart goes so far as to say: "It is deprived of the knowledge that God is at work in it" (Pr. 52).

Still, according to Eckhart, this state is not "a mere sleeping or blackout," as Forman points out.[14] One is awake and conscious. Commenting on St. Paul's experience of being carried off into the third heaven, Eckhart asserts: "If anyone had touched St. Paul with the point of a needle during the time he was enraptured, he would have known it, for his soul remained in his body" (Pr. 23). On this phenomenon Ken Wilber offers a very Eckhartian comment:

> It is not exactly that time itself disappears—it is not that consciousness goes blank into darkness. Rather, in the state of Transcendence (subtle and causal), time both collapses into the Eternal Now and continues to flow through it and from it.[15]

NOTHINGNESS

Lack of awareness is a theme that is a semantic cousin to several Eckhartian themes such as those I have presented in the preceding section, as well as the theme of nothingness, which we are broaching now. Given the centrality of nothingness in contemporary Japanese philosophy and our forthcoming discussion of it later in this book, it is important to take stock of the several senses of nothingness that are interlaced in Eckhart's writings. We find four senses, concerning respectively all creatures, the human soul, God, and mystical experience.

In Eckhart's view, "all creatures are worthless and a mere nothing (*niht*) compared with God" (Pr. 77). Moreover, finite beings are nothing by themselves and they would be actually nothing, should the Creator abandon them to themselves, because they would slip back into nothingness.

> All creatures are pure nothing. I do not say they are a trifle or they are only a little something: they are pure nothing. What has no being, is not. All creatures have no being, for their being depends on God's presence. If God turned away for an instant from all creatures, they would perish (Pr. 4).

Second, onto this ontological status of *all creatures*, which are nothing apart from receiving being from the Creator, Eckhart grafts a consideration that sounds existential (in the modern sense): it happens that the soul dramatically realizes her complete lack of existence and her utter dependency on God:

> And when she emerges into the unmixed light, she falls into her nothingness (*niht*) and in that nothingness so far from the created something, that of her own power she cannot return to her created something. God with his uncreatedness upholds her nothingness and preserves her in his something. The soul has dared to become nothing and so cannot of herself return to herself, for she has departed so far from herself before God comes to the rescue (Pr. 1).

Accordingly only the soul that has become devoid of herself can receive God. As Eckhart puts it elsewhere, "You must be dead to all things and reduced to naught. . . . if God is to make anything in you or with you, you must first be reduced to nothing" (Pr. 39).

Third, for Eckhart, God is nothing. God is no-thing; God is not *a* thing or *a* being. God does not "exist" in the restricted manner we encounter among finite beings. "God is nothing (*niht*): not in the sense of having no being. He is neither *this* nor *that* that one can speak of: He is being above all being. He is beingless being" (Pr. 82). In other words, God is Being in a sense totally different from the one we ascribe to beings. "But when I have said God is not a being and is above being, I have not thereby denied him being: rather I have exalted it in him" (Pr. 9). Elsewhere, in a single sentence, the "nameless nothingness (*nihtheit*)" is equated with an "unbecome Isness (*isticheit*)" (Pr. 83).

Last, with respect to our human acts, God is found in nothingness, that is, in an empty soul, whenever the operations of its faculties are interrupted. In this fourth sense we have a twofold intentional nothingness, namely, in regard both to the acts and to the ultimate objective of our knowing intentionality. In the first section of this chapter, we examined the texts having to do with our acts, which are suspended or brought to naught. Likewise God, the ultimate objective of our intentionality, is apprehended as nothing. "When the soul is unified and there enters into total self-abnegation, then she finds God as in nothing" (Pr. 71).

Thus, commenting on the sentence, "Paul rose from the ground and with open eyes saw nothing" (Acts 9:8), Eckhart explains:

> The light that is God is unmingled, no admixture comes in. This was a sign that it was the true light he saw, which is Nothing (*niht*). By the light he meant quite simply that with his eyes

open he saw nothing. In seeing nothing, he saw the divine nothing (Pr. 71; see Pr. 70).

Insofar as nothingness is concerned, we once again observe the connection between ontology, epistemology, and mysticism. Eckhart suggestively weaves together various cases of nothingness: the finite creatures', the soul's, and God's nothingness.

A DETACHED LOVE WITHOUT A WHY

If the soul is to identify with the divine, a condition is required: a detached love without a why.

> St Augustine says, what a man loves, that he becomes in love. Should we now say that if a man loves God he becomes God? That sounds as if it were contrary to faith. In the love that a man gives there is no duality but one and unity, and in love I am God more than I am in myself (Pr. 5a).

In union with God, there is no lack of knowing and loving. What is left behind is the knowledge and love that are associated with duality.

Transcending duality is no mere heightening of our intellectual capacities. It requires giving up "attachment" (*eigenschaft*, ownership, possession); it is the outcome of "detachment" (*abegescheidenheit*, the state of being separated from, after having parted from, everything). Addressing audiences made up of nuns, beguines, and pious laypeople, most of whom are morally converted, Eckhart does not warn against inordinate attachment to physical pleasures, but against "attachment to prayer, fasting, vigils and all kinds of outward discipline and mortification, . . . attachment to any work that involves the loss of freedom to wait on God in the here and now" (Pr. 2). According to this sermon Jesus urges both Mary and Martha to renounce any preference for particular kinds of work, be they contemplative or active, so as to be free to follow him and obey his promptings with flexibility.

The same urging recurs in another sermon:

> Anyone who seeks anything in God, knowledge, understanding, devotion or whatever it might be—though he may find it he will not have found God: even though he may indeed find knowledge, understanding or inwardness, which I heartily commend—but it will not stay with him. But if he seeks noth-

ing, he will find God and all things in God, and they will remain with him. A man should seek nothing at all, neither knowledge nor understanding nor inwardness nor piety nor repose, but only God's will (Pr. 62).

Paramount though it is, the divine will is not extrinsic. "The will of a friend with his friend's will is one will. So it is with the man who has one will with God: evil and good, joy and sorrow are all one to him" (Pr. 61). About this understanding of God's will we find a longer development in Eckhart's "Counsels on Discernment." He contends that the best of all prayers is not to ask for specifics, but to say, "Lord, give me nothing but what you will, and do, Lord, whatever and however you will in every way."[16]

Yet the divine will is intrinsic to the human will in a more intimate way than the previous texts suggested.

As long as a man is so disposed that it is his *will* with which he would do the most beloved will of God, that man has not the poverty we are speaking about: for that man has a *will* to serve God's will—and that is not true poverty! For a man to possess true poverty he must be as free of his created will as he was when he was not. For I declare by the eternal truth, as long as you have the *will* to do the will of God, and longing for eternity and God, you are not poor: for a poor man is one who wills nothing and desires nothing (Pr. 52).

Total identification with God cancels out the illusion that one's will might be distinct from the divine will. The poor man's will is so free that, in God, it pursues no external end. In a commentary on this Predigt 52, Caputo writes, "The will-lessness which Eckhart has in mind does not refer to an effortless passivity, to lassitude, but to a suspension of all teleological attitudes."[17]

Perfect obedience is practiced out of love. "You should not attach such importance to what you feel; rather, consider important what you love and what you intend."[18] For instance, love for people in need requires that meditators abandon their ecstasy and care for others. Emotions, feelings and consolations must be given up in such circumstances. "But you must know that God's friends are never without consolation, for whatever God wills is for them the greatest consolation of all, whether it be consolation or desolation."[19]

In another vernacular sermon, Eckhart points to "something that transcends the created being of the soul," something "akin to the nature of deity. . . . It is a strange and desert place, and is rather nameless than possessed of a name, and is more unknown than it is known." Again he links up this speculative statement with the radical exigence: "If you could naught yourself for an instant, indeed I say less than an instant, you would possess all that this is in itself" (Pr. 28).

The void is for the sake of plenitude. Eckhart situates freedom from self within the context of divine grace: "A man who makes himself wholly free of self for God's sake, who belongs to none but God and lives for none save God alone, is in truth by grace the same as God is by nature" (Pr. 66). In the same sermon he emphasizes the great joy that both God and the mystic experience (see also Pr. 2). In reply to the objection that we often do not feel the divine presence, he states, "Even if you think you can't feel him and are wholly empty of him, that is not the case." He proceeds to explain that God cannot but fill the vacant space created by self-emptying. For Eckhart we may receive the divine gift either in awareness or unawares (see QT 59 = Walshe 4).

Another form of detached love, which will be subsequently picked up by Heidegger and Nishitani, is the "not-asking-why." Eckhart quotes an unknown master, who affirmed, "All things have a why, but God has no why" (Pr. 59). In one of his Latin commentaries, he writes: "It is proper to God that he have no 'why or wherefore' outside or apart from himself. Therefore, every work that has a 'why and wherefore' as such is not a divine work and is not performed for God."[20]

Like God, we must perform all our activities without asking why, that is, without ranking them as means subordinated to goals or gratifications. Eckhart makes his own Seneca's saying, "if a man practises virtue for the sake of anything else but virtue, then it never was a virtue." And he comments: "If he seeks praise or anything else, he is selling virtue. One should never give up a virtue by nature for anything in the world. Therefore a good man desires no praise, but he desires to be worthy of praise" (Pr. 45). We must do all our duties in a disinterested way, not for the sake of anything in particular.

> The just man seeks nothing in his works: for those who seek anything in their works or work for any "why" are thralls and hirelings. Therefore, if you would be informed with and transformed into justice, have no ulterior purpose in your work, allow no "why" to take shape in you, as regards either time or eternity, reward or blessedness, or this or that: for in truth such works are all dead. Indeed, if you create an image of God in your mind, the works you do with that in view are all dead and your good works are ruined (Pr. 39; see Latin Sermon IV, §21).

God ought not to be reduced to the plane where results and benefits are weighed. "The end is universally the same as the beginning, or principle. It does not have a why, but is itself the why of all things and for all things."[21] "God loves for his own sake and performs all things for his own sake; that is, he loves for love, and he works for working's sake."[22] Likewise, "whoever dwells in the goodness of his nature, dwells in God's love: but love is without why" (Pr. 28).

Therefore, "The just man does not love 'this and that' in God" (Pr. 41). Or again:

> I have sometimes said whoever seeks God and seeks anything *with* God, does not find God; but he who seeks God alone in truth finds God but he does not find God alone—for all that God can give, that he finds with God. If you seek God and seek him for your own profit and bliss, then in truth you are not seeking God" (Pr. 26).

Or, more abruptly perhaps:

> Whoever sees anything *in* God does not see God. A righteous man has no need of God. What I have, I am not in need of. He serves for nothing, he cares for nothing: he has God, and so he serves for nothing (Pr. 62).

Acting without a why restores each agent to its own gratuitous mode of acting.

> In the same way as God acts, so the just man acts without why; and just as life lives for its own sake and asks for no why for which to live, so the just man has no why for which to act (Pr. 41).

Imitating God entails living and acting without ulterior motive:

> For whoever seeks God in a special way gets the way and misses God, who lies hidden in it. But whoever seeks God without any special way gets him as he is in himself, and that man lives with the Son, and that man is life itself. If a man asked life for a thousand years, "*Why* do you live?", if it could answer it would only say, "I live because I live." That is because life lives from its own ground, and gushes forth from its own. Therefore it lives without *why*, because it lives for itself. And so, if you

were to ask a genuine man who acted from his own ground, "Why do you act?", if he were to answer properly he would simply say, "I act because I act." (Pr. 5b)

In other words, "Why do you live?—Indeed I don't know—I *like* living!" (Pr. 26)

Such insistence on the sheer value and spontaneity of a living being's activities brings Eckhart very close to Zen, as we shall see later. However, in another sermon, he gives a fuller explanation which links up with the religious dimension. After stating, "There is nothing in all the world so dear and so desirable as life," he asks, "But why do you live? For the sake of living, and yet you don't know why you live. Life is so desirable in itself that we desire it for itself." Lest these thoughts sound purely secular, the preacher adds:

> What is life? God's being is my life. If my life is God's being, then God's essence must be my essence, and God's existence my existence, neither more nor less. They live eternally "with God", just on a level with God, neither below nor above. They perform all their works with God, and God with them (Pr. 6).

IS THE SOUL EQUATED WITH GOD?

The medieval notion of identity begins with Aristotle's position that in the process of knowing, the knower becomes the known. Thus Meister Eckhart writes:

> Suppose my eye, being one and single in itself, falls on the wood with vision, then though each thing stays as it is, yet in the very act of seeing they are so much at one that we can really say 'eye-wood', and the wood *is* my eye. Now, if the wood were free from matter and wholly immaterial as my eyesight is, then we could truly say that in the act of seeing the wood and my eye were of one essence. If this is true of material things, it is all the more true of spiritual (Pr. 48).

Still this starting point amounts to a mere analogy, which reaches no further than the level of Plotinus's Intellect, which does not entirely supersede duality. By identity, Eckhart means oneness in a stricter sense. Is it then Plotinus's One? Surely it is, and yet not inaccessible, but including the human soul. In fact the keynote of Eckhart's whole corpus is the identification of the human soul with God: "The soul is one (*ein*) with God and not united (*vereint*)" (Pr. 12 and Pr. 64). The apophatic vocabulary, which normally denies divine characteristics, is transferred to the human soul in order to exercise the same negating role.

On the one hand, there seems to obtain a complete identity between the human person and God: "Between man and God there is nothing foreign and aloof, and therefore man is not 'like him' but he is altogether identical with him and the very same as God is" (Pr. 77). Here Eckhart rejects mere similarity and asserts identity (see also Pr. 13). On the other hand, he clearly differentiates God and the soul: the former is uncreated whereas the latter is created (Pr. 1).

His position regarding identity is based on two Augustinian-Thomist doctrines—an ontological and a theological one, which he complements by a mystical emphasis. The ontological doctrine is that God is both transcendent and immanent or, as Eckhart phrases it in his commentary on the Book of Wisdom, both distinct and indistinct. As entirely different from all creatures, God is distinct; as continually granting being to them, God is indistinct. This view he paradoxically expresses as follows:

> Everything which is distinguished by indistinction is the more distinct the more indistinct it is, because it is distinguished by its own indistinction. Conversely, it is the more indistinct the more distinct it is, because it is distinguished by its own distinction from what is indistinct. Therefore, it will be the more indistinct insofar as it is distinct and vice versa, as was said. But God is something indistinct which is distinguished by his indistinction, as Thomas says in Ia, q. 7, a. 1, at the end.[23]

This paragraph, typical Eckhart vintage, plays on the conceptual tension between God's sameness and otherness in regard to the universe. As the only one to be the same as, that is, indistinct from his creation (since all being flows from him), God is other, or distinct. McGinn comments: "God can be at once indistinct, or immanent, in all things at the same time as and precisely insofar as he is completely distinct from, that is, transcendent to, all things."[24]

Let us also mention two variants. The first one stresses the divine indistinction, in contrast to creaturely distinction: "God is indistinct from every being, just as Existence Itself is indistinct from any being, as said above. But everything created, by the very fact that it is created, is distinct."[25] The second passage emphasizes divine immanence: "God is unseparated from all things, for God is in all things and is more inwardly in them than they are in themselves." But the interesting thing is that the preacher immediately applies this Godly condition to the human person:

> And man too should be unseparated from all things, which means that a man should be nothing in himself and wholly detached from self: in that way he is unseparated from all things and is all things. . . . And therefore, as far as you are unseparated from all things, in so far you are God and all things, for God's divinity depends on his being unseparated from all things (Pr. 77).

The second doctrine that underpins Eckhart's sense of identity between the soul and the Godhead has to do with grace. For most patristic and medieval writers, grace elevates the soul and grants it a share in divine life. The Meister teaches that "the first fruit of the Incarnation of Christ, God's Son, is that man may become by the grace of adoption what the Son is by nature." He explains that "since grace resides in the essence of the soul, not in any potency, . . . it *per se* bestows divine being."[26] Corresponding to this traditional position expressed in the just quoted Latin commentary on John, we find a bolder rendering in a German sermon which insists on the identity between the divine Word or Son and the human spirit: "In this Word the Father speaks my spirit and your spirit and every individual human being's spirit equally in the same Word. In that speaking you and I are the natural son of God just like the Word itself" (Pr. 49).

Far from being construed as pantheism, the soul's identity with God is the result of a divine gift and therefore of a human change. It is the human person which is transformed, not God. Inspired by Augustine, Eckhart has Christ say to the soul: "You will be transformed into me, but I shall not be transformed into you." And the preacher explains: "Thus it is with the soul: when she imbibes God she is turned into God, so that the soul becomes divine but God does not become the soul" (Pr. 80).

While those views are perfectly Augustinian and Thomist, in another Predigt Eckhart departs from the two-stage schema of nature and grace and daringly adds a third stage:

> But still the soul is not satisfied with the work of grace, because even grace is a creature: she must come to a place where God works in his own nature. . . . Thus the soul is united and enclosed in God, and there grace slips from her: she works no longer by grace, but divinely in God. Then the soul becomes

wondrously enchanted and loses herself, just as if you were to pour a drop of water into a butt of wine, so that she does not know herself and imagines she is God (Pr. 82).

Is Eckhart saying that the state of glory, called "the happy vision" by Aquinas, is sometimes available in this present life? It is probably better not to adopt a doctrinal interpretation of this passage, but rather construe it as part of a sermon where the preacher talks mystical psychology. What he probably means is that, beyond the normal experience of grace, the soul is so totally identified with the divine—trinitarian—work, that she is no longer aware of having any activity other than God's.

THE SOUL'S BREAKTHROUGH TO THE GODHEAD

Finally, let us try to situate in his theological-mystical context Eckhart's strange doctrine of the soul's leaving God (*deus, got*) behind and breaking through to the Deity (*deitas, gotheit*). This bold contention by Eckhart has fascinated Nishitani, among others. We begin by examining an excerpt from Predigt 52, which comes across as an apparent profession of atheism:

> While I yet stood in my first cause, I *had* no God and was my own cause: then I wanted nothing and desired nothing, for I was bare being and the knower of myself in the enjoyment of truth. Then I wanted myself and wanted no other thing: what I wanted I was and what I was I wanted, and thus I was free of God and all things.

Straying are the commentators who do not pay attention to the first words of this citation: "while I yet stood in my first cause." The Meister is referring to the Augustinian and Thomist doctrine of the divine ideas. From all eternity, "before" (from our temporal point of view) the creation of the world, there exist in the divine mind—more precisely: in the Father's Word—ideas that are exemplars and causes of all things. In his commentary on John, he remarks, "what is produced or proceeds from anything is precontained in it" and "what proceeds is in its source according to the idea and likeness in which and according to which what proceeds is produced by the source."[27] In conformity with the Plotinian grand schema of *exitus-reditus* adopted by the medievals, Eckhart equates the situation before the *exitus* with the situation after the *reditus*. Overcoming time and multiplicity, the soul realizes it is primally one with God, in the eternal now where there is no distinction between God and the world.

What is the "God" about whom Eckhart, in the same Predigt 52, suddenly and paradoxically exclaims: "Let us pray to God that we may be free of God"? The preacher distinguishes two kinds of God as follows:

> For before there were creatures, God was not "God": He was That which He was. But when creatures came into existence and received their created being, then God was not "God" in Himself—He was "God" in creatures.

We must leave behind the "God in creatures" or, as the author phrases it later in the same sermon, "taking God as the origin of creatures," so as to have access to "God in himself." So long as we are thinking about God from our viewpoint, that is, as our origin and our end, we are limited by this viewpoint. If, on the contrary, we give up all our ideas about God seen as related to us, we escape our temporal perspective and become what we were and what we shall be in the divine mind. Then, Eckhart maintains, we are God in himself.

Taking account of Eckhart's concerns, which are both precreational and eschatological, we can easily enough interpret another of his seemingly outrageous pronouncements to the effect that the divine Oneness is higher than the Trinity.

> Now if, with this power [the mind], the soul sees anything imaged, whether she sees the image of an angel or her own image, it is an imperfection in her. If she sees God as He is God, or as He is an image, or as He is three, it is an imperfection in her. But when all images are detached from the soul and she sees nothing but the One alone, then the naked essence of the soul finds the naked, formless essence of divine unity, which is superessential being, passive, reposing in itself (Pr. 83).

Is Eckhart demeaning the Trinity? Not at all. The point he is making is not tantamount to the theological falsity that the divine Unity would be higher than the Trinity. His point simply derives from the usual combination of his epistemological, theological, and mystical interests. Thus he insists that our ordinary thinking about God, which begins with images, must be superseded by a higher stage, "when all images are detached from the soul and she sees nothing but the One alone." Noteworthy is the fact that here the "images" include not only the Trinity ("as He is three") but also the divinity ("as He is God"). That which is to be left behind is neither the Trinity nor the divinity, but all images of God (not distinguished, in this passage, from concepts) that human minds can entertain.

In another sermon, Eckhart says of "the highest power, which is the intellect":

> It does not want God as the Holy Ghost nor as the Son: it flees the Son. Nor does it want God, as He is God. Why? There He has a name, and if there were a thousand Gods it would go on breaking through, it wants to have Him there where He has no name: it wants a nobler, better thing than God as having a name (Pr. 26).

Again, similarly dissatisfied with any divine attribute, the intellect moves ahead:

> It never rests; it bursts into the ground whence goodness and truth proceed, and seizes it *in principio*, in the beginning where goodness and truth are just coming out, before it has any name, before it burgeons forth, in a much higher ground than goodness and wisdom (Pr. 69).

Both sermons speak of the intellect's "breakthrough" or "bursting into" (*durchbruch*), to designate its movement away from the nameable God into the ineffable God.

In Predigt 48, that which has to be transcended is immutability (an attribute of the divinity) as well as the trinitarian relations. I will italicize the key phrases:

> Therefore I say, if a man turns away from self and from all created things, then—to the extent that you do this—you will attain to oneness and blessedness in your soul's spark (*vünkelin*), which time and place never touched. This spark is opposed to all creatures: it wants nothing but God, naked, just as He is. It is not satisfied with the Father or the Son or the Holy Ghost, or all three Persons *so far as they preserve their several properties*. I declare in truth, this light [the soul's spark] would not be satisfied with *the unity* of the whole fertility *of the divine nature*. In fact I will say still more, which sounds even stranger: I declare in all truth, by the eternal and everlasting truth, that

this light is not content with *the simple changeless divine being* which neither gives nor takes: rather it seeks to know whence this being comes, it wants to get into its simple ground, into the silent desert into which no *distinction* ever peeped, of Father, Son or Holy Ghost.

This interpretation of Eckhart is confirmed by numerous texts. For example, talking about Joseph and Mary, who lost Jesus in the crowd, and about the birth of the Word in the soul, he writes:

All the powers of the soul, and all their works—these are the crowd. Memory, understanding and will, they all *diversify* you, and therefore you must leave them all: sense-perceptions, imagination, or whatever it may be that in which you find or seek to find yourself. . . . Accordingly the question arises, whether a man can find this birth in any things which, though divine, are yet brought in from without through the senses, such as *any ideas about God as being good, wise, compassionate*, or anything the intellect can conceive in itself that is in fact divine— whether a man can find this birth in all these. In fact, he cannot. For *although all this is good and divine, it is all brought in from without through the senses* (QT 59 = Walshe 4).

Again I have italicized significant phrases which make it clear what exactly Eckhart wishes we transcend: our inevitably limited and inadequate ideas about God as trinity, unity, good, wise, compassionate.

An additional quotation on this issue shows that the lack of apprehended distinctions does not abolish the Father's and Wisdom's [the Son's] presence:

Then God is known by God in the soul; with this Wisdom she [the soul] knows herself and all things, and this same Wisdom knows her with itself; and with the same Wisdom she knows the power of the Father in fruitful travail, and essential Isness (*weseliche isticheit*) in simple unity void of all distinctions (Pr. 1).

And following Augustine, Eckhart teaches that in contrast to the "evening knowledge" that builds on distinctions, the "morning knowledge" enables us to see all created things as well as the divine Persons without distinction "in the One that is God himself."[28]

Other texts distinguish "God" and "the Godhead." Eckhart asserts: "God and Godhead are as different as heaven and earth." And after acknowledging that "all creatures speak of God," he asks, "And why do they not speak of the Godhead?" The answer is: "Everything that is in the Godhead is one, and of that there is nothing to be said." Next, an intriguing theme is introduced: "When I enter the ground, the bottom, the river and fount of the Godhead, none will ask me whence I came or where I have been. No one missed me, for there God unbecomes (*entwirt*)" (QT 26 = Walshe 56).

What is the signification of such unbecoming? We get a clue from Eckhart's "Counsels on Discernment." Speaking of detachment, he characterizes it as an attitude in which we "unbecome" (*entwerden*). The phrase is aptly translated into English by "we cease to belong to ourselves." Such a state is reached through "emptying ourselves of self."[29] What seems to be suggested here is that God's self "unbecomes" or dissolves when our ideas of God are abandoned and we realize that nothing can be said of the absolutely transcendent Godhead. We then pass from the nameable "God" to the nameless and distinctionless "Godhead."

In his German writings, Eckhart adopts the strategy of employing metaphysical themes to set up a mystical ideal for the contemplatives he addresses. Accordingly, although apparently he is making statements *about God*, we should interpret him as making statements *about the soul's insights* regarding God. Those insights are of unequal value and therefore successive: one ought to pass from linguistic distinctions about divine attributes and trinitarian Persons to nonlinguistic silence at the more advanced phase where the mystical soul identifies with the Godhead.

Eckhart's point comprises various components: a gnoseological, a theological, and a mystical one. First, he adopts Plotinus's thesis that the One is totally perfect whereas multiplicity is most imperfect. This thesis epistemologically legitimizes the fact that in contrast to "God," which must unbecome, "the Godhead" utterly lies beyond the capacities of our analytical language. Second, his theology of deification permits him to assert the oneness between God and the soul. He explains such oneness by having recourse to the identity between a seal's imprint and the wax:

> If the seal is stamped right into the wax, so that none of the wax is left over but pressed right into the seal, then it is one and the same with the seal with no difference. In just the same way the soul is wholly united with God in image and likeness, when she is in contact with Him in true understanding (Pr. 32).

Third, Eckhart's mystical intention situates this philosophical tenet in the practical setting of silent, wordless, imageless, and conceptless meditation.

CONCLUDING REMARKS

As noted at the beginning of this chapter, Eckhart's view of human life is modeled after Plotinus's grand vision of all things' return to absolute unity. More precisely it is a Christianized version of Neoplatonism, which has been enriched by the doctrine that deifying grace makes human beings one with the eternal Word, which they are not by nature (hence the differentiation between creatures and God is not canceled out). It is this doctrine of grace that permits Eckhart to stress identity between the soul and the divine, even more than Plotinus, whose mysticism is a matter of participation and union rather than of unity. Nevertheless, that emphasis on identity paradoxically goes along with the interpersonal idiom of obedience to God's will, as we saw when we outlined his view of detached love.

Eckhart could not access more than snippets of Plotinus's works, because no complete Latin translation was available at that time. Yet several elements of that great Greek thinker's thought filtered through the Neoplatonic texts that were read in the late thirteenth century. Eckhart was fascinated by what Plotinus called "the primeval, that which was from the beginning" (Ennead VI.4.14). No doubt, to his eyes this reality was the same as the "that which was from the beginning" of St. John's first letter (1:1; see Genesis 1:1). He must have been unaware that his best metaphor designating the intensity and the diffusiveness of the Good (*bullitio* and *ebullitio*, for example in his Commentary on Exodus, §16) is already present in Plotinus, who characterizes the nature of the Good imbuing all things as "boiling over with life" (VI.5.12 and VI.7.12).

However, despite such *rapprochements*, Eckhart's worldview significantly differs from Plotinus's. This is not the place to spell out all aspects of that dissimilarity. Yet one point at least is in order. In contrast to Plotinus, for whom mysticism consists in an escape from the body, Eckhart stresses the importance of incarnating the spiritual life in daily life. Thus Mary and Martha, who host Jesus at their home, are one person, uniting the contemplative and the active life in detachment and inner harmony. Like the third-century Greek philosopher, this thirteenth-century theologian relativizes temporality; but unlike the former, the latter teaches that eternity (the Gospel's "unique necessary") can be actualized in the instant, when one is busy with ordinary chores.[30] In this respect Eckhart is closer to Zen than to Neoplatonism, as will become evident in chapter 10.

In sum, Eckhart's originality is to have represented human consciousness as having become divine consciousness and as pervading daily awareness. Being a matter of nondual loving, such consciousness is the highest that can be attained on earth and yet it influences the contemplative's basic attitude in all activities, even the most ordinary.

CHAPTER 6

Schleiermacher: Consciousness as Feeling

Friedrich Schleiermacher (1768–1834) is the first modern European theologian who has attempted to base theology on self-consciousness (*Selbstbewußtsein*). His understanding of consciousness is a great achievement and yet stands in need of clarification. In this chapter I will argue that while Schleiermacher contrasts two senses of "consciousness," he actually talks about three senses. By spelling out those three different meanings, I hope to show that a threefold account of consciousness throws more light on the whole topic than the twofold division that commentators take for granted.

I shall successively review Schleiermacher's concept of feeling, his distinction between prereflective and reflective consciousness, and his construal of absolute dependence. Step by step, a detailed account of consciousness will be proposed that explicates Schleiermacher's view of human, including religious, consciousness.[1]

FEELING

Throughout his major writings, Schleiermacher consistently uses the word *Gefühl*, "feeling," to characterize prereflective consciousness.[2] For him, *Gefühl* has a meaning different from ordinary feelings such as sensations, emotions, sentiments, or unconscious states, which are often subjectivistic. It is a *Zustand*, a "mental state," that consists in "self-consciousness" (§3.2; at §35.1, it is called a *Gemüthszustand*, "a state of our heart and soul"). Schleiermacher tells his friend Dr. Lücke that he would use the word *Gesinnung*, "disposition," in H. G. Tzschirner's sense, had it not in current parlance a predominantly practical connotation.³ So he prefers to call it a *Stimmung*, a permanent "mood."⁴

In the inner life of the human self, this stable feeling is by no means merely subjective, since it has to do as much with the general (*allgemeine*) as with the individual self-consciousness.⁵ By "general," Schleiermacher means that the experience (*Erfahrung*) is "expected of everyone" (*jedem . . . zugemutet*) (§3.2). In Steffen's definition, borrowed by Schleiermacher, feeling is "the immediate presence of the whole, undivided personal existence" (§3.2, Note).⁶ Far from being subjectivistic, this sense of personal existence is always intimately bound up with the awareness of the world and the awareness of God (§30.1, §32.2).

Several commentators have pointed out that Schleiermacher's feeling of absolute dependence is not an emotion. "'Gefühl' ist nicht ein Sentiment."⁷ "By 'feeling' he did not mean an emotional quality either. Having this feeling is not in the same class with having a feeling of pleasure or of anger. It is rather a mode of self-consciousness."⁸ But *Gefühl* was bound to be mistaken by careless readers, who would hear its usual psychological ring (as in William James⁹) and be lured by the Siren's seductive sound. Schleiermacher himself led many astray by repeatedly employing *fromme Erregungen*, "pious emotions." What has often been overlooked is that having emotions or feelings (usually plural: *Erregungen, Gefühle*) belongs to the realm of the antithesis (Schleiermacher gives as examples: pleasure/pain, objective/introvertive), whereas feeling (singular: *Gefühl*) is found in the realm where the antithesis between subject and its objects is abolished (§5). Although related to pious emotions, feeling nonetheless transcends affectivity (§34).

It is noteworthy that the second edition of *Der christliche Glaube* has deleted the few affective connotations that *Gefühl* had in the first.¹⁰ For instance, the "inclination" (*Neigung*) of the first (§8) disappears in the second (§3); the "yearning" (*Sehnsucht*) of the first (§10, Corollary 3) is absent in the second (§5, where the Corollary is dropped altogether). The only seemingly affective words that remain in the second edition are "joy" and "sorrow" (*Freude und Leid*) (see §3.2). But far from being emotions, they respectively characterize the ease and the difficulty with which the feeling of absolute dependence is made present in human consciousness.

Moreover, while the first edition (at §39) uses the couple "pleasure"/"displeasure" (*Lust/Unlust*) to evoke this opposition between ease and difficulty, the second edition confines the pair "pleasure"/"displeasure" to the domain of the antithesis (§5.4, §32.1).¹¹ On the one hand, joy and sorrow are defined as two modalities *of the basic feeling* in the higher degree of self-consciousness (where antithesis is superseded), depending on the ease or the difficulty with which that consciousness is felt; on the other hand, pleasure and displeasure belong to the sphere *of emotions*, that is, to the second degree of self-consciousness (characterized by antithesis).

Anyone familiar with the intricate hermeneutical problems created by Schleiermacher's vocabulary cannot but sympathize with Paul Tillich's judgment that "Schleiermacher made a great mistake" when he used the term *Gefühl* to refer to a profound religious experience that lies beyond the realm of human emotions.[12] Then why did Schleiermacher persist in using this ambiguous word? The best answer to this question is the following: "By saying that this is a feeling Schleiermacher meant to distinguish it from knowing as well as from acting."[13] And to express this important distinction, the author of the *Christian Faith* has recourse to an expression that explicates what "feeling" is supposed to convey: "immediate self-consciousness." This phrase does not carry the ambiguity of "feeling" and should have replaced it rather than coexisted with it.

In the first edition of *Der christliche Glaube*, feeling is defined as that which allows the self to go back and forth from the realm of knowing to the realm of willing. It is seen as an intermediary, a "midpoint" (*Mittelpunkt*, §8.2; see 1821:123, 141–142, 224, 226, 232, 236–237). Friedrich Beisser calls it a "pivot" (*Angelpunkt*)[14] between knowing and willing. I would compare knowing and willing to the constituents of the self's foreground, which find their unity in a background, namely, piety.

Basing himself on Schleiermacher's lectures of 1814 in the *Dialektik*, John Thiel writes: "The transcendent ground eludes the activities of thinking and willing, but may be apprehended in the convergence of these activities."[15] The antithesis of these activities is canceled at a point of identity that Schleiermacher calls "feeling, which exists in the oscillation (*Wechsel*)" between these activities, "as the final end of thinking and the beginning of willing."[16]

Commenting on the 1822 lectures of the same work,[17] Marianne Simon remarks that the hinge between thinking and willing is, according to Schleiermacher, the locus of "non-difference" (*Indifferenz*) in which all oppositions are abolished. She interprets Scheiermacher's "zero point" (*Nullpunkt*) as a kind of "still point" (*point mort* in French) that the self experiences at the transitional moment when it has just completed its return to itself (in knowing) and is about to initiate a going out of itself (in action).[18] Or, as another commentator remarks, the indifference point is intermediate between "the having-ceased of one function and the not-yet-having-begun of the other function."[19]

However, the *Nullpunkt* is never directly reached independently of thinking and willing.[20] Each in its own distinctive way, these two activities lead to the midpoint and flow out of it. Schleiermacher speaks of *ein Übergang*, a crossing, a passage back and forth between thinking and willing. He calls it "immediate self-consciousness" or "feeling."[21]

We find an illustration of this experience in a lecture on Christian ethics, in which Schleiermacher illustrates how "primordial consciousness" can issue in a thought or in a deed:

> It becomes a thought when I reduce what is expressed to its effective ground; it becomes a deed when I find in it a summons to act in accordance with the divine will. Consider the first encounter of Andrew and John with Jesus. The influence of the divine was there first, and from that arose a thought and a deed. The thought was that we have found the Messiah; the deed was that they began to communicate with him. The primordial, from which both things arose, was the impression of the divinity of the redeemer.[22]

PREREFLECTIVE AND REFLECTIVE CONSCIOUSNESS

The consciousness we have been explicating is prereflective. Schleiermacher sets it in contrast to reflective consciousness. By doing so, fortunately he does not underwrite the misleading contrast between unconscious and conscious which so many authors have adopted. In the German-speaking world, *Bewußtsein* (consciousness) most of the time expresses only a thematic awareness. For example, we find this understanding of *Bewußtsein* in Anton Günter, Schleiermacher's contemporary.[23] For C. G. Jung also, consciousness equals reflective consciousness and can be preceded only by the unconscious.[24] Schleiermacher does not fall into this dichotomy, which leaves no room for a prereflective consciousness. He expressly affirms that his usage of the word "feeling" does not include "unconscious states" (§3.2).

Beginning with his contrast between *two* forms of consciousness, this section will investigate whether some texts of Schleiermacher would not actually suggest the presence of *three* forms of consciousness.

In a passage of the 1821 edition of the *Speeches*,[25] Schleiermacher invites his readers to an exercise in self-awareness: "I must direct you to your own selves. You must apprehend a living movement. . . . What you are to notice is the rise of your consciousness . . ." (1821:41). The experience he attempts to evoke seems to have three properties. First, the knowing subject and the known object are one: "The more definite your image, the more, in this way, you become the object, and the more you lose yourselves" (42). Second, the self is one, since it encompasses in its own consciousness the whole gamut of what is perceived: "And how are you for yourselves? By the unity of your self-consciousness, which is given chiefly in the possibility of comparing the varying degrees of sensation" (43). Third, the self is one with the Infinite: "Your whole life is such an existence for self in the Whole" (43).

The exact nature of these traits and of their connections remain vague; but the purpose of Schleiermacher's rhetorical *Speeches* is not to offer a philosophical analysis, but to evoke for his readers a unitary experience that approximates prereflective consciousness.

A few pages further on, Schleiermacher returns to prereflective consciousness as he remarks about reflective consciousness, called "contemplation": "this contemplation presupposes the original activity" (47).[26] Humans are conscious of this original activity, since "all knowledge is recollection" (44), namely, recollection of inner phenomena that had to be conscious from the start, albeit prereflectively, since they can be subsequently recalled. Or, more metaphorically: "Uninterruptedly, like a sacred music, the religious feelings should accompany his active life" (59).

The *Christian Faith* also sheds light on consciousness. At §3.2, a distinction is introduced between two kinds of self-consciousness. One of them is feeling, or immediate self-consciousness (*unmittelbares Selbstbewußtsein*). The other is "that consciousness of self which is more like an objective (*gegenständlich*) consciousness, being a representation (*Vorstellung*) of oneself, and thus mediated by self-contemplation." There is no significant difference between the adjectives *objektiv* and *gegenständlich* in these contexts, for they both mean a consciousness of an object, an object-oriented consciousness. In the *Dialektik* the vocabulary is almost the same: as immediate self-consciousness, *Gefühl* is different from the *Ich*, from reflective self-consciousness, more accurately from "*reflected* self-consciousness," *verschieden von dem reflektierten Selbstbewußtsein*.[27]

In all those writings (the *Speeches*, the *Dialektik*, the *Christian Faith*), Schleiermacher operates with a twofold scheme, namely, a contrast between prereflective (called "immediate") and reflective (called "objective") consciousness. Unfortunately, this duality leaves in the shadows another form of consciousness, which I would situate in between the two other forms.

Schleiermacher does not ignore this third form of consciousness, which coexists with all our human operations. The *Dialektik*, for instance, adumbrates it when this work presents the *Gefühl . . . als ein überall durchgehendes und begleitendes*, "as something that pervades and accompanies everywhere." What feeling or immediate self-consciousness accompanies is "a moment of thinking or willing" (*einen Moment des Denkens oder des Wollens*).[28] Schleiermacher adds that although feeling often appears to be a bare minimum, it can never be reduced to zero. It goes along with every moment, no matter whether thinking or willing predominates.

It would be helpful to detach and situate this third kind of self-consciousness (called consciousness B) halfway between immediate self-consciousness (consciousness A) and reflected self-consciousness (consciousness C). More precisely, I would argue that in some passages of Schleiermacher's writings immediate self-consciousness is subdivided into what I call consciousness A and consciousness B.

A moment ago, an excerpt from the *Dialektik* was quoted that highlighted consciousness B as accompanying consciousness C. In the same §51 of the *Dialektik*, Schleiermacher points out that there are two aspects in the ever-abiding feeling. He writes: "our self-consciousness is always affected by the external multiplicity, but at the same time it is also affected by the transcendent ground in itself, which cancels all multiplicity." He adds that "we cannot separate the religious side of feeling from the side that is turned outward."[29] I take "the religious side" to be consciousness A and "the side that is turned outward" to be consciousness B, which accompanies consciousness C.

The first edition of *Der christliche Glaube* spells out a distinction between feeling as we find it in the knower and the doer with respect to any *particular* state of affairs, and the pious feeling that expresses the relation of the thinking and acting person to the *universal* order. On the one hand, there is consciousness C, namely, a feeling we can notice in connection with the particular objects that we find in each of the two domains. For example, with respect to knowing, we observe that

> Every cognitive phase, irrespective of domain or object, is accompanied by a feeling which expresses the knower's certainty about this determinate state of affairs ... at the same time it expresses the knower's disposition (*Neigung*) toward the determinate object, and thus it is dependent upon this disposition.

A similar feeling obtains with respect to doing, where

> every determinate particular doing emerges from a feeling which refers particularly to the domain of that doing, a feeling which, if it operates undisturbed, produces the uprightness of

this doing without requiring piety to this end, as in the feeling for one's family, professional feeling, the feeling of patriotism, and even universal human love.

On the other hand, we find consciousness B. First, with respect to knowing,

> there is another feeling of conviction (*Überzeugung*) which can accompany all acts of knowing alike, irrespective of their object, since it expresses especially the relation of every cognitive sphere to the whole and to the highest unity of all cognizing, and thus refers to the highest and most universal order and harmony; and no one will refuse to call this a pious feeling.

Again, this time with respect to doing, we mark

> a feeling of the relation of its determinate domain to the totality of action and to the highest unity of action. Likewise no one will refuse to recognize such a feeling as pious, which thus expresses the relation of a person as agent to that universal order and harmony.

From this he concludes: "It is evident how pious feeling can co-exist with knowing and doing, accompanying both" (§8.3).

What is helpful here is the difference between two kinds of feeling. First Schleiermacher describes the kind of feeling that is part and parcel of our particular activities as we engage in knowing and acting. Second he describes a kind of feeling, the "pious feeling," which unifies the spheres of knowing and doing. On the one hand, then, we have an aspect of consciousness C: the intellectual "certainty or conviction" in our knowing and the ethical "resolve" in our doing (as the parallel §5.2 of the second edition phrases it). On the other hand, we have consciousness B as our sense that we are related to a totality of cognition and action.

In §5.1 of the second edition of the same work, Schleiermacher recasts the distinctions in a new framework, namely, the three grades of human consciousness. In the context of our discussion, we can leave aside the first and lowest grade. Schleiermacher considers this to be the confused, animal consciousness, which is ours as infants or as half-awake adults. The second and third grades of consciousness are directly significant for our purposes. The second grade is "sensible" (*sinnlich*) self-consciousness, whose "determinations ... develop from our relations to nature and to man." It belongs to "the realm of reciprocal action." It is consciousness C, the one that deals with objects and thus functions in the realm of antitheses.

Of the third and highest grade of consciousness, Schleiermacher writes:

> This is not the consciousness of ourselves as individuals of a particular description, but simply of ourselves as individual finite existence in general; so that we do not set ourselves over against any other individual being, but, on the contrary, all antithesis between one individual and another is in this case done away (§5.1).

Still, this highest grade of consciousness, which is permanent in us, is somehow connected with the second grade:

> It is impossible to claim a constancy for the highest self-consciousness, except on the supposition that the sensible self-consciousness is always conjoined with it (§5.4).

It seems that there is an ambiguity in Schleiermacher's highest grade of consciousness. It comprises two things: first, the sense that our intellectual and ethical activities are unified; second, the sense that these unified activities have a source or a ground. For the sake of clarification, I would submit that the first belongs to consciousness B, while the second derives from consciousness A. On the one hand, consciousness B has to do with the synthesizing of our activities, which was presented in the first section of this article, when attention was drawn to feeling as the conscious experience of an inner midpoint, pivot, passage back and forth between thinking and willing. On the other hand, consciousness A consists in the feeling of absolute dependence, which relates us to the origin of our unified consciousness and which will be discussed shortly.

From the texts examined in this section, then, we can surmise that Schleiermacher talks about not two but three basic forms of consciousness:

A. the unobjectifiable consciousness that amounts to "piety" and, as we shall see in the next section, is construed by Schleiermacher as the feeling of absolute dependence;
B. the in-itself-unobjectified-yet-objectifiable integrating consciousness that accompanies our particular acts of knowing and willing, and that enables us to pass from knowing to willing (and vice versa); and

C. object-oriented consciousness, which objectifies beings that are given in perception and which can also account for consciousness A and B.

ABSOLUTE DEPENDENCE

The difference between consciousness A and consciousness B will become clearer if we pay close attention to §4 of the *Christian Faith*, where Schleiermacher introduces the concept of absolute dependence. In the previous section, he characterizes consciousness B as he reiterates "the assertion that piety is a state in which Knowing, Feeling, and Doing are combined" (§3.5). But he goes beyond §3 as he points to our openness (=consciousness A) to the common source of knowing and doing.

In order to do so, he introduces a basic distinction, between "abiding-in-self" and "passing-beyond-self" (*Insichbleiben* and *Aussichheraustreten*). On the one hand, Feeling is sheer "abiding-in-self" and therefore "it belongs altogether to the realm of receptivity" (§3.3). On the other hand, both Knowing and Doing are forms of "passing-beyond-self" (although Doing is more entirely so).

Schleiermacher then explains "how a Doing can arise from a Knowing" (and vice versa): it cannot "except as mediated by a determination of self-consciousness." Such a determination, or Feeling, is the central pivot, so that "the piety is just the determination of self-consciousness which comes in between the two" (§3.5). Thereupon follows the demonstration that this fundamental determination is "the consciousness of being absolutely dependent" (§4, thesis).[30]

§4.1 wants to account for the fact that, in self-consciousness, there is an identical and a variable element. Two kinds of consciousness are presented as inseparable.

> In any actual state of consciousness, . . . we are never simply conscious of our Selves in their unchanging identity, but are always at the same time conscious of a changing determination of them (*In keinem wirklichen Bewußtsein, . . . sind wir unsres Selbst an und für sich, wie es immer dasselbe ist, allein bewußt, sondern immer zugleich einer wechselnden Bestimmtheit desselben*) . . . every consciousness of self is at the same time the consciousness of a variable state of being (*jedes Selbstbewußtsein ist zugleich das eines veränderlichen Soseins*).

In the same paragraph, the permanence is ascribed to "the I" (*das Ich*, translated as "the Ego"), whereas the variability is generated by a factor called an "other" (the German *andere* must be translated here not with an uppercase but with a lowercase "o"). It is in interaction with "this other" (*dieses andere*) that determination takes place.

The pair, "unchanging identity"/"changing determination" is then rephrased as "a self-caused element"/"a non-self-caused element" (*ein Sichselbstsetzen/ein Sichselbstnichtsogesetzthaben*),[31] as "a Being"/"a Having-by-some-means-come-to-be" (*ein Sein/ein Irgendwiegewordensein*), or again as "the existence of the subject for itself"/"its co-existence with an other" (*das Sein des Subjektes für sich/Zusammensein mit anderem*) (§4.1). There are semantic shifts in these equivalences, but the meanings are sufficiently close so as not to weaken the demonstration Schleiermacher is engaged in.

The second part of §4.1 begins as follows: "Now to these two elements, as they exist together in the temporal self-consciousness, correspond in the subject its *Receptivity* (*Empfänglichkeit*) and its spontaneous *Activity* (*Selbsttätigkeit*)." The verb "correspond" (*entsprechen*) *seems* to suggest that activity and receptivity respectively characterize the first and the second member of the previously mentioned pairs. But a careful reading of §4.2 can dispel this first impression. Schleiermacher shows that both activity (the movement from within) and receptivity (the movement from without) are present in each member of the pairs. From the point of view of consciousness, then, receptivity becomes the "feeling of Dependence" (*Abhängigkeitsgefühl*) and activity becomes the "feeling of Freedom" (*Freiheitsgefühl*). The former sums up the receptive determinations of self-consciousness, whereas the latter sums up the active determinations.

Schleiermacher proceeds to claim that the element of receptivity is always the primary one, and for two reasons: first, because we cannot think away our coexistence with the "other" that ever affects us in some way, and second, because all our actions are given their direction from a prior moment in which something is known and responded to (see §4.1). These two reasons are most noteworthy, for they clearly exclude the idea of a dependence that would be individualistic or merely passive. On the contrary, absolute dependence encompasses both our relatedness and our spontaneous activity. Indeed, without the presence of the other as influencing us or as being influenced by us, and without our dynamic aliveness as due to what Schleiermacher will later call "God-consciousness" (§106.1), neither the feeling of partial dependence nor the feeling of partial freedom would occur. Thus both of these feelings combine into a consciousness of "reciprocity" or "interaction" (*Wechselwirkung*) when the self and its environment act upon each other (see §4.2).

At this point, Schleiermacher engages in a masterful demonstration.

> Now let us suppose the totality of all moments of feeling, of both kinds, as one whole: then the corresponding Other (*Andere*, which only at this stage comes with a capital "A") is also to be supposed as a totality or as one . . . .

Then,

> we think of the total "outside" as one, and moreover (since it contains other receptivities and activities to which we have a relation) as one together with ourselves, that is, as a *World*.

This situation, which is basic to our human condition, is "an equipoise" between the two "limits" that are dependence and freedom (§4.2).

In the next paragraph, Schleiermacher dismisses the possibility, among humans, of a feeling of *absolute* freedom. To exclude it, he brings back the reason already mentioned:

> For if the feeling of freedom expresses a forthgoing activity, this activity must have an object which has been somehow given to us, and this could not have taken place without an influence of the object upon our receptivity.

Therefore, this feeling of *relative* freedom presupposes a prior receptivity, expressed in a feeling of dependence.

Now what about the other alternative? Is there a feeling of *absolute* dependence? Schleiermacher answers affirmatively. But one must observe that this feeling does not have any limited object, because such an object would imply "a counter-influence" on the part of the human subject and hence a feeling of relative freedom. The feeling of absolute dependence, or of being acted upon by an Other on which we do not act, is determined by something much larger than a limited object.

> But the self-consciousness which accompanies all our activity, and therefore, since that is never zero, accompanies our whole existence, and negatives absolute freedom, is itself precisely a consciousness of absolute dependence; for it is the consciousness that the whole of our spontaneous activity comes from a source outside of us . . . (§4.3).

It is important to notice that the feeling of absolute dependence is basic both to the feeling of relative dependence and to the feeling of relative freedom. It is not the result of some one-sided emphasis on the passive side of human existence, as Hegel mistakenly thought.[32] On the contrary, the feeling of absolute dependence encompasses both the active and the passive aspects of the self's interactions in the world.[33]

Schleiermacher's characterization of the feeling of absolute dependence should make it clear that, since it has to do with Transcendence, it does not consist in consciousness B, which is immanent to the unity of all human subjects in the world. Does it consist in consciousness A? As I shall explain in my assessment, it is inspired by consciousness A and yet requires consciousness C in order to be expressed. At any rate, it seems to me that this characterization does support a clear distinction between consciousness A and B, as well as the superseding of the twofold schema by a threefold one, to which we now return.

THREE KINDS OF CONSCIOUSNESS

What can be drawn from this exposition of Schleiermacher's thought on consciousness? The readers may need to hark back to the differentiation of consciousness into A, B, and C, at the end of our section entitled "Prereflective and Reflective Consciousness."

First, does Schleiermacher present the three forms of consciousness? As a matter of fact he does talk about the three of them, but he does not situate consciousness B halfway between consciousness A (unobjectifiable, received in the feeling of absolute dependence) and consciousness C (object-oriented, which objectifies beings that are given in perception, and which can also objectify consciousness B). Either he contrasts A with C, or B with C, apparently without realizing that A and B ought to be expressly distinguished.

The few extracts from his writings that we have scrutinized suggest that consciousness B is indeed different from consciousness A. It is presented as accompanying all human acts of knowing and willing, and integrating them. In this essay it has been characterized as a consciousness which is in itself unobjectified and yet can be subsequently objectified. It is in itself unobjectified because, in contrast to consciousness C, it does not amount to an awareness of objects, but to the deeper consciousness of how our acts take place and are interrelated. Nonetheless it is objectifiable inasmuch as, by grasping the links between the various operations it permeates (such as sensing, perceiving, conceptualizing, judging, willing), we can represent it faithfully.

In light of those clarifications, let us summarize again our account of the three forms of consciousness:

Consciousness A is the fount or ground of consciousness B and C. Schleiermacher correctly sees it as the unobjectifiable source whence the two basic modes of worldly consciousness (knowing and willing) derive.

Consciousness B, which accompanies all cognitive and affective acts, is in itself prereflective, but it can be objectified and thus become a part of consciousness C; were it lacking, we would have no reflective self-knowledge at all. It is the integrating point where the two basic modes of worldly consciousness converge.

Consciousness C, which intends the world, encompasses perception, conceptualization, judgment, and volition; it can also reflect on self-consciousness and objectify it.

In the second place, we must ask: both in the case of consciousness B and A, is Schleiermacher right in saying that self-consciousness is immediate? Consciousness B is given in one's acts; that is to say, it is prereflective awareness of one's self as living and operating. It is immediate in the sense that it accompanies the subject's operations, prior to reflecting upon them. However, when it has been mediated and objectified by concepts and judgments available in language, it becomes a part of consciousness C.

If we now consider consciousness A, we find that it is indeed immediate, and even more immediate than consciousness B, since it is not accompanied by any definite thought or act. Beyond the subject / object division, which is typical of the realm of antithesis, one simply rests in the still point. But since this point is prior to any reflection, we must affirm, pace Schleiermacher, that consciousness A is not *self*-consciousness. Only *post factum*, namely, *after* ordinary consciousness has been restored, does one realize that one was immersed in a totally unobjectifiable consciousness. The awareness of this shift to and from A, however, belongs to consciousness B.

In the third place, can consciousness A be characterized as an experience of absolute dependence? Such a characterization leaves much to be desired. When Schleiermacher opposes "the view that this feeling of dependence is itself conditioned by some previous knowledge about God" (§4.4), he fails to take into consideration the fact that there is no feeling or consciousness of absolute dependence unless preceded by some idea of absolute dependence. Far from being an immediate experience, the conviction of absolute dependence is *an assertion* that, whether believed or demonstrated, requires a minimum of understanding (at least grasping the relation of cause to effect). Since this conviction is always intellectually mediated and objectified, it belongs to consciousness C.

This point is confirmed by Schleiermacher's own insistence that absolute dependence is always felt in connection with consciousness C: "It is as a person determined for this moment in a particular manner within the realm of the antithesis that he is conscious of his absolute dependence." As he explains, "if the feeling of absolute dependence in general were the entire content of a moment of self-consciousness, . . . it would lack the definiteness and clearness which spring from its being related to the determination of the sensible self-consciousness (§5.3).

Thus, consciousness C validly states that humans permanently stand in a relation of absolute dependence in regard to a "Whence." Far from directly flowing from religious experience, such an interpretation stands for itself intellectually. As a matter of fact, Schleiermacher's various lectures on *Dialektik*, from 1811 until 1831, and his Introduction of 1833 developed the epistemological metaphysics that he used in his *Glaubenslehre*.[34] Of course the fact that, from the *Speeches* onward, Schleiermacher paid attention to his own consciousness must have influenced the very presence of this theme in his philosophy. Moreover, by locating consciousness A on the spectrum of human consciousness, he allows his readers to envision it as the best way to live out absolute dependence in unobjectified meditation or prayer.

In the fourth place, can we be more precise about the relation prereflective/reflective? The distinction between consciousness A and B allows us to incorporate the fact that the former rules out any reflection on it while one still is in it, whereas the latter does not. However, consciousness B can be mindful of consciousness A and thus meaningfully situate it (such situating is less than objectifying in the sense of comprehending it) among the various kinds of consciousness. As soon as we talk about consciousness A, we are no longer in it. But when we talk about consciousness B, we remain in it, since it accompanies all our mental operations, including our reflecting on the consciousness that we have of them. Talk about consciousness A and B is, strictly speaking, consciousness B remembering consciousness A and explicating both A and B in consciousness C. In other words, A always remains prereflective, whereas B transits between the prereflective and the reflective.

Notwithstanding his brilliant analysis of human consciousness, Schleiermacher seems to have unwittingly conflated consciousness A with consciousness B and pronounced the undifferentiated compact to be immediate self-consciousness, which he equated with God-consciousness. But the distinction between A and B enables us to unravel the mystical and nonmystical traits of immediate self-consciousness. On the one hand, consciousness A is mystical because it consists in being derived from a divine source. On the other hand, consciousness B, although not unrelated to the divine source, is in itself secular: it expresses the unity of all selves as a whole throughout their knowing and willing activities.

Having sorted out the differences between the three basic forms of consciousness, we can see more clearly the status of consciousness A as the core of religious experience. We can also appreciate the intermediary and yet paramount role of consciousness B as integrative. And finally, we can acknowledge the importance of consciousness C for a philosophy of religion that wants to situate consciousness A and B with respect to the objectified world in which we live.

CONCLUDING REMARKS

A twentieth-century disciple of Schleiermacher's, Georg Wobbermin, who has attempted to develop his master's theology, writes:

> Schleiermacher conceives of the objective consciousness in the sense of perceptual objectivity. The discovery that there is also a non-perceptual comprehension of objects was made later. Schleiermacher does not reckon at all with any such process. He thought only of perceptual objectivity, more precisely, of the reflective processes of the mind in which it results.

It is from the model of perceptual objectivity that Schleiermacher wanted to characterize, by contrast, the kind of consciousness typical of religious feeling. "Hence he added the qualification 'immediate,' lest anyone be led to think of a self-consciousness which is more like an objective consciousness. . . ."[35]

Schleiermacher's use of the perceptual metaphor is consistent with his somewhat modified Kantianism. For him, knowledge is obtained in accord with the two Kantian stages: first, the direct contact or impression that occurs in perceiving or intuiting; and second, objectification or conceptualization. However, realizing that religious experience is different from ordinary knowledge, he decides to characterize it not as objectification, since this stage is obviously at one remove from religious experience, but as perception. Not as sense perception, of course, but as another kind of perceiving, intuiting, being impressed, or being determined. The weakness of this strategy resides in the fact that his analogy, as well as Wobbermin's, is perceptual. Being the lowest component of human knowing, perception cannot be fruitfully employed as the *principal* paradigm for religious analogy.

Our careful reading of Schleiermacher's *Dialektik* and of his *Glaubenslehre* has signaled the presence of three layers in his archeology of consciousness: first, reflective knowledge (= consciousness C); second, consciousness accompanying all our acts (= consciousness B); and third, religious experience (= consciousness A). Except in a few passages, he clearly distinguishes only the first layer from the two others, which he lumps together. Let us now revisit these layers and their elements.

First, in our object-oriented knowledge, more is involved than perception and conceptualization. When the human mind intends the world, the results that it achieves are not, *pace* Kant and Schleiermacher, mere constructs like percepts and concepts; intentionality also reaches out to reality by inquiring, getting insights, verifying the status of its partial discoveries.

With respect to the second layer, Schleiermacher rightly asserts that we are capable of more than knowing what lies outside of us. He points to a consciousness that accompanies all our acts of knowing and doing and that is in itself prereflective and unobjectified. About it, he asks a very Aristotelian question:

> Through our search for supreme principles, do we want first to posit ourselves as being in possession of something? We rather presuppose it as existing already and want simply to attain the consciousness of it; it exists in all our knowing but previously in an unconscious way and only under the form of activity; it is indeed something actually at work, but it is not also taken up into consciousness.[36]

And in the following lecture, Schleiermacher avers: "In order to come to know one must nonetheless have some prior knowing of that knowing" (§6).

In the *Glaubenslehre* Schleiermacher returns to the importance of the prereflective "I," in which the transition between thinking and willing takes place and which constitutes the living unity of human consciousness (§3.4). He underlines the significance of this unobjectified self-consciousness which lies at the source of all our operations. It is not unlike what Aristotle writes about the ever abiding human wonder and about the desire for happiness (in both cases a permanent "feeling" indeed, in Schleiermacher's sense of the word *Gefühl*). It could be compared to Thomas Aquinas's principles of understanding and of practical reason.

Schleiermacher does distinguish self-consciousness and self-knowledge. The former is prereflective, whereas the latter is a case of reflective knowledge. Unfortunately, his account of self-knowledge does not take into consideration some indispensable acts of which we are conscious. These conscious acts are questioning, acquiring insights, making grounded judgments, loving in a way that is impregnated with meaning and truth. Furthermore, as we saw in our examination of the first layer, his construal of objectification, which applies both to our knowledge of others and to our self-knowledge, leaves much to be desired insofar as the role of insights and judgments is underplayed.

As far as the third layer is concerned, Schleiermacher correctly explains why immediate self-consciousness is not the outcome of finite causality and therefore is directly received in absolute dependence (§4). But even so he fails to elaborate the critical-realist epistemology in which this religious experience acquires its full significance. Far from totally escaping the realm of knowledge, absolute dependence and its "whence" can be meaningfully and truly referred to in insights, judgments and propositions that, for all their purely analogical and negative character, are nevertheless intellectually more valid than he imagined.

Despite the richness of his observations on immediate self-consciousness and absolute dependence, Schleiermacher merely detects and hazily adumbrates what has been presented here as the second layer, namely, consciousness B, which accompanies all our acts and states. Because it stands halfway between the other two layers (reflective knowledge and mystical experience), this consciousness B is the key to a right assessment of the other two. It is not a consciousness-*of*, typical of intentionality, but a consciousness-*in*, that is, present in all our acts and states.

Of course Schleiermacher realizes that. But failing a successful explication of consciousness-in, he cannot show all its import for a philosophy of religion. Apparently unaware of how this consciousness B can be fully explicated, he has a hard time situating consciousness A within a frame of reference derived from consciousness B and reflectively developed by consciousness C. He does not offer much more than a simple contrast with reflective knowledge wrongly construed as perception-conceptualization. Furthermore, he interprets religious experience as another kind of perception, pronounced different from ordinary perception and yet too similar, in my estimation, since it is seen as an intuition.

Undoubtedly, however, Schleiermacher is convinced that religious consciousness amounts to much more than perception. As we saw, he asserts that "the highest degree of feeling is the religious one."[37] Noteworthy also is the fact that he locates this religious feeling at the origin of both knowing and doing, that is to say, in the very ground of the soul.

PART III

A Dialogue with Zen Philosophy

CHAPTER 7

Western Views of the Self

In this chapter I single out a concept that becomes problematic in mystical experience: the human self. By "self" I mean a person, that is, a self-conscious individual with all its actual characteristics, comprising both those owing to the human species and those amounting to its idiosyncrasies. I employ the term "ego" as an equivalent for "self," and not in the technical sense that we find in Freud (as distinct from superego and id), or in Jung (as distinct from self), but rather in the precise sense we have found in Sartre (as the reflected "I" that is more restricted than the self's overall experience).

The questions that trigger this investigation of the self are the following. In consciousness A, do mystics lose their sense of self? Do they assert that there is no human ego, or do they merely cease being aware of their own self, beyond consciousness B? Is the ego of consciousness C (consciousness-of) which is rejected always a false self? Or is it the genuine sense of identity of consciousness B (consciousness-in) that is being transcended?

I will delineate, in the first place, the pictures of the self that the Scottish philosopher David Hume (1711–1776) and the American philosopher William James (1842–1910) find untenable. The former argues that the self cannot be adequately represented, whereas the latter endeavors to overcome the concept of an unrelated self. In the second place, I will examine the well-argued case that Lonergan and others make for the existence of a genuine self. In the third place, mainly with the help of Sally King, I will discuss how the self may be transcended. Finally, an interpretation will be offered.[1]

ARGUING AGAINST THE SELF

Hume raises an objection to the philosophical validity of self-awareness. In accord with his view of knowledge, he considers our belief in the self to be a fiction. He argues as follows. For the self to exist, the idea we form of it must correspond to an unchanging and unitary reality that holds the stream of experience together. But our experience merely consists of *discrete* impressions, also called perceptions, such as pain and pleasure, grief and joy, passions and sensations.

About our idea of self, he asks with skepticism:

> from what impression cou'd this idea be deriv'd? . . . But self or person is not any one impression, but that to which our several impressions and ideas are suppos'd to have a reference. If any impression gives rise to the idea of self, that impression must continue invariably the same, thro' the whole course of our lives; since self is suppos'd to exist after that manner. But there is no impression constant and invariable.[2]

Hume confines himself within a narrow model of human knowledge, namely, the view that ideas are nothing but pale replicas of sense impressions.[3] Given this perceptualism, he obviously cannot accept as real anything besides those impressions. He states:

> The mind is a kind of theatre, where several perceptions successively make their appearance; pass, re-pass, glide away, and mingle in an infinite variety of postures and situations. . . . They are the successive perceptions only, that constitute the mind; nor have we the most distant notion of the place, where these scenes are represented, or of the materials, of which it is compos'd.[4]

If knowledge is merely a matter of perception through impressions, obviously there is no abiding self to be perceived. As he admits, "I never can catch *myself* at any time without a perception, and never can observe any thing but the perception."[5] In other words, we might speak of many selves in rapid succession, indistinguishable from our many perceptions. Later in the same section Hume explains that the objects we conceive of are continually changing; but the fact that they are related by association, habit, and belief, makes us commit the mistake of confusing their ever shifting relations with an identity or sameness. Hence the fictitious notions of soul, self, or substance. Since the bond that links our impressions amounts to a manifold of extraneous connections, the bond between our ideas, which derive from those impressions and which constitutes the notion of a permanent self, must be pronounced an illusionary one.

Hume overlooks the kind of questions that human intentionality spontaneously raises, namely, questions for understanding and for judgment. He also does not take into consideration the kind of consciousness that accompanies all our cognitive acts and that is continuous (except, of course, in dreamless sleep or coma). Correct as he surely is regarding the inconstancy of impressions, he nevertheless ignores the intentional consciousness present throughout all those impressions as well as throughout all other human activities. I will say more on this topic in the next section.

For his part, James disagrees with Hume's contention that experience generally consists of discrete elements that are extrinsically related. *The Principles of Psychology* asserts that in our unbroken stream of consciousness, whenever we talk to ourselves or to others, all the parts of any sentence are apprehended together. For example, in the phrase, "The pack/of cards/is on/the table," the four time-parts that constitute the saying do not correspond to four objects that would be distinctly perceived, at least at first. It is only in a second, reflective stage that we can isolate these four separate components. From the unified meaning of this perceptual experience, James proceeds to his conviction that the "I" cannot be a mere empirical aggregate. The things we refer to "must be thought together, and in one *something*, be that something ego, psychosis, state of consciousness, or whatever you please."[6] Still, he rightly insists, and Sartre would concur, that this sense of an enduring "me" is not yet the reflective ego.

Nonetheless, even as early as in *The Principles of Psychology*, James is reluctant to commit himself to this commonsense view of the self, which he does not consider to be a philosophical truth. He declines to speak of the self from a metaphysical point of view, namely, as a substantial Soul or a timeless pure Ego, however defined by rationalist or idealist thinkers. He begs us to note that in this book he writes psychology.

It is from this latter point of view that we should read the following description, phenomenologically so accurate, of what he calls "the self of all the other selves."

> If the stream [of consciousness] as a whole is identified with the Self far more than any outward thing, a *certain portion of the stream abstracted from the rest* is so identified in an altogether peculiar degree, and is felt by all men as a sort of innermost

centre within the circle, of sanctuary within the citadel, constituted by the subjective life as a whole. Compared with this element of the stream, the other parts, even of the subjective life, seem transient external possessions, of which each in turn can be disowned, whilst that which disowns them remains.[7]

Later in his reflections, James rejects outright the notion of an apprehending self defined in opposition to its apprehended contents. In his battle against the dualism knower/known, he objects to the dissociation between the subjective and the objective poles. He denies that consciousness could exist as a spiritual entity or substance set over against the material objects that are grasped. He opts for a new, nonidealist monism according to which everything, thoughts and things, is "pure experience." Thus, in the brief summary he gives us of his piece, "Does 'Consciousness' Exist?" he states, "Thoughts and things are absolutely homogeneous as to their material, and . . . their opposition is only one of relation and of function."[8]

While his version of monism remains unconvincing, nevertheless he interestingly moves in the direction of a perceptual nonduality. Hence the definition of "Experience" he provides for Baldwin's *Dictionary* in 1902: "Psychic or mental: the entire process of phenomena, of present data considered in their raw immediacy, before reflective thought has analysed them into subjective and objective aspects or ingredients."[9] However, coming *before* the distinction subject/object, this primordial nonduality is not yet mystical consciousness, as indicated in the section on Lonergan in chapter 3.

In James's article, "Does 'Consciousness' Exist?" Eric Voegelin sees a confirmation of his own experiences of participation in a reality that is fundamentally homogeneous, beyond any division subject/object. He writes,

> The term *consciousness*, therefore, could no longer mean to me a human consciousness that is conscious of a reality outside man's consciousness, but had to mean the In-Between reality of the participatory pure experience that then analytically can be characterized through such terms as the poles of the experiential tension, and the reality of the experiential tension in the *metaxy*.[10]

James's intuitions regarding a larger self were anticipated by Plotinus. However, whereas the American philosopher wavered about the existence of the self, the Greek philosopher did not doubt it.[11] I agree with James's repudiation of consciousness as a sort of spiritual stuff placed alongside a material stuff made up of objects. In part one of this book, we have repeatedly heeded the warnings of those who asserted that consciousness cannot be seen or observed. The conscious human subject is definitely neither a perceptible body nor even an imaginable immaterial entity. The danger, of course, is to reify such explanatory concepts as consciousness, the self, the empirical "I," or the transcendental ego. Only an analogical sense allows us to speak of consciousness as a higher degree of being, irreducible to weird subjective entities.

While the later James voices dissatisfaction about his treatment of consciousness in *The Principles of Psychology*, he seems to have never realized that his empiricism begs what Mark D. Morelli calls "the fundamental question of the spontaneous sources of the normativity of the flow of consciousness."[12] As we saw Lonergan demonstrate in chapter 1, the structuring of our flow of conscious intentionality is normative, since any attempt to question the interrelated acts of that structure must implement them. And this remark brings us to our next section, where we find Lonergan and other thinkers arguing for the self.

ARGUING FOR THE SELF

In this section the argument in favor of the self comes principally from Lonergan's magnum opus, *Insight*, to which I referred in chapter 1.

Lonergan mentions John Locke only briefly and negatively, on two separate pages of *Insight*. In the second of those pages, talking about his own understanding of the self as a central form, Lonergan writes:

> The difference between our central form and Aristotle's substantial form is merely nominal. For the Aristotelian substantial form is what is known by grasping an intelligible unity, an *unum per se*. However, since the meaning of the English word 'substance' has been influenced profoundly by Locke, since the Cartesian confusion of 'body' and thing led to an identification of substance and extension and then to the riposte that substance is underneath extension, I have thought it advisable, at least temporarily, to cut myself off from this verbal tangle (462).

I will follow this piece of advice, while asking the readers to expect, under the pen of several Japanese writers, this distorted construal of substance which is, as Lonergan correctly states, a modern view having little to do with Aristotle's *ousia*.

Notwithstanding the justifiably negative character of the remark by Lonergan, which I have just quoted and which has to do with Locke's defective epistemology, we find a passage in the English philosopher's great work, *An Essay concerning Human Understanding*, where the latter adumbrates human consciousness in a way that surprisingly resembles Lonergan's own account of consciousness. Locke points to

> that consciousness, which is inseparable from thinking, and as it seems to me essential to it: It being impossible for any one to perceive, without perceiving, that he does perceive. When we see, hear, smell, taste, feel, meditate, or will any thing, we know that we do so. . . . For since consciousness always accompanies thinking, and 'tis that, that makes every one to be, what he calls *self*.[13]

Besides mentioning the accompanying character of such consciousness, Locke indicates its unifying role:

> For it is by the consciousness it has of its present Thoughts and Actions, that it is *self* now, and so will be the same *self* as far as the same consciousness can extend to Actions past or to come . . . : The same consciousness uniting those distant Actions into the same *Person*.[14]

There is an intimate connection between such self-consciousness as tying countless acts and states, and the sense of self that derives from this unifying inner experience. For Locke this continued self is the seat of personal identity. Let the readers be reminded of the observations on the unity of consciousness that were gleaned from Brentano in my first chapter, and from Helminiak in my second chapter. Both note that since our mental activities are inwardly perceived as existing together, they constitute a real unity.

Lonergan's input on our understanding of the self comes from two sections of *Insight*. In the first, he expounds the concept of a thing, a being endowed with continuity; and in the second, he talks about the unity of consciousness.

In chapter 8 of *Insight*, entitled "Things," Lonergan tells us that besides the kind of insight that grasps relations between data (which he calls experiential and explanatory conjugates), there is another kind of insight that grasps a unity, identity, whole in data. In other words, instead of considering data from an abstractive viewpoint, we take them in their concrete individuality and in the totality of their aspects. "Thus, the dog Fido is a unity, and to Fido is ascribed a totality of data whether of color or shape, sound or odor, feeling or movement" (271). Consequently, we may truly attribute characteristics to Fido, as to any reality or "thing."

A distinguished Lonergan scholar aptly sums up the kind of understanding that enables us to discover a thing:

> Insight is that bridge or pivot, not as an abstractive insight, but as a concretizing insight that grasps the whole in the parts, the one in the many, the perduring identity in the differences, the unity in the relations.[15]

Lonergan mentions three facts about things:

> Thus, things are conceived as extended in space, permanent in time, and yet subject to change. They are extended in space, inasmuch as spatially distinct data pertain to the unity at any given instant. They are permanent in time, inasmuch as temporally distinct data pertain to the same unity. They are subject to change, inasmuch as there is some difference between the aggregate of data at one instant and the aggregate of data on the same unity at another instant (271).

Then the author underscores the importance of the concept of thing: "Without the notion of the thing there can be no notion of change" (272). If we do not grant the presence of a concrete unity of data at the beginning of a process, and of the same, albeit altered, unity of data at the end, how will we be able to identify any precise change? Furthermore, he states that the notion of the thing is necessary for the continuity of scientific thought. Scientific progress requires that explanatory systems evolve from previous ones. To achieve this development, we must link up ensembles of correlations with concrete, relevant data (as opposed to a selection of data which would rule out pertinent ones and thus exclude the very possibility of comparing the systems). And such data, whether described or explained, need the notion of the thing as identical, indeed whose identity demands better, more encompassing theories (272–273).

Lonergan concludes this first section of his chapter 8 with the pronouncement, "no thing itself, no thing as explained, can be imagined" (275). Explanation goes beyond observation; in that scientific phase, which comes after common-sense description, we prescind from all observers and all observables.

The author expands this assertion in section 2 of the same chapter on "Things." He maintains that things are not necessarily bodies. The latter are objects of sensory extroversion. All together, they appear as the "already out there now real." Far from being a linguistically constituted world, bodies make up the spontaneous environment of animals, or of human beings insofar as they have not attained the stage in which they are committed to functioning in an intelligible and verified world. To confuse a thing with a body is to amalgamate "an intelligible unity grasped in data as individual" with an "already out there now real" (277).

Such was Hume's mistake, when he insisted that only the perceptible was "real." By contrast, for Lonergan, reality is not the object of extroversion, but what has been intelligently explained and verified. However, he readily concedes that for us human beings as well as for animals, the biological pattern of experience, based on extroversion, is absolutely indispensable for our maintenance and survival. He simply rejects the confusion between that pattern, for which bodies are paramount, and the intellectual pattern, for which things are central. Accordingly, a thing is not a "substance," if we construe this term as a body.

The same carefulness not to succumb to the literalness of imaginary representations is required as we now approach what Lonergan writes about consciousness as normally unified in the human agent. (The readers may want to turn back to my section on consciousness according to Lonergan, in chapter 1.) In chapter 11 of *Insight*, section 3, he highlights the unity of consciousness.

He sees the unity of consciousness at once on the objective and on the subjective side. What happens on the side of the object is this:

> The contents cumulate into unities: what is perceived is what is inquired about; what is inquired about is what is understood; what is understood is what is formulated; what is formulated is what is reflected on; what is reflected on is what is grasped as unconditioned; what is grasped as unconditioned is what is affirmed (349).

On the side of the subject, the author notes:

> Conscious acts are not so many isolated, random atoms of knowing, but many acts coalesce into a single knowing.... Not only is the percept inquired about, understood, formulated, reflected on, grasped as unconditioned, and affirmed, but also

there is an identity involved in perceiving, inquiring, understanding, formulating, reflecting, grasping the unconditioned, and affirming (349).

There is, then, a single field of consciousness. If our objective contents and our subjective inner acts were basically discontinuous, there would be no transition between them, and thinking would be abolished. In a state of utter confusion, we would be incapable of asking questions about our perception and our understanding.

Lonergan concludes that "a single agent is involved in many acts," and that "concretely, consciousness pertains to the acting agent" (350). The single field of consciousness includes not only a person's living states and activities, but also the person qua consciously living, the one who says "I" (to others and to oneself), thus using the grammatical first person singular. Similarly Zahavi rightly equates "the self-givenness of lived consciousness" with a "first-personal givenness."[16] I am not only a thing, but a consciously acting thing or self.

Elsewhere, Lonergan states that "consciousness . . . constitutes and reveals the basic psychological unity of the subject as subject."[17] In the words of Joann and Walter Conn:

> The self experienced in consciousness does not exist without consciousness (e.g., in a coma). The "I" who understands, judges, and decides is not only revealed to itself in consciousness but is capable of understanding, judging, and deciding only through consciousness. The self is constituted as an "I" by consciousness. In short, consciousness is not only cognitive, it is also constitutive of the very reality of the self-as-subject.[18]

Or, as Zahavi aptly says, "The object is given through the act, and if there is no awareness of the act, the object does not appear at all."[19]

Daniel Helminiak, whose remarks on consciousness have been heeded in chapter 2, echoes Lonergan's, Locke's, Brentano's, and Husserl's affirmation of the self as he underscores the fact of "experienced continuity":

> To be able to report your experiences is to have a sense of self. Nonreflecting awareness "of" oneself as the experiencing subject links the flow of ongoing experiences as the experiences of a somebody. So nonreflecting consciousness is the key to the human sense of personal continuity and identity.[20]

With respect to some Eastern views that the "I" is nothing, Helminiak states:

> the "I" is nothing insofar as it is no thing; it is not an object. "I" is not something in contrast to which a person may stand. Rather, "I" is the one who does the standing. "I" is subject precisely as subject; it is nothing like anything else. This realization does not imply that, because "I" is no thing, "I" must therefore not be real or not exist, as some philosophies might suggest. Rather, "I" is not in the same way as other things are, so "I" may appear not to be real (as other things are), that is, appear not to exist. Yet one can show how "I" both exists and is real. It exists and is real because, on the basis of the data of nonreflecting consciousness, it can be correctly affirmed.[21]

This text is helpful, inasmuch as it clearly demarcates accurate from mistaken representations of the self. But do Lonergan and Helminiak go far enough? To add one adjective to the phrase just used by Helminiak, on the basis of the data of *mystical* nonreflecting consciousness, could we not say that not only the false self but even the genuine self, as represented by Lonergan and his followers, must be transcended?[22]

TRANSCENDING THE SELF

In chapter 3, we have seen that Lonergan speaks of the realm of transcendence or of religious interiority as the furtherance of ordinary interiority. For him, mystical consciousness is the prolongation of ordinary consciousness. We must now situate this state within his overall account of self-transcendence, which comprises several levels.[23]

As we noted earlier, we human beings, like animals, respond to the stimuli of our physical habitat, which come from "bodies." The fact that we adjust to our environment and even modify it (as some higher animals do) shows that far from being locked up in ourselves, we begin to transcend ourselves. Lonergan calls "empirical" this first level of activity.

On the second, "intellectual" level, we ask questions for intelligence. As language enables us to understand and relate things and properties, we go beyond the narrow strip of space-time accessible through perception and we construct a worldview, in which the questions "what," "how," and "why" get at least provisional answers.

On the third, "rational" level, we ask questions for reflection. We are critical of any idea, hypothesis or system, and we want to ascertain whether or not this really is so. We seek what is independent of the subjects that we are. We want to know, not what we would be inclined to think or say, but what is the case. We doubt, verify, and enunciate judgments of fact.

On the fourth, "responsible" level, we ask questions for deliberation. We are not content with mere knowledge; we want to shape our behavior by finding what the right response should be in a particular situation. We ask whether the contemplated course of action is worthwhile, not just apparently good but truly good. We end up with judgments of value and decisions.

Finally, looking at the fourth level from the standpoint of our affective states, we discover that we are invited to love not only finite human beings or things in a responsible manner, but also to love in an unrestricted fashion. In itself, this mystical state constitutes a withdrawal from the objectified world into a "cloud of unknowing." Lonergan considers that our capacity for self-transcendence is entirely actualized when our being becomes being-in-love. Then our conscious intentionality, namely, our capacity to reach out to all echelons of reality, is radically fulfilled. We feel a deep-set joy and a radical peace.

In sum, according to Lonergan, as we mount from level to level, on the one hand, we are aware of being a fuller self and, on the other hand, we become more detached and disinterested. We can reach beyond ourselves in five fundamental ways, that is, as we successfully become involved with higher and higher degrees of reality: experience, understanding, judging, acting, and unrestrictedly loving.

Sally King reports the same complementarity between becoming a fuller, richer, and therefore different self and forgetting oneself. Totally transcending the self presupposes a meditative or mystical state in which one experiences "a radically altered sense of self," as she puts it.[24]

> the mystic path entails radical self-transformation, precisely in that one's sense of who and what one is is overturned at its foundation. This being the case, how could a mystic be expected to determine what is self and what is other in a mystical experience? The self is in fact becoming other-than-what-it-was (274).

King maintains the subsistence of the self as she recognizes "an existential grounding of the individual," in "an experience that leaves one existentially grounded." Such grounding has to do with the affective side of mystical experience.

> There is also an element of axiological grounding: an encounter with absolute value. . . . Mystics frequently report feelings of bliss, ecstasy, or of serene joy, deep peace; Otto speaks of the fascination of the numinous. Such reports are evidence of a grounding in values produced by mystical experience, an experiential encounter with a source of superlative, intrinsic value. Again, such language fits the Tao even inasmuch as it is Nonbeing. It even fits emptiness—not in the sense that emptiness as such possesses value, which is impossible since it is only a tool, but in the sense that the transformation engendered by the discipline of emptiness possesses value (275).

King recognizes that emptiness is not vacuous but engenders a priceless transformation.

In her book entitled *Buddha Nature*, King contrasts "a fundamentally deluded or warped perspective upon oneself and reality" with the state of enlightenment. Whereas unconverted people lack genuine freedom because their actions are driven by karma, the converted people have the joy of realizing that their particular behaviors possess reality and value. Far from robbing a person of individuality, conversion or enlightenment manifests the Buddha nature in concrete deeds. Being no entity of any kind, the Buddha nature, in effect, amounts to all acts of charity and altruism.[25]

In the previously quoted article, however, she indicates that in the mystical experience, we lose the awareness of being a subject in the presence of an object. What is being transcended is the self, or the subject:

> In the moment in which we 'have' our experience (or, as a Buddhist might say, we 'are' our experience), there is, experientially, no subject experiencing an object. There is just experiencing (272).

In another piece, King suggests that *sunyata* (emptiness) may be viewed as "an anti-concept, a self-surpassing surpasser."[26] She explains:

> Emptiness itself must be realized as empty. That is, one does not properly understand emptiness if one grasps on to emptiness as the true principle which reveals things as they really are. The truth of this anti-concept 'emptiness' is its functioning to pre-

vent grasping on to any concept, including itself, as the truth. It is language which shows the relativity and limitations of language (456).

Which is to say: "The anti-concept . . . contains in its nature a non-stasis which prevents this grasping activity of the mind, forcing it to continue moving, never coming to rest in a conceptual place" (457). In our next three chapters we will scrutinize this notion of *sunyata*.

CONCLUDING REMARKS

What part of oneself has to be transcended? In the first place, the false self, that is, the human individual as either self-enclosed in its sensory immediacy, or self-assertive and thereby isolated, or warped because it fails to pursue its relevant questions and thus remains distorted by bias, oversights, misjudgments, or bad decisions. This inauthentic self lives without moral conversion and without the psychic healing that both supports and derives from its ethical renewal.

In the second place, self-transcendence means the fact that the authentic self is so interested in things, persons, and God that it is less preoccupied with itself and that, at least most of the time, it forgets itself. Experientially, then, the ego is superseded in the measure that it is less self-aware in everyday life. In chapter 1, the insistence on conscious intentionality, on the part of Brentano, Husserl, Sartre, and Lonergan, provided a rational explanation for this built-in tendency to get interested in others and to relate to them with insight, truth, and respect.[27] This self-forgetfulness requires the firm individuality which can stand up for unpopular values and resist group pressure and bias.

In the third place, self-transcendence consists in leaving behind another kind of inauthentic situation: the case of morally good people who nevertheless restrict their experience to that of an ego immersed in subject/object relations. As they overcome this restriction, they are aware of their consciousness, whether secular or mystical, and they decide to cultivate it so as to attain a more complete religious conversion.

In the fourth place, self-transcendence is attained when ordinary consciousness gives way to an entirely different state, which may be called "emptiness." A person then experiences the total unawareness typical of mystical consciousness. How can that consciousness be unawareness? It is there as consciousness, and yet it remains totally unadverted to (hence unaware). To revert to the categories of my

Introduction, it is the highest form of consciousness-in, which rules out any consciousness-of or awareness.

An instance of such an experience is the second of the three reports given by Forman, which I introduced at the beginning of chapter 3. Let me add a few more sentences.

> Eventually, even the thin boundary that had previously separated individuality from unbounded pure consciousness began to dissolve. The "I" as a separate entity just started to have no meaning. The boundaries that I put on myself became like a mesh, a net; it became porous and then dissolved; only unbroken pure consciousness or existence remains. Once I let go of the veil of individuality, there is no longer "I perceiving" or "I aware."[28]

Still, at the same time, we are entitled to maintain the existence of the self. Price, whose helpful remarks we garnered in chapter 3, rightly affirms that the conscious self is the ground and possibility of any state or activity. But this ground, a capacity also called the human spirit or intentionality, derives from another ground, the divine ground. "The ground of consciousness refers to the source or transcendent ground of this capacity."[29] Moreover, the fact that mystical consciousness is not a consciousness-of and therefore goes beyond the experience of subject/object invites us to reify neither the self nor its divine source. Yet it does not suggest the abolition of the ontological difference between finite and infinite consciousness. The very presence of divine consciousness in us is an adequate explanation for the sense that mystics have of some kind of identification or oneness in mystical experience.

CHAPTER 8

Japanese Views of the Self

Most of the Zen-inspired philosophers have shown great interest in the Self that is the result of enlightenment, namely *satori, kensho*. In contrast to the Self, the limited, individual self appears as an alienated self. The existential plight of this illusionary ego strikes the Buddhist thinkers so much that it is difficult to detect, in their works, neutral accounts of the self—accounts that would be comparable to the one we found in Lonergan. And yet occasionally we find remarks by Japanese writers that can be situated within the compass of those neutral accounts, that is, halfway between the inauthentic self and the fully enlightened Self.

SUZUKI

Daisetz Teitaro Suzuki (1869–1966) makes one of those remarks that connect the Buddhist understanding of Self with the Western interest in a nonegocentric self. In "The Sense of Zen," he talks about the experience of the adolescent who discovers sexual attraction.

> This is the first time the ego really comes to recognize the "other." I mean the awakening of sexual love. . . . Love makes the ego lose itself in the object it loves, and yet at the same time it wants to have the object as its own. . . . What I want to emphasize in this connection is this: that through the awakening of love we get a glimpse into the infinity of things. . . . When the ego-shell is broken and the "other" is taken into its own body, we can say that the ego has denied itself or that the ego has taken its first steps towards the infinite.[1]

These are merely first steps, and they overlap with the beginnings of self-transcendence, which was described in the previous chapter.

Let us continue our search by collecting a few useful observations by Suzuki on the difficulty of acknowledging the Self. In a lecture on Zen Buddhism, he offers remarks that have to do with methodology. Because scientists are wary of being "subjective," they cannot help us get acquainted with the Self.

> Scientific knowledge of the Self is not real knowledge as long as it objectifies the Self. The scientific direction of study is to be reversed, and the Self is to be taken hold of from within and not from the outside. This means that the Self is to know itself without going out of itself.[2]

Accordingly, people who wish to know themselves must explore the realm of their subjectivity.

Suzuki pursues his criticism of the scientists (including theologians and philosophers) who crave for misplaced or misconstrued objectivity.

> They forget the fact that a person invariably *lives* a personal life and not a conceptually or scientifically defined one. . . . Objectivity or subjectivity is not the question here. What concerns us most vitally is to discover by ourselves, personally, where this life is, how it is lived.

And again: "The Self knows itself from within and never from the outside."[3] Except for the tendency to rule out precise definitions, this program (and even some of its wording) sounds the same as Lonergan's.

In an exchange with Thomas Merton, Suzuki dismisses a low-quality kind of consciousness, called "egocentric consciousness," and a reductive representation of the ego, called "a thingish ego-substance."[4] If it is Descartes' thinking substance that is rejected, we may nod, while adding that since Heidegger, such a repudiation of substance has become commonplace in many quarters of Western philosophy.

Still, in his famous book, *Mysticism: Christian and Buddhist*, Suzuki gives us an original account of the relations between the "empirical" and the "transcendental ego."[5] The first is the relative ego that is dependent on others and therefore has no freedom; the second ego (I wish Suzuki would have called it the Self, as we saw him do before) is "the creative agent" (131) that expresses itself in the empirical ego and that is the source of its consciousness. Of course, those egos are not two juxtaposed selves, but rather two perspectives upon the self. As Suzuki asserts in an article, the relative self (*ki*) and the absolute self (*ho*) are one.[6]

Suzuki asks a fascinating question, "What is it, then, that makes it [the empirical ego] feel free as if it were really so independent and authentic? Whence this delusion?" (129) In other words, why does the empirical ego mistakenly view itself as a transcendental ego? To answer, Suzuki distinguishes "two aspects of relationship, outer and inner":

> Objectively speaking, the empirical or relative ego is one of many other such egos. It is in the world of plurality; its contact with others is intermittent, mediated, and processional. Inwardly, its contact or relationship with the transcendental ego is constant, immediate, and total. Because of this the inner relationship is not so distinctly cognizable as the outer one (130).

Given that "this inner cognition is not the ordinary kind of knowledge which we generally have about an external thing" (130), it is difficult to identify it in its distinctness.

> The object of ordinary knowledge is regarded as posited in space and time and subject to all kinds of scientific measurements. The object of the inner cognition is not an individual object. The transcendental ego cannot be singled out for the relative ego to be inspected by it (130).

Hence the frequent confusion between the two aspects of the ego:

> When this unique relationship between the transcendental ego and the relative ego is not adequately comprehended or intuited, there is a delusion. The relative ego imagines itself to be a free agent, complete in itself, and tries to act accordingly (131).

This explanation sheds light upon the process whereby the human ego absolutizes itself. We have here, in my opinion, the contrast between Schleiermacher's consciousness C and consciousness A, namely, between the objectified and the unobjectifiable consciousness. In his *Introduction to Zen Buddhism*, Suzuki equates "absolute emptiness" with a "state of consciousness, about which we cannot make any logical statement." Further on in that book, he adds, "*Satori* is the sudden flashing into consciousness of a new truth hitherto undreamed of."[7]

We may want to ask, however, is there some room, in Suzuki's analysis, for consciousness B? Let us recall that consciousness B is that immediate self-acquaintance that we have in our states and acts, which quickly translates itself into self-awareness.

To answer our question, let us pay attention to what Suzuki says, in the same book, about *prajna*, wisdom:

> The ego must be caught not from outside but from within. This is the work of *prajna*. The wonder *prajna* performs is to catch the actor in the midst of his action, he is not made to stop acting in order to be seen as actor. The actor is the acting, and the acting is the actor, and out of this unification or identification *prajna* is awakened. The ego does not go out of himself in order to see himself. He stays within himself and sees himself as reflected in himself. But as soon as a split takes place between the ego as actor and the ego as seer or spectator, *prajna* is dichotomized, and all is lost (40).

In *Studies in Zen*, Suzuki explains that *prajna* is a global intuition that takes in the whole, whereas *vijnana* amounts to reason, or discursive understanding, and is concerned with parts.[8] Even though *prajna* is more comprehensive than consciousness B since it also includes consciousness A, nonetheless we find several traits of consciousness B in the excerpt just quoted. Let me suggest the following rephrasing: the actor is the acting, consciously being himself in the midst of his action, prior to being aware or seeing himself reflected in himself.

Does the split of which the author speaks take place unavoidably? Inasmuch as the awareness involves images, yes; inasmuch as the understanding of one's states and acts goes deeper than the imagination and terminates in true judgments, no. True judgments entail an identity between the mind and the thing affirmed. Regrettably Suzuki does not seem to have honed his epistemology enough to be capable of making this clear distinction between the representation as imagined and the representation as understood and correctly asserted. This latter representation, which is the result of several insights, adds much to the former as it states its actual meaning. Thus consciousness C does at times rightly pronounce true judgments, even about such difficult matters as consciousness B and consciousness A. But Suzuki operates with a caricature of consciousness C. Underestimating its abilities, he finds it incapable of giving a correct account of consciousness B and A.

All the same, let us follow him as he interestingly unpacks, again in *Mysticism: Christian and Buddhism*, what *prajna* contains:

Buddhists generally talk about the egolessness (*anatta* or *anatmya*) of all things, but they forget that the egolessness of things cannot really be understood until they are seen with the eye of *prajna*-intuition. The psychological annihilation of an ego-substance is not enough, for this still leaves the light of *prajna*-eye under a coverage (41).

He insists, "The enlightenment-experience therefore means going beyond the world of psychology, the opening of the *prajna*-eye, and seeing into the realm of Ultimate Reality" (42).

Obviously Suzuki has moved beyond psychology and beyond the psychological self-presence that is constitutive of consciousness B, into consciousness A, or mystical consciousness. And of course, for a Zen practitioner like himself, "Ultimate Reality" means *sunyata*, emptiness. Although emptiness, also called absolute nothingness, will be the theme of our next chapters, let us continue listening to Suzuki as he shares with us his understanding of *sunyata*. Doing so has the advantage of completing my presentation of his views and of preparing the way for the forthcoming chapters.

At this point, a caveat is in order: I will not raise the question of whether the construals of *sunyata* offered by Suzuki, Nishitani, and Hisamatsu accord or not with anterior Zen-Buddhist views (such as Dogen's for instance). I will simply take those accounts at their face value to compare them with Western perspectives on the same realities.

Let us begin with the experiential side of emptiness, called *satori*. In "Satori, or Enlightenment," Suzuki tells us that there is an analogy for it in the "eureka!" exclamation: "when a difficult mathematical problem is solved, or when a great discovery is made, or when a sudden means of escape is realized in the midst of most desperate complications." Then he introduces a qualification:

> But this refers only to the intellectual aspect of satori, which is therefore necessarily partial and incomplete and does not touch the very foundations of life considered one indivisible whole. Satori as the Zen experience must be concerned with the entirety of life. For what Zen proposes to do is the revolution, and the revaluation as well, of oneself as a spiritual unity.[9]

The eureka expresses an insight that most of the time does not affect one's whole life, whereas *satori* does. After all, there is an "existential" ambience in Zen, not in the European sense, of course, but according to a specific mood that we shall find more fully explicated by Nishitani and Hisamatsu. Suzuki adds:

> The state of "Great Doubt" (*tai-gi*), as it is technically known, is the antecedent. It must be broken up and exploded into the next stage, which is looking into one's nature or the opening of satori (102).

Suzuki also points out that *satori* has something in common with the Western understanding of conversion. This term, however, cannot be applied to the Buddhist experience in its usual Christian, or more precisely Protestant sense:

> The term has too affective or emotional a shade to take the place of satori, which is above all noetic. The general tendency of Buddhism is, as we know, more intellectual than emotional, and its doctrine of Enlightenment distinguishes it sharply from the Christian view of salvation (85).

Hence the "impersonal tone" of the Zen experience (106–107), a central feature that is discussed more at length by Nishitani. Although both Suzuki, Nishitani, and Hisamatsu occasionally mention love, it is not one of their principal themes.

For Suzuki, *sunyata* does not lie beyond the empirical ego or beyond this universe. If we thought it did, we would still be caught up in duality. *Sunyata* is at the same time the object and the subject of enlightened knowledge. "Knowing and seeing *sunyata* is *sunyata* knowing and seeing itself; there is no outside knower or spectator; it is its own knower and seer.... We are *sunyata*."[10] Accordingly it encompasses everything in a creative manner:

> That is why *sunyata* is said to be a reservoir of infinite possibilities and not just a state of mere emptiness. Differentiating itself and yet remaining in itself undifferentiated, and thus to go on eternally engaged in the work of creation—this is *sunyata*, the *prajna*-continuum.[11]

One of the effects of Zen is the release of positive energies. In *Mysticism: Christian and Buddhist*, Suzuki explains that this phenomenon is not "something sheerly of privative value" but "something filled with infinite possibilities." The egolessness of all things "displays positive constructive energies ... by creating a world of altogether new values" such as wisdom and love (42). This experience amounts to an unblocking. "Zen liberates all the energies properly and naturally stored in each of us, which are in ordinary circumstances cramped and distorted so that they find no adequate channel for activity."[12]

This noetic liberation consists in seeing things in their "suchness" (*tathata*), or "isness," as Suzuki also suggests,[13] that is, as they actually are, shorn of the interpretation we superimpose upon them. He considers this ability as positive, as affirmative of reality:

> While *sunyata* may erroneously appear to be negativistic, there is nothing in the concept of *tathata* that would suggest the idea of negativity. *Tathata* is the viewing of things as they are: it is an affirmation through and through. I see a tree, and I state that it is a tree; I hear a bird sing and I say that a bird sings; a spade is a spade, and a mountain is a mountain; the fowls of the air fly and the flowers of the field bloom: these are statements of *tathata*. . . . If *sunyata* denies or rejects everything, *tathata* accepts and upholds everything; the two concepts may be considered as opposing each other, but it is the Buddhist idea that they are not contradictory, that it is from our relativistic point of view that they seem so. In truth, *tathata* is *sunyata*, and *sunyata* is *tathata*; things are *tathata* because of their being *sunyata*.[14]

In "Self the Unattainable,"[15] Suzuki says of the Self that "it is like a zero that is equal to, or rather identical with, infinity" (16). He explains, "When it is stripped of all its trappings, moral and psychological, and when we imagine it to be a void, it is not really so; it is not 'negativistic.' There must be something absolute in it" (17). And in another essay contained in the same volume, he writes:

> But what Zen teaches is neither nihilism, nor its opposite. What Zen speaks of as the *satori* experience, as enlightenment, is this immediate seeing into the reality or suchness of things. This suchness is nothing other than emptiness, which is, after all, no-emptiness. The reality is beyond intellection, and that which lies beyond intellection we call emptiness.[16]

Again in the same collection, Suzuki explains the same reality, this time starting with a helpful metaphor:

> A field without an inch of growing grass in it, symbolizes *sunyata*, the ultimate reality of Buddhist philosophy. *Sunyata* is

literally "emptiness." To say that reality is "empty" means that it goes beyond definability, and cannot be qualified as this or that. It is above the categories of universal and particular. But it must not therefore be regarded as free of all content, as a void in the relative sense would be. On the contrary, it is the fullness of things, containing all possibilities.[17]

If we return to the dialogue reported in Merton's book, *Zen and the Birds of Appetite*, we find that same insistence on the equation between emptiness and fullness.

> Zen emptiness is not the emptiness of nothingness, but the emptiness of fullness in which there is "no gain, no loss, no increase, no decrease," in which this equation takes place: zero = infinity (133–134).

Moreover, for Suzuki *sunyata* requires total detachment. He affirms: "To be absolutely nothing is to be everything. When one is in possession of something, that something will keep all other somethings from coming in" (109). Accordingly he construes this "nothing-everything" as bringing together opposing concepts.

Commenting on chapter 3 of the biblical book entitled *Genesis*, he contrasts Innocence with Knowledge of good and evil. He defines them as follows:

> "Innocence" is to be taken as the state of mind in which inhabitants of the Garden of Eden used to live around the tree of life, with eyes not opened, all naked, not ashamed, with no knowledge of good and evil; whereas "Knowledge" refers to everything opposite of "Innocence," especially a pair of discriminating eyes widely opened to good and evil (104, n. 2).

Then, equating Innocence with Original Light and Knowledge with Ignorance, he states:

> The so-called opposition between Innocence and Knowledge or between Ignorance and the Original Light is not the kind of opposition we see between black and white, good and evil, right and wrong, to be and not to be, or to have and not to have. The opposition is, as it were, between container and the contained, between the background and the stage, between the field and the players moving on it. The good and the evil play

their opposing parts on the field which remains neutral and indifferent and "open" or "empty." It is like rain that falls on the just and on the unjust. It is like the sun rising on the good and on the evil, on your foes and on your friends (105–106).

Elsewhere, Suzuki distinguishes a relative and an absolute affirmation. Whereas the former does not integrate the negative, the latter unifies all the opposites.

To be free, life must be an absolute affirmation. It must transcend all possible conditions, limitations, and antitheses that hinder its free activity. . . . The point is to make one realize what I call an absolute affirmation. Not merely to escape the antithesis of "yes" and "no", but to find a positive way in which the opposites are perfectly harmonized.[18]

Concerning such reconciliation of antitheses, we may want to heed a warning by Suzuki:

The fact that Zen is not a philosophy makes it avoid demonstrating its experience after the manner of a discursive exposition. The masters appeal to what may be designated as a negative, ironical method of treatment. They are always afraid of being one-sided, and consequently they sometimes assert and deny simultaneously, or praise while seemingly devaluating. They are, as it were, fond of contradicting themselves.[19]

Again: "The negative side is at the same time the affirmative side, which means that negation is affirmation. It is a contradiction, flatly. But still that very contradiction is in fact the truth."[20] Therefore: "Ignorance is what we ought to have in order to get enlightenment. If in fact any time we see *ignorance*, there is also enlightenment underneath."[21]

This integration of the opposites does not take place on the earthly or moral plane. If it did, it would remain a relative affirmation. And since our psychological awareness is always infected with dualism, we should not even think of enlightenment as an "experience." In words that would please Eckhart, Suzuki remarks, "The Zen Master therefore will tell us to transcend or 'to cast away' the experience itself."[22]

Before bringing this section to an end, two objections are worth considering. First, Suzuki protests that Zen is not mystical. This point is extremely well discussed by Jan Van Bragt in chapter 2 of *Mysticism Buddhist and Christian*. He notes that after having published in 1957 a book entitled *Mysticism: Christian and Buddhist,* Suzuki surprised many readers when he declared, eight years later, "Zen has nothing 'mystical' about it or in it."[23]

Van Bragt mentions three elements that can explain this abrupt assertion by Suzuki. First, the theoreticians of Zen who recognize mysticism in Christianity and not in Buddhism identify a part of Christianity as mystical, while their own religion does not set apart a separate aspect as distinctively mystical. Second, they state that whereas Christians view the area of the mystery or of the mystical as another world, Zen never leaves the everyday world. And third, Zen, which is "cool" and detached, does not share the highly personal and passionate character of Christian mysticism.[24]

Yet, asked by Winston King about his denial of mysticism in Zen, Suzuki makes a distinction:

> If mysticism is defined as something immediate, without any medium, it's alright; but when it is understood to be something hidden "behind" what we actually see, then Zen is not mysticism.... Yes, Zen differs from mysticism. In *mystical* experience there is something mystically experienced, that special experience which is something different from all ordinary experiences. But in Zen, *ordinary* experience itself is mystical experience.[25]

So it seems that Suzuki is willing to reconcile himself with the idea that Zen is mystical, provided we acknowledge that it differs from the standard Christian understanding of mysticism.

On this issue I want to offer a remark in connection with my enterprise in this book. Suzuki is unclear about which authors count as representatives of the standard Christian understanding of mysticism. Could we characterize Eckhart by the kind of mysticism that Suzuki says he does not find in Zen? Obviously not, as Suzuki himself admits in *Mysticism: Christian and Buddhist.* (He nevertheless goes awry as he does not distinguish enough Eckhart from Zen authors.) Let me emphatically assert that Zen is mystical in the sense I have adopted in my Introduction (mysticism as distinct from prophecy), in the characterization presented in chapter 3, and in the understanding found in Plotinus, Eckhart, and Schleiermacher (under a diversity of terms, of course), which part 2 has expounded. Indeed, an important current of Western mysticism falls in the same category as Zen, so that both traditions can be truly said to be mystical.

The second objection concerns the relevance of the phrase "mystical consciousness" to Zen. Most of the time, Zen authors use the word "consciousness" to designate a lower state of mind. Rarely, however, some of them employ the term in a positive sense. Thus Suzuki, in *An Introduction to Zen Buddhism*, commenting on "absolute emptiness," affirms, "This state of inner consciousness, about which we cannot make any logical statement, must be realized before we can have any intelligent talk on Zen."[26] Later in the same book, he distinguishes "relative consciousness" from the consciousness attained in *satori*. He writes, "*Satori* is the sudden flashing into consciousness of a new truth hitherto undreamed of."[27]

Interestingly, in his Foreword to Suzuki's work, *An Introduction to Zen Buddhism*, the great psychoanalyst Carl G. Jung uses the word "consciousness" (*Bewußtsein*, the very word we found in Schleiermacher) successively in its rich sense, to characterize *satori* (13–17), and in its restrictive sense, to characterize relative consciousness (21, 23, 27). And as expected, he proceeds to underline the role of the unconscious in the stages preparatory to enlightenment (20–23, 28).

NISHITANI

Nishitani Keiji (1900–1990) has a single view of consciousness, which is always restrictive, and a twofold view of the self, which is firstly narrow and secondly broad. In *Religion and Nothingness*[28] he explains that when we look at things from the standpoint of the ordinary self (also called the ego), we become subjects that see things merely as objects. We set up a separation between the "within" (the subjects) and the "without" (the objects). He calls this standpoint "the field of consciousness," in which the self-conscious self occupies center stage (9) and is inevitably self–centered (183, 204).

According to him, the big mistake committed by the self-conscious ego is to take representations too seriously. It fails to apprehend the reality of things because it reduces them to the status of concepts or representations. What happens to things also happens to the self. Like represented things, this self as represented is "a self that is separated from things and closed up *within* itself alone" (10). A few pages further on, Nishitani states:

> At this level, even the self in its very subjectivity is still only *represented* self-consciously as self. It is put through a kind of objectivization so as to be grasped as a being (16).

Or again:

On all other fields [namely, besides the field of *sunyata*] the self is at all times reflective and, as we said before, caught in its own grasp in the act of grasping itself, and caught in the grasp of things in its attempt to grasp them (155).

Nishitani depicts knowledge in terms of ocular vision. The knowledge that the reflective self vainly attempts to attain is reduced to being "a *refraction* of the self bent into the self" (154). Elsewhere, in a denunciation of "sheer subjectivism," like Suzuki he contends that self-knowledge cannot go beyond merely projecting our conscious acts and states onto a mental screen:

> Where the self is investigated from the standpoint of self-consciousness, it internally makes itself into a screen, as it were, upon which it observes the stream of consciousness—the various sensations, emotions, desires, representations, conceptions and the like, arising and disappearing.[29]

To unravel this difficulty, we may want to distinguish between an inadequate and an adequate representation of our conscious acts and states. Nishitani does not seem to envision the possibility of the latter. For him, like for Sartre, any attempt at representing the self ends up in failure. For me, as I indicated in my discussion of Suzuki's views, a valid kind of self-knowledge can be achieved in true judgments. Thanks to correct understanding of what we are, we become better human beings. And yet I ungrudgingly grant that this self-understanding pales in comparison with mystical insight, which is almost entirely ineffable. Consequently I agree with Nishitani every time he extols the "self-awareness" typical of religious enlightenment, while disagreeing with him about his disparagement of "self-consciousness," because this disparagement is marred by an inadequate cognitional theory.

With this inadequate account of self-knowledge, he must have recourse to paradoxical language as he proceeds to characterize the subjective epistemological condition that makes the knowledge of things possible. Like a sort of negative postulation, this precondition is called a "not knowing of the self" (156). "There the self is what is *not* the self" (157).

Besides this very limited self—let us call it self1, another self—let us call it self2, may emerge. "Only when the self breaks through the field of consciousness, the field of *beings*, and stands on the ground of nihility is it able to achieve a subjectivity that can in no way be objectified" (16). Notice that the contrast lies, not between subjectivity and nonsubjectivity, but between represented subjectivity and a subjectivity beyond objectification.

As with Suzuki's two egos, self1 and self2 are not two ontologically different persons; rather, they are two distinct perspectives upon the same self. Nishitani comes out clearly about this:

> In this kind of existential conversion [the emergence of self2], the self does not cease being a personal being. What is left behind is only the person-centered mode of grasping *person*, that is, the mode of being wherein the person is caught up in itself. In that very conversion the personal mode of being becomes more real, draws closer to the self, and appears in its true suchness. When person-centered self-prehension is broken down and nothingness is really actualized in the self, personal existence also comes really and truly to actualization in the self (71).

This renewed understanding of "person" dovetails with Sally King's remarks, reported in our preceding chapter. There are two very different modes of being person. That which is good in the former mode loses its self-centeredness and reappears, entirely reconfigured, in the later mode—the infinite self. As Nishitani writes in an article, "the obliterated self is brought to life by the power of that embrace [by God or Buddha] and is reborn: thus death for the self immediately becomes rebirth."[30] Or, more at length:

> This is the ground of absolute affirmation. The self that one confronts when one is reborn after the self itself has died is the self on the ground of this absolute affirmation. Returning here, for the first time one accepts oneself absolutely. Here one can approve of one's existence as good in and of itself. This also means truly reaching the certainty of self.[31]

Whenever Nishitani talks about self1, he speaks of "consciousness," which encompasses consciousness C and B, albeit pejoratively viewed; and whenever he undertakes to characterize self2, he speaks of "awareness," which amounts to consciousness A. In the former case, the conscious subject remains caught up in the dualism oneself/other:

> to the degree that we regard the usual, conscious self (what Buddhism calls the self of discrimination) as the self itself, it goes without saying that everything that is not the self will be seen as 'other.'[32]

In the latter case, Nishitani includes at once "the awareness of our true self-nature" and of "the selfness of each and every thing" (*Religion and Nothingness*, 106). The two come about simultaneously and in unison, because the separation between oneself and all the other things is abolished. Moreover, the two of them are understood to be unknowable: what appears is "the self-awareness that the selfness of things and the self are utterly beyond the grasp of cognition" (136).

Let us go back to the negative approach mentioned earlier. "This self that is not a self, the self emerging into its nature from out of non-ego, is the truly *original self*" (257). Yet, this original self turns out to be much more than a negative postulation, since it is positively glimpsed in the field of *sunyata*. This will be the topic of chapter 10.

CONCLUDING REMARKS

Suzuki's and Nishitani's "consciousness" is tantamount to the consciousness-of that is typical of our commonsense way of operating in everyday life. The empirical ego, or self1, is the "I" about which I have a consciousness-of. It is an inauthentic self, since it is merely represented. Suzuki and Nishitani do not appeal to consciousness-in (Lonergan's "consciousness") to elucidate the authentic self that is constituted by consciousness in its states and operations. For them (except in a few texts by Suzuki), all forms of consciousness are instances of the inauthentic self, which they construe as a reflective self. They fail to locate an authentic individual self, halfway between the false self and the transcendent Self.

An expert in the Kyoto School, Hans Waldenfels, remarks that Nishitani has in mind the modern Western self-centered ego and apparently does not know that there exists another Western understanding of the person as open to communication with others, which owes much to Boethius and Richard of St. Victor.[33] Had he become acquainted with that understanding, Nishitani might have differentiated his account of the person into three kinds of self instead of two: the inauthentic, the authentic, and the mystical.

I would contend that there is continuity between the authentic self and the mystical self. Wilber situates this continuity in a context of personal evolution:

> The self, that is, eventually *disidentifies* with its present structure so as to *identify* with the next higher-order emergent structure. More precisely (and this is a very important technical

point), we say that the self detaches itself from its *exclusive* identification with that lower structure. It doesn't throw that structure away, it simply no longer exclusively identifies with it. The point is that because the self is differentiated from the lower structure, it *transcends* that structure (without obliterating it in any way), and can thus *operate* on that lower structure using the tools of the newly emergent structure.[34]

Still, Suzuki's transcendental ego, or Nishitani's self2, is the equivalent of Lonergan's mystical consciousness, at the fourth level of conscious intentionality. In chapter 10, when we examine the notion of emptiness, we shall return to Nishitani's account of "awareness," which, in Lonergan's vocabulary and mine, actually is the highest state of "consciousness."

As the seat of consciousness, the human self is not self-contained. It can realize that it derives its light and dynamism from an encompassing Self or luminous Source. Accordingly why should there be any contradiction between affirming the existence of the individual self and recognizing its awareness of belonging to a broader sphere of consciousness? The self may be, at the same time, convinced of being ontologically distinct from anything else and of being continuous with the Ground from which it derives. On the one hand, it affirms its identity by excluding ("I am *not* x, y, z); on the other hand, it recognizes its belonging by letting itself be included ("my real home is the infinite X").[35]

In sum, we may want to distinguish relative and absolute self-knowledge. The former can be a sound account of one's conscious acts and states as well as of one's individual and yet not unrelated identity. As we observed, Suzuki has a little place for it, whereas Nishitani does not recognize it. He incorporates into consciousness A what is good in consciousness B, without differentiating them. It is absolute self-knowledge that is of utmost interest to them.

CHAPTER 9

Western Views of Nothingness

The notion of nothingness has been less prominent in the West than in Zen Buddhism. All the same, this chapter begins by recalling its significance for Plotinus and Eckhart, which was outlined in part 2. Thereafter the lion's share is granted to Martin Heidegger (1889–1976), who is convinced that "nothing" has a central place in human experience. At the outset of that long section on Heidegger, I say a few words about Jacob Böhme (1575–1624) and Friedrich Schelling (1775–1854), whose reflections on nothingness and groundlessness precede Heidegger's. Incidentally, Nishitani wrote his graduation thesis on Schelling and translated the latter's important work, *Of Human Freedom*, on which Heidegger lectured. Last, I report the reception of Plotinus, Eckhart, and Heidegger by Nishitani.[1]

PLOTINUS AND ECKHART

As we saw in part 2, both Plotinus and Eckhart at times assert that the One is nothing. For the former there is definitely no question of attributing being to the One; for the latter, being can *and* cannot be ascribed to God, depending on what concept of being is entertained. On the one hand, if "being" is taken as unrestricted, it can be applied to God. On the other hand, if "being" is understood as similar to finite beings, it cannot be predicated of God.

Heidegger aptly expounds how it is that for Eckhart no determination can be predicated of God and that consequently God can be pronounced pure nothing:

> When Meister Eckhart says "God" he means Godhead, not deus but deitas, not ens but essentia, not nature but what is

above nature, the essence—the essence to which, as it were, every existential determination must still be refused, from which every additio existentiae must be kept at a distance. . . . Thus God is for himself his "not"; that is to say, he is the most universal being, the purest indeterminate possibility of everything possible, pure nothing. He is the nothing over against the concept of every creature, over against every determinate possible and actualized being.[2]

If the Infinite is said not to "exist" because the current meaning of existence implies limitation, this in no way relegates it philosophically *beneath* the plane of beings. On the contrary, for both Plotinus and Eckhart, the One is *above* beings. Hence it bears noting that the One is fullness of life. As already observed, it is fascinating that independently from each other both authors have recourse to the metaphor of "boiling over" with life.

Accordingly, for them the nothingness of the One does not amount to an atheistic assertion. Nothingness is not naught, or simply nonexistent. Sufficient to prove this nonatheism is their stance of ultimate concern vis-à-vis the one they name the Good. Again for both, the most important thing in human life is to partake of that supreme goodness. Finally this primal Source cannot be a mere naught, since everything emanates from it.

Eckhart contrasts God and his creatures in a manner that we do not find in Plotinus, who does not have the idea of creation. For the medieval thinker, creatures are nothing in comparison with the Creator. Furthermore, they are also nothing in the sense that they do not possess being on their own and they continuously depend on God for their subsistence.

Nothingness takes on an additional sense for Plotinus and Eckhart. Both stress the absence of knowledge and of self-awareness in the state of union or identity with the One. Since the human faculties are inactive, one experiences a void, an emptiness, in a word: nothing. The soul becomes nothing in that state of complete self-forgetfulness.

HEIDEGGER

Martin Heidegger was highly interested in Japanese philosophy. He met with Nishitani in Freiburg and asked him many questions. He also read at least one of Suzuki's books and remarked to a friend, "If I understand this man correctly, this is what I have been trying to say in all my writings."[3]

Heidegger also acknowledges having drawn some inspiration from Meister Eckhart. In chapter 5, we found an instance, namely, "life without a reason why." However, Heidegger profoundly reworked the themes he borrowed from his illustrious German forerunner.[4] So, in regard to the role of nothingness, we expect from him a treatment that is quite different, not only from Plotinus's, but even from Eckhart's. Moreover, Heidegger's approach to nothingness is indebted to the seventeenth-century mystic Jacob Böhme and to the nineteenth-century philosopher Friedrich Schelling, on whom he lectured in 1936.[5]

In chapter 1 of the first of his "Six Theosophic Points,"[6] Böhme speaks of the eternal "unground" (*Ungrund*), which is an eternal nothing (*Nichts*) (§7–9). It is the same as "the hidden eternal wisdom of God, which resembles an eternal eye without essence" (§11), and the same as "the eternal will" (§12). Such unground has "no ground nor limit" (§12). Given that essences are limited, Böhme repeatedly states that the unground is "without essence," being the source of all the essences. He explains, "It is its own, and yet also in comparison to Nature is as a nothing (understand, in comparison to palpable being, so to speak); though it is all, and all arises from thence" (§14). While "in the unground there is no manifestation, but an eternal nothingness" (§29; see §19), Böhme speculates that in the Trinity "that which is eternally grasped in wisdom, the grasp comprehending a basis or centre in itself, passing out of the ungroundness into a ground, is Son or Heart" (§15), and "the going within itself to the centre of the ground is Spirit" (§16). In other words, the divine unground is more primordial than its manifestation in the Son. Three centuries after Eckhart, Böhme seems to echo his German intellectual forebear, who distinguished between "the Godhead" (with no distinctions) and "God" (with the trinitarian distinctions).

A similar duality within the Godhead recurs in Schelling's thought. He speaks of a "primal ground" (*Urgrund*) or the "groundless" (*Ungrund*), which is more primordial than the "basis" (*Grund*). The first aspect is the "absolute indifference," without distinctions, which "has no predicates except lack of predicates, without its being naught or a nonentity."[7] The second aspect (not a temporal stage) appears as "duality immediately breaks forth" (88). The indifference is the "neutrality" (*Gleichgültigkeit*) found in God as long as we make abstraction of creation (90). The basis amounts to a divine potentiality that accounts for the tension, within the created universe, between "this aroused creature-will (the possible principle of evil)" and "the will of love." The former will is "the condition upon which alone the will of love could be realized" (83). The latter is "life and love and personal existence" (89), also called "beneficence" (90).

For our purposes, let us note that Böhme and Schelling have in common the dialectic of two aspects in God: the *Ungrund* and the *Grund*. Böhme contrasts the nothing with the trinitarian differentiations, whereas Schelling contrasts the absolute indifference with the duality. Heidegger is intrigued by the ambiguity of such a quest for the ground. We shall see how he originally transforms the concept of *Grund* by differentiating it into the *Urgrund*, the *Abgrund*, and the *Ungrund*.

Because of Heidegger's evolution in his thinking, this presentation of his views on being and nothingness will follow a chronological order. In Heidegger's *Being and Time (Sein und Zeit,* 1927),[8] we find the most remarkable case of "the phenomenon of the *equiprimordiality (Gleichursprünglichkeit)* of constitutive items" (131). That is to say, being *(Sein)* and the nothing *(das Nichts)* are equally primordial in human thinking as well as in the reality to which thinking points. The nothing exercises a specific role within the basic experience of anxiety *(Angst)*. In contrast to fear, which refers to specific objects, anxiety makes us confront something "completely indefinite." "That in the face of which one has anxiety is characterized by the fact that what threatens is nowhere *(nirgends)*" (186; see the whole of §40). Anxiety is about the world, which could be reduced to naught. Consequently anxiety has to do with "the utter insignificance" of all entities within the universe (187). And this insignificance has profound repercussions upon us since it removes any possibility of spontaneously ascribing meaning to our quest: "our concernful awaiting finds nothing in terms of which it might be able to understand itself; it clutches at the 'nothing' of the world" (343).

Accordingly, *Dasein* (the "being-there" of the questioning person) loses its "everyday familiarity" with entities around itself.

> In anxiety one feels uncanny *(unheimlich,* unhomelike). Here the peculiar indefiniteness of that which Dasein finds itself alongside in anxiety, comes proximally to expression: the "nothing and nowhere". But here "uncanniness" also means "not-being-at-home" *(das Nicht-zuhause-sein)* (188).

How is uncanniness connected with nothing?

> Uncanniness . . . puts Dasein's Being-in-the-world face to face with the 'nothing' of the world; in the face of this 'nothing', Dasein is anxious with anxiety about its ownmost potentiality-for-Being" (276).

Anxiety is also about death, which spells the end of one's existence. "In this state-of-mind, Dasein finds itself face to face with the 'nothing' of the possible impossibility of its existence.... Being-towards-death is essentially anxiety" (266). Again: "The 'nothing' with which anxiety brings us face to face, unveils the nullity by which Dasein, in its very basis, is defined; and this basis itself is as thrownness into death" (308).

In *History of the Concept of Time*, a series of lectures given in 1925, contemporaneous with the redaction of *Sein und Zeit*, Heidegger describes *Angst* (here translated as "dread") and *Nichts* in a more vivid manner.[9]

> Because that of which dread is in dread is this nothing in the sense of "nothing definite and worldly," the nothing amplifies its proximity, that is, the possibility of the can-be (*Seinkönnen*) and of "being able to do nothing against it." This absolute helplessness in the face of the threatening, because it is indeed indefinite, because it is nothing, offers no ways and means of overcoming it.... It is not this or that concern which is threatened, but *being-in-the-world as such*.

He explains, in a particularly helpful way: "The of-which and the about-which of dread are both Dasein itself, more accurately, the fact that I am, that is, 'I am' in the sense of the naked being-in-the-world" (291). And further on:

> But dread is dread of this being itself, such that this being-in-dread-of-it is a being in dread about this being. But this implies that Dasein is an entity for which in its being, in its being-in-the-world, "it goes about its very being" (*es geht um sein Sein selbst*), for which, that is, its very being is at issue. This is the sense of the selfsameness of the of-which and the about-which of dread which has just been expounded (292–293).

The reality in question is the dread *of* the self *about* the self, about its naked existing. (The adjective "naked" or "bare," repeated in those pages, is reminiscent of Eckhart.) As we see, in *Being and Time* and *History of the Concept of Time* Heidegger underscores the experiential character of that fundamental situation.

Let us examine excerpts from a few essays by Heidegger, collected in *Pathmarks*.[10] In his 1929 essay, "What Is Metaphysics?" Heidegger reintroduces the theme of the "nothing" in a context where the limitations of science are underlined. He tells us that science only investigates beings, and besides those, nothing. Yet what seems at first a rather casual and innocuous sense of "nothing" soon opens up a new dimension, foreign to science. Heidegger asks:

> What about this nothing? . . . However, why do we trouble ourselves with this nothing? The nothing is rejected precisely by science, given up as a nullity. . . . If science is right, then only one thing is sure: science wishes to know nothing of the nothing. Ultimately this is the scientifically rigorous conception of the nothing.

Yet science cannot do without the nothing. Ironically "when science tries to express its own proper essence it calls upon the nothing for help. It has recourse to what it rejects" (84).

The author is fascinated by the nothing. Far from being the "nullity" rejected by science, "the nothing is what we are seeking." He defines it as follows: "The nothing is the complete negation of the totality of beings" (86). Or equivalently: "it is nonbeing pure and simple" (85). It appears that the role of nothing is to have us relativize every being (*das Seiende*, any entity) and to pose the question of being (*Sein*). So we are invited to proceed in three stages.

The first stage consists in realizing, through experiences such as boredom or love, that "we certainly do find ourselves stationed in the midst of beings that are unveiled somehow as a whole." Still this sense of the whole is only a first step. "But just when moods of this sort bring us face to face with beings as a whole they conceal from us the nothing we are seeking" (87).

Therefore a second stage is in order, which may happen "only in a correspondingly originary attunement that in the most proper sense of unveiling makes manifest the nothing." We need to enter into another basic mood, "the fundamental mood of anxiety" (88). Pervaded by a peculiar calm, "a kind of entranced calm" (90) very different from fear and not opposed to joy (93), anxiety plays its part whenever we feel uncanny as things recede from us.

> The receding (*Ent-gleiten*, withdrawal) of beings as a whole, closing in on us in anxiety, oppresses us. We can get no hold on things. In the slipping away of beings only this "no hold on things" comes over us and remains.
>
> Anxiety makes manifest the nothing.
>
> We "hover" in anxiety. More precisely, anxiety leaves us hanging, because it induces the slipping away of beings as a whole (88).

As beings slip away, we are released from our entanglement among them, we undergo a liberation from them. Heidegger explains: "The nothing itself does not attract; it is essentially repelling. But this repulsion is itself as such a parting gesture toward beings that are submerging as a whole" (90). Thanks to the manifestation of the nothing, the human self is revealed to itself as it adopts a stance towards beings and towards itself.

Da-sein means: being held out into the nothing.

Holding itself out into the nothing, Dasein is in each case already beyond beings as a whole. Such being beyond beings we call *transcendence* (91).

The fundamental mood of anxiety, which unveils the nothing, is not a matter of logical negation. "Unyielding antagonism and stinging rebuke have a more abysmal source than the measured negation of thought" (92). Such experiences are more profound than the dialectic of a Hegelian intellect, in which affirmations and negations succeed one another. "The nothing does not remain the indeterminate opposite of beings but unveils itself as belonging to the being of beings" (94).

We thus come to the third stage, where the nothing exercises the function of releasing the question of being, which is intimately bound up with the question of the nothing.

Only because the nothing is manifest in the ground of Dasein can the total strangeness of beings overwhelm us. Only when the strangeness of beings oppresses us does it arouse and evoke wonder. Only on the ground of wonder—the manifestness of the nothing—does the "why?" loom before us (95).

Heidegger sums up the three-stage journey as follows:

It is of decisive importance, first, that we allow space for beings as a whole; second, that we release ourselves into the nothing, that is to say, that we liberate ourselves from those idols everyone has and to which they are wont to go cringing; and finally, that we let the sweep of our suspense take its full course, so that it swings back into the fundamental question of metaphysics that the nothing itself compels: Why are there beings at all, and why not far rather Nothing? (96)

Let us draw a few indications about nothingness from Heidegger's lecture course of 1935, entitled *Introduction to Metaphysics*,[11] given after the essay on which I have just been commenting and before the other pieces of *Pathmarks*, to which I shall return. In addition to the themes already present in *Sein und Zeit* and in other writings of the 1920s, the author introduces the concept of ground. Starting with the question about the problematic status of the whole of what is, he differentiates three possibilities:

> What is put into question comes into relation with a ground. But because we are questioning, it remains an open question whether the ground is a truly grounding, foundation-effecting, originary ground (*Ur-grund*); whether the ground refuses to provide a foundation, and so is an abyss (*Ab-grund*); or whether the ground is neither one nor the other, but merely offers the perhaps necessary illusion of a foundation and is thus an unground (*Un-grund*) (3).

At this stage it remains undecided whether the ground will turn out to be an originary ground or an abyss. What is certain, however, is that Heidegger militates against the illusion of the unground, into which many philosophers fall, because they do not pursue the question of being and they stay in the state called the oblivion of being. "How are we even supposed to inquire into the ground for the Being of beings, let alone be able to find it out, if we have not adequately conceived, understood and grasped Being itself?" (35) But how can we avoid the illusion of the unground if we are unwilling to experience the abyss? Here as in "What Is Metaphysics?" Heidegger points to the fact that we hover in anxiety, as we question "the ground for the wavering of the beings that sustain us and unbind us, half in being, half not in being, which is also why we cannot wholly belong to any thing, not even to ourselves" (31).

> With our question we establish ourselves among beings in such a way that they forfeit their self-evidence *as beings*. Insofar as beings come to waver within the broadest and harshest possibility of oscillation—the "either beings—or nothing"—the questioning itself loses every secure foothold. Our Dasein, too, as it questions, comes into suspense, and nevertheless maintains itself, by itself, in this suspense (31).

Again we realize that the question is twofold: indissociably about being and nothing, although we tend to avoid the latter in order to seize the former directly:

If we want to lay hold of Being it is always as if we were reaching into a void. The Being that we are asking about is almost like Nothing, and yet we are always trying to arm and guard ourselves against the presumption of saying that beings *are not* (38).

In a very important work, *Contributions to Philosophy (From Enowning)*, composed right after *Introduction to Metaphysics*, that is, in 1936–38 and posthumously published in 1989,[12] Heidegger emphasizes the proximity of ground to abground in human experience, as he asks, "Why is Da-sein the ground and abground for historical man?" (222). He affirms, "Ground needs ab-ground" (266). Successively stressing the prefix and the noun, he proclaims, "*Ab*-ground is Ab-*ground*" (265). There can be no ground without ab-ground as the privation of ground: "Ab-ground is the staying-away of ground. . . . Ab-ground is the hesitating refusal of ground" (265). In this §242, he returns to the tripartite differentiation into ur-ground, ab-ground, and un-ground. While un-ground is characterized as the place where ab-ground is totally dissembled, both ur-ground and ab-ground are intimately interlaced, as the positive and negative sides of the same "enowning" (*Ereignis*), namely, the movement whereby Be-ing (*Seyn*) is appropriated as well as unattained, since it is "un-possessive."[13]

In *Contributions* the Dasein is still important, as the author insists on the decision, on the leap (214). Yet the revealing-concealing movement from *Seyn* (understood as truth) is more underlined than in Heidegger's previous writings. Rich metaphors are introduced, such as self-withdrawing, self-sheltering, concealing, not-granting, on the part of Being. One of those metaphors is of particular interest to us, namely, emptiness. "Not-granting is not nothing but rather an outstanding originary manner of letting *be* unfulfilled, of letting *be* empty—thus an outstanding manner of enopening" (265).

Here again ab-ground plays a crucial role: "ab-ground is the primary clearing for what is open as 'emptiness'" (265). Notice the link with grounding and ab-groundness in the following sentences:

> The only thing that matters is to determine what is ownmost to emptiness itself—that is to say, to think the ab-groundness of abground, i.e., how ab-ground grounds. Actually, that is always to be thought only from within the ur-ground, from enowning, and in enacting the leap into its resonating turning (266).

Emptiness is also fullness:

> "Emptiness" is actually the fullness of what is still-undecided, what is to be decided, what holds to ab-ground, what points to ground, to the truth of being.
>
> "Emptiness" is the fulfilled distress of the abandonment by being, but this already shifted into what is open and thereby related to the uniqueness of be-ing and its inexhaustibility (266).

The author multiplies the phrases that highlight the complementarity, indeed the unity, of being and nothing. He calls the latter "that alone which has equal rank with be-ing—because it continues to belong to be-ing" (173). He states, "The more originarily being is experienced in its truth, the deeper is the *nothing* as the abground at the edge of the ground" (228). This unity amounts to the inseparability of the affirming and the nihilating.

> The open of the ab-ground is not groundless. Ab-ground is not—like a groundlessness—the no to every ground but rather the yes to the ground in its hidden expanse and remoteness (271; see 174).

We are invited "to experience the nihilating (*das nichtende*) in be-ing itself" because "be-ing belongs to the not" (188). As William Richardson points out, "Heidegger emphasizes the radicality of the not that permeates the abyssal depth of the grounding process without reducing it to a gross nihilism."[14]

In the lectures of 1941, entitled *Basic Concepts*,[15] Heidegger notes that on the one hand, being is the most reliable aspect of our life since everything presupposes it, and on the other hand, it offers no foundation and no ground among beings since we cannot base any mundane expectation on it (52–53). As far as the nothing is concerned, the author explains that it is not a third vis-à-vis beings and being, and yet, pace Hegel, it is not to be simply identified with being. "Nothing is in a certain way the other to being" (60). Still, in their respective uniqueness, being and nothing are the same (60–61).

Towards the end of his *Parmenides*, a lecture course from the winter semester 1942–43,[16] Heidegger evokes, in words that resemble the Zen language, the "simple wakefulness in the proximity of any random unobtrusive being, an awakening that all of a sudden sees that the being 'is'" (149). He adds, "To think Being requires in each instance a leap, a leap into the groundless from the habitual ground upon which for us beings always rest" (150). He carefully demarcates the groundless from our ordinary understanding of a ground:

> Being, however, is not a ground but is the groundless. It is called such because it is primordially detached from a "soil" and "ground" and does not require them. Being, the "it is" of a being, is never autochthonous in beings, as if Being could be extracted from beings and then stood upon them as on its ground. It is only beings in relation to beings that are autochthonous. Being, the never autochthonous, is the groundless. This seems to be a lack, though only if calculated in terms of beings, and it appears as an abyss in which we founder without support in our relentless pursuit of beings. In fact we surely fall into the abyss, we find no ground, as long as we know and seek a ground only in the form of a being and hence never carry out the leap into Being or leave the familiar landscape of the oblivion of Being (150).

Let us now return to the other essays in *Pathmarks*. In his "Letter on 'Humanism'" (1946) Heidegger maintains that for him "being" differs from God: "'Being'—that is not God and not a cosmic ground" (252). Apparently this position would distance him from Plotinus and Eckhart. However, in Dasein's experience of self-transcendence towards being—its "ek-sistence"—the nihilation (the "no") is inseparable from the affirmation (the "yes") of the ineffable being.

> It remains to ask, granting that thinking belongs to ek-sistence, whether every "yes" and "no" are not themselves already eksistent in the truth of being. If they are, then the "yes" and the "no" are already intrinsically in thrall to being. As enthralled, they can never first posit the very thing to which they themselves belong" (273).

We find an explanation for this incapacity to posit, in Heidegger's "Postscript to 'What Is Metaphysics?'" (1943):

> Unlike beings, being cannot be represented or brought forth in the manner of an object. As that which is altogether other than all beings, being is that which is not. But this nothing essentially prevails as being (233).

In other words: "The nothing, as other than beings, is the veil of being" (238).

And he summarizes his essay on metaphysics as follows:

> This lecture thinks out of an attentiveness to the voice of being and into the attunement coming from this voice, attuning the human being in his essence to its claim, so that in the nothing he may learn to experience being (234).

The function of the nothing with respect to the question of being is again highlighted in his "Introduction to 'What Is Metaphysics?'" (1949): "The question must begin from that which is not a being. And this is precisely what the question names, and it capitalizes the word: the Nothing" (290).

In "On the Question of Being," (1955), he reminds us that "it is by no means easier to say 'being' than to speak of the nothing" (309). In a manner that brings thinking about being close to mysticism, he contends:

> No information can be provided concerning the nothing or being or nihilism, concerning their essence or concerning the essential (verbal) unfolding of such essence (nominal), that might lie ready before us in the form of propositional statements waiting to be seized (310).

And after reiterating the point of "What Is Metaphysics?" he is emphatic about the inseparability of being and nothing:

> Only *because* the question "What is metaphysics?" from the start recalls the surpassing, the *transcendens*, the *being of beings*, can it think the "not" of beings, *that* nothing which is equioriginarily the Same as being (318).

At the same period as "On the Question of Being," that is, in 1955–56, Heidegger gave a lecture course and an address published as *Der Satz vom Grund*.[17] He argues that besides the reason (*Grund*) that can be found as an answer to the "why" questions of science and technology, genuine philosophy consists in a quest for another kind of reason (*Grund*) (125–129). In an implicit reference to Eckhart and an explicit reference to Angelus Silesius, who speaks of a rose which exists "without why" (35–38, 41), Heidegger naturally identifies the second kind of ground with being:

> The principle of reason speaks of the being of beings. What does the principle say? The principle of reason says: *to being*

> there belongs something like ground-reason. Being is akin to grounds, it is ground-like (49).

And once more he makes sure we do not confuse the two ways of grounding:

> Being "is" in essence: ground/reason. Therefore being can never first have a ground/reason which would supposedly ground it. Accordingly, ground/reason is missing from being. Ground/reason remains at a remove from being. Being "is" the abyss in the sense of such a remaining-apart of reason from being. To the extent that being as such grounds, it remains groundless (51; see 111).

Lastly, in his 1957 lecture entitled "The Principle of Identity," Heidegger asserts that a leap in thinking is required so that we may move away from Being, "interpreted as the ground (*Grund*) in which every being as such is grounded." In a brisk manner his questions and answers alternate:

> Where does the spring go that springs away from the ground? Into an abyss (*Abgrund*)? Yes, as long as we only represent the spring in the horizon of metaphysical thinking. No, insofar as we spring and let go. Where to? To where we already have access: the belonging to Being.[18]

A few pages further on, he reiterates that "this abyss is neither empty nothingness nor murky confusion, but rather the event of appropriation (*Er-eignis*)" (39). We recognize here the "enowning" of *Contributions to Philosophy*: the mutual owning-belonging between Dasein and Being, which necessitates the repudiation of the traditional, metaphysical sense of grounding.

To recapitulate: By "nothing," Heidegger means neither a mere logical negation nor some entity or object. Instead, he points to the possibility that beings as a whole might not have existed or might cease to exist. Hence the question concerning the beingness of beings, which is not yet being but nevertheless shows that Dasein is open to being and receives from it its basic freedom. But if the nothing is to play its role, one must consent to enter a state of anxiety, in which Dasein finds itself hanging over the abyss of nothingness. In this fundamental mood, the person can no longer hold on to things or values that might otherwise have served as idols. The nothing thus de-substantializes everything.

Because of the possible nothingness of all beings, the ineffable nature of being (still unknown and yet ineluctable) is unveiled while remaining veiled. The de-grounding nothing ensures that the grounding being will never be captured. Thus, as a perceptive commentator puts it, "Negativity is the condition of all positivity."[19]

Finally, we may want to ask, is there a parallelism between Eckhart and Heidegger on "nothing"?[20] Yes, and that parallelism is at least threefold. First, because "nothing" is neither a mere nullity nor a determinate something, the two authors attach an enormous importance to it. Second, the sense of "nothing" emerges in a fundamental experience—either Eckhart's detachment of the soul from all beings, or Heidegger's anxiety of Dasein in the midst of beings. In both cases, one finds oneself cut off, or differentiated from the realm of beings (*abegescheiden*, writes the former; *unterschieden*, writes the latter). Third, both thinkers equate pure nothing with pure Being, albeit with different meanings, since the medieval preacher is a theist whereas the German philosopher is an agnostic.[21]

NISHITANI AS INTERPRETER OF PLOTINUS, ECKHART, AND HEIDEGGER

Judging by his texts translated into English, Nishitani discusses Plotinus's views much less often than Eckhart's or Heidegger's. Nevertheless, in "Religious-Philosophical Existence in Buddhism," he situates Plotinus with respect to the Buddhist concept of *anatman*, "no-self." Nishitani submits that while the earlier European concept of *subjectum* is the basis for each individual existence, *anatman* is a non-*subjectum*. In Plotinus, it would appear that the One and Matter are two types of non-*subjectum*, since the One lies beyond the subject and Matter lies beyond physical substance. And yet, "both the One and Matter have the character of a *subjectum*. Both possess a certain ground in themselves, so that we are forced to conceive of them as a *subjectum*."[22]

Nishitani criticizes this search for a ground or foundation in a non-*subjectum* which is thereby reduced to a *subjectum*: "each non-*subjectum* of this sort offers us a foundation upon which we can ground ourselves. We are always striving zealously to identify ourselves with this foundation." He adds, "It is precisely such a non-*subjectum*, apparently offering man a firm foundation, that actually hinders him from penetrating himself and coming to an essential understanding of himself" (3).

According to Nishitani, such a transmutation of what is intended as a non-*subjectum* into what actually acquires the characteristics of a *sub-*

jectum plagues not only Plotinus's One, but also the God of much Western thinking, and even Nietzsche's nothingness, which becomes an original principle of that sort.

> This tendency to imagine the non-*subjectum* as something—that is, to think of it once again as having the nature of a *subjectum*—is so deep-rooted that it is already present at the emergence of the basic concepts mentioned above [One, Matter, God, Nothingness]. That is why these fundamental concepts necessarily contain an element of ambiguity. What is to be explained by them by its very nature actually lies beyond the scope of subject and the scope of substance, outside the "sensed" and "intelligible" world (4).

Is Nishitani's criticism of Plotinus fair? I do not think so. For the Greek philosopher, it is *nous*, Intellect, that is the *hypokeimenon*, the underlying substrate or *subjectum*. The One resides totally beyond the scope of subject, substance, substrate, or Intellect.[23] While Plotinus would rightly dismiss the criticism leveled at him by the Japanese thinker, he would nonetheless appreciate and underwrite the latter's approach to a non-*subjectum* entirely beyond the ken of any *subjectum*. He would like Nishitani's metaphor of the non-*subjectum* as "the absolutely open" (6).

Likewise, Nishitani misconstrues Plotinus's thought in a passage of *Religion and Nothingness* where he affirms that "such an absolute One does not pass through the field of nihility before making its appearance" (143). Plotinus clearly locates the One beyond the realm of what exists, hence in nihility.

Next, let us examine Nishitani's reading of Meister Eckhart. In *Religion and Nothingness*, how does he deal with the Meister's paradoxical sayings? Most of the time, he registers their fine nuances.

As a first example, let us observe that he interprets Eckhart correctly with respect to his contention that we must go beyond "God" to "the Deity." While the former can be said to be a "substance" according to the form in which he discloses himself to us, the latter resides beyond any form.

> Eckhart speaks of the godhead, or the "essence" of God, in terms of an altogether formless, absolute "nothingness" wherein God is on his own home-ground beyond any of the forms in which he discloses himself to his creatures, and in particular beyond the "personal" forms through which he reveals himself to man (115).

Further on, Nishitani seems to be quoting Eckhart twice, without saying so, when he writes that the field of *sunyata* "would appear as the field of a wisdom that we might call a 'knowing of non-knowing'" (121) and that "in the self in itself, as it is on the home-ground of the self, there is an essential *not-knowing* that is one with the *knowing* of the self" (154).[24]

In a longer passage on Eckhart, right after introducing the twin themes of God's birth in the soul and of the breakthrough to the Godhead, Nishitani proceeds to construe Eckhart's sayings in terms of nothingness.

> Absolute nothingness signals, for Eckhart, the point at which all modes of being are transcended, at which not only the various modes of created being but even the modes of divine being—such as Creator or Divine Love—are transcended (61).

In an article, Nishitani has recourse to a Buddhist image according to which, in the experience of emptiness, all the differentiated components are like waves that do not move apart from the water and thus are water. Variety is at the same time unity. And he thinks that Eckhart's phrase, *ein einzic ein*, "a single One," amounts to the same intuition.[25]

Such absolute nothingness, however, does not characterize God only, but the human soul as well. For Eckhart, insofar as the soul inhabits the desert of the godhead, it is selfless.

> Here the soul is completely deprived of its egoity. This is the final ground of the soul, its *bottomless ground*. Although it marks the point at which the soul can for the first time return to be itself, it is at the same time the point at which God is in himself. It is the ground of God (*Religion and Nothingness*, 62; see 99).

Nishitani speaks of "the absolute death of ego" and of "our absolute death-*sive*-life" (63; see 90). He suggestively equates "the absolute death of ego" with Eckhart's *Abgeschiedenheit*, detachment (63; see 106; he uses the modern German rendering here). Thanks to this realization, the human self identifies with God's nothingness.

This experience goes further than the existentialist stance:

> The "nothingness" of godhead that Eckhart sees at the very ground of God himself must be said to be still more profound than the nihility that contemporary existentialism has put in the place of God (65).

Furthermore, according to Nishitani, Eckhart's position lies ahead even of Nietzsche's: beyond the God pronounced dead, one can find "the nothingness of godhead" (66).

Earlier in the book, in a dialogue with Augustine which could have been carried out equally well with Eckhart, Nishitani sees in the Christian doctrine of the *creatio ex nihilo* an omnipresence of God that "deprives us of a locus to stand in self-existence" and thus casts us out "into the middle of a desert of death" (38; see 37–40 and 75). Interestingly, Eckhart teaches that the soul has no "locus" and dwells in a "desert." Nishitani explains:

> That a thing is created *ex nihilo* means that this *nihil* is more immanent in that thing than the very being of that thing is "immanent" in the thing itself. This is why we speak of "absolute immanence." It is an immanence of absolute negation, for the being of the created is grounded upon a *nothingness* and seen fundamentally to be a nothingness. At the same time, it is an immanence of absolute affirmation, for the nothingness of the created is the ground of its *being* (39).

It is in the immanence of the human self that both Eckhart and Nishitani find transcendence (90).

Another theme of Eckhart's, namely, existence without a why, which was elaborated by Heidegger in *The Principle of Reason*,[26] as we indicated earlier in this chapter, also recurs in Nishitani, who writes:

> On the field of sunyata, fact as primal fact, that is fact as the very fact it is in its own true reality, is groundlessly itself.... It is simply itself, cut off from every How and Why and Wherefore (158).

Later in his book, Nishitani remarks, "It is the point that Meister Eckhart calls *Leben ohne Warum* ('life without a reason why')" (180; see 283).

Lastly we can notice an allusion to a tenet of Eckhart's that was mentioned in chapter 5, namely, our existence in the divine mind before the universe came to be, in Nishitani's remark about "the self of each man as at bottom preceding the world and things" (159).

To conclude these reflections about Eckhart and Nishitani: I see two main differences between them in their respective approaches to nothingness. First, Eckhart's literary genre belongs to speculative mysticism, with rare personal allusions, whereas Nishitani's approach is more distinctively existential and experiential (in the Zen sense). Second, although Eckhart repeatedly points to the nothingness of God, of the world, and of the human soul, he does not systematically develop his insights. By contrast, Nishitani's contribution is more differentiated, as we shall find out in chapter 10.

To shift to Heidegger's influence upon Nishitani, who studied under the German master in the 1930s, we may safely affirm that it is omnipresent in the Japanese thinker's writings where he brings together his Zen tradition and Western perspectives. Even when Heidegger's name is not mentioned, his vocabulary is used. As we shall see in the next chapter, Nishitani radicalizes the nihilism of Nietzsche and Heidegger, in particular the understanding of the abyssal ground found in the Dasein.

How does he assess Heidegger's contribution on nothingness? According to Nishitani's book, *Religion and Nothingness*, Heidegger goes way beyond the duality subject/object by uncovering the ground of their relationship—a ground that nullifies both subject and object.

> What seems to make things and ourselves unreal in fact makes them emerge more really. In Heidegger's terms, the being of beings discloses itself in the nullifying of nothingness (*das Nicht nichtet*) (109, a quotation, without reference, of "What Is Metaphysics," 90).

In "Reflections on Two Addresses by Martin Heidegger," Nishitani states that the "nowhere" of *sunyata* lies beyond the alternative of "to be" and "not to be," in a dimension beyond duality. Deeply attracted to Heidegger's assertion that the earthly magnitude of man and the emptiness of its meaning together constitute a single truth, Nishitani comments, "Heidegger's saying about the 'truth' of their togetherness may be interpreted as hinting not only at a negative truth but rather more at a positive one."[27] Thereby, he reads Heidegger as synthesizing the affirmation and negation, in line with the basic insight of *sunyata*.[28]

In *Religion and Nothingness*, Nishitani also praises Heidegger for having surpassed the other brands of contemporary existentialism in expressing the human sense of being deprived of all basis, "the groundlessness (*Grundlosigkeit*) of existence lying at the ground of self-existence" (96).

In Nishitani's judgment, however, the German philosopher does not completely leave behind the view "that simply sets nothingness over against existence as a mere conceptual negation." Heidegger seems to represent nothingness as "something outside of the existence of the self and all things," as some "thing" adjacent to human existence (96).

Fred Dallmayr questions Nishitani's construal of Heidegger's thought in this respect.[29] He contends that we do not find in Heidegger's works an equation of nothingness with logical negativity or with some realm outside human existence. All the same, Dallmayr grants that in *Being and Time* nothingness is still viewed mainly from the vantage point of *Dasein* and that this approach may account for Nishitani's objection. Nevertheless, in "What Is Metaphysics?" the German philosopher insists, as we saw, that the nothing is neither a logical concept nor something extrinsic, but lies within the Dasein's own intrinsic abyss. And in *Contributions to Philosophy*—Dallmayr could have added "On the Question of Being," 317—far from accepting an antithesis or reciprocal exclusion, Heidegger highlights the mutual implication and intertwining between being and nothing. Having made these remarks, Dallmayr helpfully notes that *Contributions to Philosophy* approximates the "sive" which for Nishitani, as will be seen in the next chapter, characterizes the field of *sunyata*.

Interestingly, Nishitani considers Heidegger as someone whose words point in the direction of a mystical way, that is, as a thinker open to mysticism.[30] He would agree with John Caputo who sees a "mystical element in Heidegger's thought," yet without treating his writings as mystical literature.[31]

CONCLUDING REMARKS

In this chapter comparisons have been made between the views of nothingness put forth by Western writers such as Plotinus, Eckhart, Böhme, Schelling, and Heidegger. We have also examined how Nishitani interprets those views. For all those religiously inclined persons, the experience of nothingness preconditions their redefinition of self and their access to an entirely new kind of consciousness, however they call it. In our next chapter we shall complete our characterization of the encounter between some Western and some Japanese thinkers regarding nothingness.

CHAPTER 10

Japanese Views of Nothingness

In this final chapter, I introduce the positions of two Japanese thinkers on nothingness: Nishitani Keiji and Hisamatsu Shin'ichi.[1] Beginning with Nishitani, I describe first his approach to nihilism, and second, his views on absolute nothingness. Third, I consider Hisamatsu's clarification of what he calls Oriental nothingness.

NISHITANI'S APPROACH TO NIHILISM

Nishitani's interest in nothingness depends on two factors. First, the centuries-long fascination of Mahayana Buddhism with *sunyata*, emptiness, to which pride of place is given in Buddhist thought. He caught this fascination through the practice of Zen.[2] Towards the end of his life, in a short piece entitled "Encounter with Emptiness," he summed up his philosophical enterprise:

> I am thinking of making philosophy work as the thinking of basic non-thinking, just like the everyday labor of working the field and pulling the weeds in the mode of "taking the spade in the hand while staying empty-handed," directly revealing absolute nothingness. From such a standpoint I wish to clarify the many problems of our day.[3]

I will return to this metaphor of the empty hand.

Second, according to what he confesses in his book on Nishida Kitaro, his mentor at Kyoto University, as a young man he engaged in a philosophical quest by facing the issue of his own emptiness and despair, and by asking the question of the meaning of human life in a most earnest fashion.[4] In another work, *The Self-Overcoming of Nihilism*, Nishitani tackles the problem of nihilism in its historical and communal aspects, in dialogue with Western thinkers, mainly with Nietzsche. Furthermore, he claims that nihilism characterizes not only Western, but Japanese culture as well.[5] In an article, he submits:

> Until now the standard of values, the ultimate foundation of all principles has rested in God—or Buddha, maybe. Nowadays the ultimate foundation of all value standards has become fragile, a situation which we describe as nihilism and which is really the most fundamental problem of our age.[6]

In *Religion and Nothingness* Nishitani acknowledges that Nietzsche does a great service to philosophy by uncovering the emptiness that lies at the core of modern civilization. After stressing the significance of Nietzsche's diagnosis, he sets out to show that *sunyata* is the only answer to the cultural plight described by Nietzsche. As a mere concept, however, *sunyata* obviously cannot measure up to that which is experienced in Zen. Therefore Nishitani insists that we need "a real appropriation," which is more than "philosophical cognition" or "theoretical knowledge." This real appropriation consists in the "self-awareness of reality," which includes "both our becoming aware of reality and, at the same time, the reality realizing itself in our awareness" (5).[7]

The spiritual journey that Nishitani maps out consists of two basic standpoints, the first of which is subdivided. Hence, we have, in an order of increasing profundity, first, the nothingness (in Japanese: *mu*) or nihility (*kyomu*, hollow nothingness) of twentieth-century positivism and existentialism; second, the nihility of Nietzsche's later thought and of Heidegger's reflections on nothingness and being; and third, *sunyata*, the emptiness (*ku*) of Buddhism, reinterpreted by Nishida as absolute nothing (*zettai mu*).[8]

First, there is an experience of nothingness both in the positivistic worldview deriving from modern science and in existentialism. These two stances represent the extreme poles (intellectually interactive and yet, in the end, totally thrown apart) of objectivism and subjectivism. In science, the universe is represented as devoid of finality and of any personal agency. By contrast, a typical existentialist thinker such as Sartre contends that the *néant* (nothingness), being the part of the person that is not objectifiable, allows the self to choose itself freely. For all the fundamental questions regarding the meaning of life and death that Sartre expresses, nevertheless he does not overcome the viewpoint of the self-conscious ego (30–35, 65).

Second, according to Nishitani, after registering the groundlessness of all values and the ensuing nihilism and atheism, Nietzsche takes up a position beyond the confines of the ego as he affirms life.[9] His construal of *amor fati* displays an acceptance of the whole historical, evolving universe. Heidegger, for his part, having assumed many of his predecessor's insights, escapes the limitations of Husserlian subjectivity and goes deeply into the relation of nothing to being.

Third, with respect to *sunyata*, Nishitani sees it as emptiness-plenitude, negation and affirmation, the great doubt in concentration (*samadhi*) and the enlightenment of suchness (*tathata*), where every thing presents itself and is received in nonattachment. This is what we now must examine.

NISHITANI'S CHARACTERIZATION OF "ABSOLUTE NOTHINGNESS"

It is important not to expect from Nishitani a presentation of *sunyata* which would purport to be literally faithful to a single tradition. What we are going to discover is something more original, which is the result of the author's several concerns, as just outlined in the former section. Let us pay attention to the Preface to his book, *Religion and Nothingness*, where he states his intention of dealing, not with particular brands of religion, but with religion as such, whose status has become very problematic in our world. Consequently, his references to specific doctrines are fluid enough, given his interest in letting light emerge out of novel cross-denominational and cross-philosophical comparisons.

About his recourse to Buddhist concepts, he writes:

> This does not mean that a position is being taken from the start on the doctrines of Buddhism as a particular religion or on the doctrines of one of its sects. I have borrowed these terms only insofar as they illuminate reality and the essence and actuality of man. Removed from the frame of their traditional conceptual determinations, therefore, they have been used rather freely and on occasion—although this is not pointed out in every case—introduced to suggest correlations with concepts of contemporary philosophy (xlix).

Given the richness of those suggested correlations as well as the sheer intellectual beauty and clarity of many passages (oftentimes discussed and rewritten with his translators, see xlii), I will quote him amply.

In the approach to emptiness adopted in *Religion and Nothingness*, we find a definite existentialist tone, evinced by the experiences to which Nishitani alludes at the beginning of his first chapter, entitled "What Is Religion?" They are situations such as a bad turn of events, an illness, death, or sin—elsewhere he brings up the possible experience of a nuclear catastrophe[10]—which entail a fundamental negation of our life, existence, and ideals, and bring the meaning of life into question.

> Questions crowd in upon one: Why have I been alive? Where did I come from and where am I going? A void appears here that nothing in the world can fill; a gaping abyss opens up at the very ground on which one stands. In the face of this abyss, not one of all the things that had made up the stuff of life until then is of any use (3).

The realization goes even further:

> In fact, that abyss is always just underfoot (3). . . . Our life runs up against death at its every step; we keep one foot planted in the vale of death at all times. Our life stands poised at the brink of the abyss of nihility to which it may return at any moment. Our existence is an existence at one with nonexistence, swinging back and forth over nihility, ceaselessly passing away and ceaselessly regaining its existence (4).

Hence a first characterization of nihility: "Nihility refers to that which renders meaningless the meaning of life" (4). For Nishitani, religion begins with the awareness of nihility, when "we become a question to ourselves," when "our very existence has turned into a question mark" (4). And having discussed whether, and for whom, mountains and streams, flowers and forests, the entire visible universe, atoms, energy, economic relations, food and children, a piece of Greek sculpture would count as realities, he defines nihility: "Nihility is absolute negativity with regard to the very being of all those various things and phenomena just referred to" (7).

Giving another illustration, Nishitani points to a fundamental uncertainty:

> Contained in the pain of losing a loved one forever is a fundamental uncertainty about the very existence of oneself and others. This doubt takes a variety of forms and is expressed in a variety of ways. For instance, Zen speaks of the "self-presentation of the Great Doubt" (16).

In this experience self-identity is disclosed:

> To that extent the realization of nihility is nothing other than the realization of the self itself. It is not a question of observing nihility objectively or entertaining some representation of it. It is, rather, as if the self were itself to *become* that nihility, and in so doing become aware of itself from the limits of self-existence (16).

This paragraph sheds light, I hope, on what had remained somewhat enigmatic in the treatment of self2, as I called it in chapter 8. Affirming that "the being of the self itself is *nullified* along with the being of everything else," Nishitani explains that "it is nullified but not annihilated" as "all being becomes a single great question mark" (17).

The full insight into nihility requires a radicalization of anxiety and doubt. As he puts it in an article I have already cited, "doubt changes into a foundational doubt which conjoins the world and the self into one primal doubt: each is transformed and fused into the so-called Great Doubt."[11] Or, to return to *Religion and Nothingness*:

> The Great Doubt comes to light from the ground of our existence only when we press our doubts (What am I? Why do I exist?) to their limits as conscious acts of the doubting self. The Great Doubt represents not only the apex of the doubting self but also the point to its "passing away" and ceasing to be "self." It is like the bean whose seed and shell break apart as it ripens: the shell is the tiny ego, and the seed the infinity of the Great Doubt that encompasses the whole world. It is the moment at which self is at the same time the nothingness of self, the moment that is the "locus" of nothingness where conversion beyond the Great Doubt takes place. For the Great Doubt always emerges as the opening up of the locus of nothingness as the field of conversion from the Great Doubt itself. This is why it is "Great" (21).

Like Suzuki, Nishitani warns against the mistake of psychologizing this realization:

> It would be an error to regard the self-presentation of the Great Doubt as a kind of psychological state that takes place in the course of religious practice, as even a great number of religious people seem to see it nowadays. In the state of Doubt, the self

is concentrated single-mindedly on the doubt alone, to the exclusion of everything else, and *becomes* the pure doubt itself (samadhi). This much is certain, since it is no longer a question of a self that doubts something on the field of consciousness, but rather a point at which the field of consciousness has been erased.

The author concedes that the concentration on the doubt produces its own psychological state. But he is emphatic that it must be interpreted as more than a mere psychological state, since the "mind" of "single-mindedness" is reality (19).

Further on, again like Suzuki, Nishitani makes the connection between sunyata and tathata:

All attachment is negated: both the subject and the way in which "things" appear as objects of attachment are emptied. Everything is now truly empty, and this means that all things make themselves present here and now, just as they are, in their original reality. They present themselves in their suchness, their *tathata*. This is non-attachment (34; see 90).

In the short piece I quoted at the beginning of this chapter, Nishitani illustrates the experience of being empty:

Nothingness or emptiness is "not having a single thing". . . . When the spade, the work, and the worker are one, there is no spade, no work, and no worker. This is the realization of emptiness; this is what is meant by the empty-hand. . . . And what one can take in hand while remaining empty-handed is certainly not only the spade, but equally the pen when writing, or the cigarette when smoking, or the wheel when driving. Therein always appears immediate reality in everyday life, and precisely this is the ultimate reality for Eastern thinking. . . . The basic "non-thinking" is the same as being "empty-handed."[12]

In a chapter of a book composed by several authors, Nishitani contrasts two ways of envisioning a thing. First, looking at it "outside" us as an object or a substance; second, letting it be itself, allowing it to present itself "spontaneously," in its "complete individuality." In the latter case, far from being separated, things are "interpenetrating and reciprocal."[13]

In an article to which I previously referred, he explains that "every single thing is manifest entirely as it is, as clearly and distinctly as what one sees in one's own hand." And regarding the abolition of duality, he offers an illuminating metaphor: "'I' directly see 'myself' in the appearance of every single thing just as it is, as though two mirrors were mutually reflecting one another."[14]

In the second chapter of *Religion and Nothingness*, entitled "The Personal and the Impersonal in Religion," the author attempts to bring religion and science closer "by locating a point beyond the opposition of personal and impersonal" (45). For him, religion sees the world as having a goal, thanks to the personal presence of God, whereas science sees the world as nonteleological and impersonal.

He goes beyond the opposition of personal and impersonal by describing "a non-differentiating love that transcends the distinctions men make between good and evil, justice and injustice" (58). In a sentence in which Ignatius of Loyola would have recognized his understanding of *indiferencia*, Nishitani writes, "the indifference of love embraces all things in their most concrete Form—for example, good men and evil men—and accepts the differences for what they are" (58). The mode of being that this love represents is tied in with the non-ego.

> Hating one's enemies and loving one's friends are sentiments typical of human love. They belong to the field of the ego. Indifferent love belongs rather to the realm of non-ego (59; see 274).

Accordingly Nishitani speaks of a quality of *transpersonality* (60). He characterizes this viewpoint, beyond the opposition personal-impersonal, as follows:

> It is what we should call an "impersonally personal relationship" or a "personally impersonal relationship." The original meaning of *persona* probably comes close to what we are speaking of. In Christianity, the Holy Spirit has this characteristic. While being thought of as one *persona* of the Trinity, it is at the same time the very love of God itself, the breath of God; it is a sort of impersonal person or personal nonperson, as it were (40-41).[15]

As for Heidegger, for Nishitani also, "absolute nothingness" reveals the person. This nothing is neither a thing or an entity, nor a mere subjective experience. "This 'nothingness' is no objective being; neither is it subjective nothingness."[16] In contrast to the "nihility" of nihilism, far from being a negation, a mere concept, a nothingness only in thought, it is "a nothingness that is lived" in "an existential conversion." The conversion unveils "the actual self," "the original self" (70), "the sheer self itself" (71), which I have called self2. There is no actual self without nothingness. "Person is constituted at one with absolute nothingness as that in which absolute nothingness becomes manifest" (71).

Such a realization has nothing to do with any abolition of human individuality. The author cautions against this misrepresentation:

> In this kind of existential conversion, the self does not cease being a personal being. What is left behind is only the person-centered mode of grasping *person*, that is, the mode of being wherein the person is caught up in itself. In that very conversion the personal mode of being becomes more real, draws closer to the self, and appears in its true suchness (71).

Indeed, what happens is "an encounter between Person and Person on the ground where an absolute resolution of each self can take place."[17] He explains:

> To sum up, what is opened up in a Zen encounter is a place which in every way serves as the ultimate locale for a meeting between people. When two Persons who have each returned to their own original source meet, no matter when this takes place, it is on such a ground; this will never change. In Buddhist doctrine this is called "a place of only Buddhas and Buddhas." The phrase in Christianity, *communio sanctorum* (the interchange of saints) probably corresponds to the same thing.[18]

Or, as he states elsewhere, "The I *is* the Thou, even as the Thou *is* the I. . . . I and Thou blend completely into one another."[19]

In an endnote to chapter 2 of *Religion and Nothingness*, Nishitani indicates that all contradictory opposites should be considered as inseparable, provided we realize that "the oneness in question here is absolutely nonobjective and absolutely nonobjectifiable." He writes:

> An understanding is only possible existentially, through immediate experience within human Existenz and principally through experience in the realm of religion. In order to express this sort of unity, the terms "life-*sive*-death," "affirmation-*sive*-negation," and so forth have been adopted here (289, n. 8; see Glossary, "Sive," 303).[20]

Thus "person" is both negated and affirmed, illusory and real, nothing and being, "personal-*sive*-impersonal, impersonal-*sive*-personal" (74).

In chapter 3, the author begins with modern science, which he considers to be the clearest case of impersonality.[21] Science has voided the universe of any *telos*, end, goal, either set by a divine agent or pursued by human agents. Technology, the offspring of science, has brought about the mechanization of both man and world, and consequently the loss of the human. Accordingly the contemporary worldview is impersonal. Nishitani thinks that this depersonalization has given rise to a reassertion of personality, under the guise of the ego, by modern philosophers. The final outcome has been existentialism, which is subjectivistic, ego-centered, and nihilistic.

Here is how Jan Van Bragt, the translator of *Religion and Nothingness*, summarizes the first section of chapter 3:

> Nishitani offers us a deep-probing and rather Heideggerian analysis of the relationship of technology and the human. The same human being who has succeeded in emancipating himself from the laws of nature and has learned to control them, precisely by a total and interiorized submission to these laws,—in a new and curious reversal of controller and controlled, on the one hand, comes to be mechanized himself and, on the other, ends up finding himself totally estranged from nature, with the result that he throws himself head over heels into an irrational freedom and has no ground left to stand on. Nihility has opened up under his feet.[22]

Yet, in Nishitani's opinion, the combined impact of science and existentialism constitutes a great opportunity for enlightenment, provided we are willing to descend into the abyss of nihility.

This abyss is found in the human self. One of Nishitani's recurrent themes is that the field of *sunyata* lies "on the near side," in immanence, where we discover genuine transcendence. "Such a field cannot lie on a far side, beyond *this* world and *this* earthly life of ours, as something merely transcendent" (90). Pursuing this illusory transcendence would make us miss the opportunity to encounter absolute nothingness in contemporary nihilism. In the face of nihility, escapism into pure being (or even into pure emptiness) is the temptation that may lure the traditional religions.[23]

Nishitani maintains that we need the orientation to life, with the purposiveness and personality that characterize the traditional religions.[24] And he insists that we also need the opposing orientation to death, with its meaninglessness and impersonality. We need at the same time the "life-oriented axis" of the traditional religions and the "death-oriented axis" of the scientific viewpoint. Indeed,

> the emergence of any given thing in the Form of its true suchness can be considered as the point at which the orientation to life and the orientation to death intersect. Everything can be seen as a kind of "double exposure" of life and death, of being and nihility (93).

As a commentator who highlights the dynamic character of the interaction puts it, "the self is situated right in the *middle* of the swing between life and death. The self, in other words, is found at the "*sive*" of life-*sive*-death and death-*sive*-life."[25]

It is crucial to realize that we have been "shackled" either to being or to nothingness. The attachment to either being or nothing goes along with the fact that we have not actually negated both being and nothing. "It is here that emptiness, as a standpoint of absolute non-attachment liberated from this double confinement, comes to the fore." This standpoint is "the stance of the 'sive'." Here Nishitani helps us de-reify both being and emptiness. Having de-reified them, we see them as belonging to "a relationship of *sive* by which both being and emptiness are seen as co-present from the start and structurally inseparable from one another" (97). As Paul Swanson declares, "the point is to go beyond the extremes of nihility and substantive Being."[26]

Nishitani lists three possible answers to nihilism. First, the position of the traditional religions or of Plato, which looks to a world beyond this one. "It is a far side viewed perpendicularly from the earth upward. It consists only of a 90° turn from the preoccupations of ordinary, everyday life" (104). Second, the position of nihility. "It is as if we were looking down from a position *on* the earth to what lies *under* the earth, turning 90° in the opposite direction of the Platonic or the Christian sense." Third, the standpoint of emptiness, which may be said to comprise two phases. Here is the first:

> The standpoint of emptiness makes its appearance in a kind of 180° turn, as a field that simultaneously comprises both the 90° turns of the formally opposing orientations upward to heaven and downward to under the earth (105).

And here is the second phase:

> Furthermore, when the standpoint of emptiness is radicalized—and the corresponding orientation is one in which emptiness itself is also emptied—this is like a 360° turn. Front and back appear as one. The point at which emptiness is emptied to become true emptiness is the very point at which each and every thing becomes manifest in possession of its own suchness. It is the point at which 0° means 360°. And thus, in spite of its being originally an absolute near side, or rather for that very reason, it can also be an absolute far side. For only 0° can at the same time be 360° (105–106).

In sum, Nishitani distinguishes three fundamental standpoints: traditional religiousness, nihility, and emptiness. As regards the first, he highlights its shortcomings while acknowledging its resources. As for the second, he shows its historic significance (in modern science, Sartre, Nietzsche, Heidegger, and other thinkers), with a wealth of information and of nuances. As for the third, he considers *sunyata* as the proper response to the issue of nihilism. He affirms: "Zen has not only posed the problem, it has also given an answer. We don't know 'where to seek the mind.' This realization itself is the point where we can have peace of mind for the first time."[27]

I have already quoted several passages from Nishitani's fourth chapter, entitled "The Standpoint of Sunyata." Let us revert to it in order to perfect our understanding of *sunyata*.

The author talks about the original "selfness" of a thing, what a thing is in itself.[28] Although Nishitani does not mention *tathata* ("suchness") in this context, I think he is expressing the same insight here. In contrast to being known as an object and a substance, a thing can be purely itself only in the field of *sunyata*. Moreover, far from being isolated, things support and interpenetrate each other, as he maintains in his chapter 1. Such a fundamental relationship he calls "circuminsessional." This means that "all things are master and servant to one another."

> To say that a certain thing is situated in a position of servant to every other thing means that it lies at the ground of all other things, that it is a constitutive element in the being of every other thing, making it to be what it is and thus to be situated in a position of autonomy as master of itself. It assumes a position

at the home-ground of every other thing as that of a retainer upholding his lord (148).

As John Maraldo puts it, "a thing can be itself only in interdependence with other things, and can be defined only in reference to other things."[29]

In its selfness a thing is not reduced to its function, to its effect upon other things, and it has no effect upon itself. As Nishitani states, "Fire does not burn fire," "The sword does not cut the sword," "The eye does not see the eye" (125). He calls this "an action of non-action" (116). Since fire does not burn itself, the fact that it burns other things beckons us to its original unburning. "Combustion has its ground in non-combustion. Because of non-combustion, combustion is combustion" (117).

Notice the Eckhartian and Heideggerian vocabulary of "ground." The author also speaks of the "home-ground" of every thing (125, 146). But from the viewpoint of ordinary knowledge, this ground is "abyss," "bottomlessness" (122), "bottomless abyss" (143).

Earlier we noted that for Nishitani nihilism comes before the fundamental conversion, "the turnabout from the Great Death to the Great Life" (231). Accordingly, nihility, as "purely negative (antipodal) negativity," has a "transitional character" (137). It is still relative, that is, related to the substances that it negates. The final resting place is "absolute nothingness" or the emptiness of *sunyata*, the "home-ground." Of such emptiness, he writes:

> It is not simply an "empty nothing," but rather an *absolute emptiness*, emptied even of these representations of emptiness. And for that reason, it is at bottom one with being, even as being is at bottom one with emptiness (123).

The last two chapters of *Religion and Nothingness*, which bear on time and history, are not directly relevant to our present inquiry. In my Conclusion I will say a word about Nishitani's attempt to make sense of history from the standpoint of *sunyata*. However, I will conclude this presentation of his views by calling attention to the last section of his book. There he compares the attitude of St. Francis of Assisi with the Buddhist compassion resulting from *sunyata* and extending to all living things.

St. Francis "referred not only to his fellow men but to all things as his kin" (281). As he was about to have an infected eye cauterized, he turned and addressed the cautery:

> My Brother Fire, noble and useful among all other creatures, be kindly to me in this hour, because formerly I have loved thee for the love of Him who created thee. But I pray our Creator who created us, that he will so temper thy heat that I may be able to sustain it (283).[30]

After which, Francis made a sign of the cross over the cauterizing iron. Nishitani offers a suggestive interpretation of this traditional Christian gesture:

> Could it not be that the sign of the cross made over the relationship between oneself and others signals the opening up of a field where self and others are bound together in divine *agape*, where both are made into a nothingness and "emptied out," and that this is where the encounter with others takes place? (283–284)

The extraordinary phenomenon that occured is that the fire did not cause him any pain. As Francis told his religious brothers, "In truth I say unto you, that I have felt neither any pain nor the heat of the fire." Nishitani reports the Japanese saying, "Once you annihilate the mind, even the burning fire is cool." And he comments:

> Fire was indeed encountered as brother. In this encounter, the fire was in the home-ground of the fire itself, where "Fire does not burn fire" and where "Fire is not fire, therefore it is fire." And there St. Francis, too, was truly at the home-ground of his own self, as a "self that is not a self."

Surely this episode is the high point of *Religion and Nothingness*. Nishitani concludes that "in the circumincessional relationship [a misprint for "circuminsessional"] a field can be opened on which contradictory standpoints . . . are both radicalized precisely by virtue of their being totally one" (284).

HISAMATSU'S CHARACTERIZATION OF "ORIENTAL NOTHINGNESS"

Like Nishitani, Hisamatsu Shin'ichi (1889–1980) approached awakening through the personal experience of the Great Doubt, as the Zen

Buddhists call it. In a short biography, his disciple Abe Masao abundantly quotes from a memoir in Japanese by Hisamatsu, entitled "Memories of my Student Life."[31] Raised in a devout Shin Buddhist family, Hisamatsu lost his naive religious belief when he came in contact with critical reason towards the end of his high-school years. He subsequently took up the study of philosophy under Nishida Kitaro at Kyoto University. At that time he practiced Zen and achieved enlightenment, namely, *kensho* (seeing one's Nature).

Among Hisamatsu's most important essays is his piece in two parts, entitled "Ultimate Crisis and Resurrection."[32] He operates with the now familiar disjunction between the self (in its two forms, physical and mental) and the formless Self, which is the dimension of depth. In connection with the Self, he mentions width, namely, the Self as expanding to the entirety of the human race, "standing on a perspective of *brotherly love for all humanity*, while still paying due respect to the particularity of all nations and races" (12). The third dimension is length, both chronological and spatial, which "means *forming history* on the basis of the other two dimensions of man's being" (13).

The author argues that "true religion ought to be something that is possessed of the above structure" (13) and he proceeds to characterize genuine religion. To be authentic, contemporary religion must stem from modern humanism, that is, from the autonomous, critical mind which, going to the bottom of his predicament, breaks through the confinement of rationality while retaining autonomy. Genuine religion must evolve out of a criticism of humanism itself (17–18). However, autonomy is retained because, far from being saved by someone else, the self profoundly awakens to its original Self (28; see 37–40). As Hisamatsu writes elsewhere, "Autonomy is not simply negated; rather, through its own negation, it brings its original nature to complete realization."[33]

His starting point is the following question:

> *Where in man does one find the "moment" whereby he needs religion?* Where in mankind—not in a particular individual—does one find the reason that religion must exist? . . . In other words the problem is: Where in man does one find the "moment" which prevents man from remaining merely man? Where is the objective reason for which man cannot abide at ease with merely being man? (16)

In a dialogue with the theologian Paul Tillich, whose mother-tongue was German, the interpreter indicates that Hisamatsu uses the German word, *Moment*, variously translated as *Motif*, that which moves, *kairos*, the right condition at the right time, the right occasion.[34]

That moment is Hisamatsu's fulcrum, by which his whole account of religion as emptiness is launched. The locus that is the starting point is man's basic, ultimate antinomy, inherent in human reason itself. The first aspect of that antinomy is sin, in the sense of original sin. At the level of reason, we can never be free from sin. Unfortunately, at this stage, the author does not explain this first aspect. He equates it with the antinomy rational/irrational and merely affirms, "*sin ought to be extended to include the problem of reason per se*" (20). Yet he introduces a second aspect—death, which throws light on the nature of the antinomy.

> There is no death as such alone; *death, after all, is not to be separated from life*. It is death as the other side of life. In this sense, one must say that death is invariably *of the nature of life-and-death* (22–23).

Given this antinomy of "origination-and-extinction" or "existence-and-nonexistence," the solution cannot consist in acquiring "a life which has the nature of life alone." Such an attitude would amount to turning our back on the human condition. By contrast "one should fear not death but life-and-death." Hence a second sense for "death": "*the meaning of death ought to be deepened to the extent that* not mere death but *life-and-death is death*. . . . This is what is called *Great Death* in Zen" (23). It is not death that is the problem, but the antinomic and insuperable situation of life-and-death.

In the actual, concrete person, the two cases of ultimate antinomy (life-and-death and rational/irrational) never move apart. They are one in the following manner.

> To ask why the ultimate antinomy of life-and-death becomes pain or suffering in us is already a question based on the judgment of reason. Not only because one feels that pain is detestable but because *one judges* that it is to be detested, does liberation from pain come to be a really objective problem (24).

At the same time, the antinomy is "fundamentally subjective" (25). When someone is confronted with the basic antinomy, that person's whole subjectivity is at stake, since "*what is being doubted is the very doubter himself*." One has become the "great doubting-mass" spoken of in Zen. In this situation, "doubting . . . means *something total*, in which emotional anguish and volitional dilemma, as well as intellectual doubting, are *one fundamental subject*" (26).

Abe has a helpful note about Hisamatsu's notion of "subjective":

> "Subjective" (*shutai-teki*) does not indicate "subjective" (*shukan-teki*) in the epistemological sense as opposed to "objective" (*kyakkan-teki*). Rather, it refers to the dynamic existential self involved in responsible, self-determined action of a moral, ethical, or religious nature.[35]

In another article, Hisamatsu says that in the experience of the antithesis, we acquire, not a scientific knowledge, but a "fundamentally subjective knowledge," which he characterizes as "knowledge-at-work," like the artisan's know-how.[36] Such is the "subjective knowledge of ethics" (9), although it is only in "*live* philosophy" or "*live* religion" that "man must achieve his ultimately unified, fundamental subjectivity" (11).

To go back to the great doubting introduced in "Ultimate Crisis and Resurrection," Hisamatsu describes the resolution in the following terms.

> For the overcoming of this doubting-mass, the bottom of man ought to be broken through. The way of breaking through it is only this—to be awakened to the True Self, the self in whom the doubting-mass is resolved. Here is a leap. The self in ultimate antinomy cannot become the True Self with continuity. Only when the self which is ultimately antinomic breaks up, does the Self of Oneness awake to itself (27–28).

In the second part of his essay, the author tells us that we must move from relative worries to ultimate worries. The latter "*derive from the following two which constitute man's actual way of being. That is, first, man is a being involved with values; and second, at the same time, man is a conditioned, time-space being*" (42). The vocabulary has changed somewhat, but we recognize the two aspects of the basic antinomy, now called "value and anti-value" (41) and "existence and non-existence" (44). In the second dialogue with Paul Tillich, it is called "good and evil" and "being and nonbeing" (113–118).

Again, Hisamatsu portrays salvation as overcoming the duality of the basic antinomy. Let us recall that in the first part of his article, he asserts that we must go, not beyond death, but beyond the duality of life-and-death. Here he declares:

> This awakened state is also we ourselves, but it is neither the self of existence-nonexistence nor the self of value-antivalue. It

is the self of non-"existence-nonexistence," non-"value-anti-value." It goes beyond all definitions, beyond all forms. It is, as it were, the Formless Self. By our awaking to this Formless Self, we overcome the ultimate antinomic self and come to be saved from the ultimate antinomy (49).

Transcending the antinomy thus consists in "transcending the negative-affirmative" (52).

In this extremely dynamic process, the self is both negated and affirmed.

> That Self, awakened, *flows backward* into the unawakened self and fills it. The original Self becomes the fountainhead, and *the way of being of the ordinary self becomes what has come out of that fountainhead*. Or contrariwise, the ordinary self *returns to the fountainhead*. Thus does positiveness or affirmativeness arise. That direction, which is the opposite of the one toward the original Self, brings about a positive continuity with it. Previously there was *the self-negating continuity from the unawakened self to the awakened Self*. Now, on the contrary, there is effected *the affirmative, positive continuity from the awakened Self to the unawakened self*. That comes to mean *resurrection or resuscitation of the self*. It is only here that one can speak of absolute affirmation (52).

In the last section of the essay, the author sums up his philosophy as "F.A.S." (62–63). The Formless Self (referred to as "F") stands on the standpoint of All mankind (referred to as "A") and creates history Supra-historically (referred to as "S"). As in the case of the self, which is taken up by the Self, there is a concern to link formless awakening to historical creativity, by showing the influence of the former upon the latter.

In a piece by Hisamatsu from which we have already drawn, namely, "Ordinary Mind," we find a variation on his theme of the antinomy. He writes, "there is necessarily within history a negating 'Moment' which negates history itself." He explains: "History is history in that it is contradiction which is none other than unity, non-being which is none other than being" (25). He propounds the solution:

> It means that history, as abyss and ultimate contradiction, dissolves itself, dies to itself (the Great Death), and casts itself off totally, in a fundamentally subjective manner. This is the ultimate "overcoming," the ultimate unification (27).

And he demarcates his position from Hegel's:

> The casting off and self-dissolution of the ultimately contradictory subject of history and its freeing of itself with the emergence of the unhindered, Self-abiding, fundamental subject, is not achieved in the movement of history, that is, through the historical dialectic. It is accomplished at the root-source of history, which is prior to the birth of history (28).

A few pages earlier, the same insight was expressed in terms of being and non-being:

> Being, while it is the self-limitation of absolute nothingness, is also, insofar as it must be negated, "non-being." It is in this sense that that which is actual in history is said to be being which is none other than non-being (21).

There is an interplay of immanence and transcendence in this negation-affirmation:

> This subject of history, in that it eternally creates that which is historically actual, is "absolute being" and of immanent character, but at the same time, in that it eternally negates its self-limitation, it is "absolute nothingness" and of external and transcendent character (22).

His assertion, "that which is actual is of the character of negation that is none other than affirmation" is explicated as follows:

> By negating that which has been transformed into being, it comes to acquire the creative character of self-limitation. If the subject of history were fixed as some particular being, its self-limitation would become deterministic, and its creativity in history could not but be annihilated (22).

The author thus grounds historical creativity (ruling out determinism) in "the root-source of history."

This relation of limited creativity to its root-source is paralleled by a beautiful metaphor implied in the title of the article, "Ordinary Mind." In its initial note, the translator jots down, "*Heijoshin* (lit., 'quelled or tranquil, constant mind'; here rendered as 'ordinary mind')" (1). And the author soon spells out the relation of inconstancy to constancy:

There is a sense in which an ordinary thing is a "synthesis." Synthesis, as synthesis, is in any case a unity of contradictions, a quelling of them. Synthesis finds itself when and where its contradictions are quelled; it then is smoothed out, and settles into position. Settled, it becomes quiet. It finds repose, gains constancy, and attains the present. In the present there is stability and composure. Since in ordinariness there is the quality of the present, man, in his ordinariness, can feel at ease and live his life (3).

This experience sounds quite psychological and indeed, in my opinion, it has a psychological component. Still, it is more than psychological. In the dialogue with Paul Tillich, to which we have already referred, Hisamatsu declares: "For the kind of consciousness meant here, we rather use such terms as 'No-Mind' or 'No-Consciousness'." One of his interpreters remarks, "Zen awareness is not a state of mind," and the other interpreter adds, "[It is] without *nen*. This 'nen' is somewhat difficult to translate; it means a unit of consciousness" (part 1, 93).

Hisamatsu unpacks his insight:

> Concentrating upon something—whatever it is—is not the type of concentration I mean. What I mean is a concentration that is not a concentration on anything, strange as this may sound. In this respect, it differs from ordinary concentration. It is a concentration in which "that which concentrates" is no other than "that which is concentrated upon" (96).

One of the interpreters then says:

> When everything has been "broken-through," "negated," or "emptied," however, and there is "Nothing," that mode of concentration without any object—what may be called an "objectless concentration"—is the sort of concentration one has to come to (96).... Dr. Hisamatsu adds that needless to say, it is also subjectless (97).

In the third dialogue, the same interpreter states:

> Zen's "Nothingness" is not a matter of intense concentration upon "some-thing" with the consequent negative blocking-out of the consciousness of everything else. Neither is it, as frequently it is misunderstood to be, a suspension or cessation of total consciousness (part 3, 110).

Throughout this dialogue we notice a profound disagreement between Tillich and Hisamatsu regarding the relation of the finite to the infinite. The former construes that relation in terms of participation: the finite partakes of limitless being. The latter affirms, "Zen's 'nonduality' is not 'participation'" (107). From the viewpoint of Zen, participation involves duality.

Almost everywhere in Hisumatsu's writings we come across the traditional Buddhist insight into the indissociability of the formless and all forms. For example:

> Zen thus may be said to have two aspects: one is the aspect of the true emptiness of the True-Self which, unbound by any form, is completely free from all forms; the other is the aspect of the wondrous working of the Self which, unbound by any form, actualizes all forms.[37]

Here is a variant:

> Oneness and manyness—or, unity and diversity—are mutually indispensable moments within the basic structure of man. They must necessarily be one with each other and not two. Oneness without manyness is mere vacuity without content; manyness without oneness is mere segmentation without unity (41).

And he quotes a Zen expression, "Within Nothingness (there is contained) an inexhaustible storehouse" (42).

In the only book by Hisamatsu available in English so far, the author explains Japanese paintings in terms of the relation of the formless to innumerable artistic forms. He proposes that "it is always the Formless Self that is, on each and every occasion, the creative subject expressing itself." For him, one of the characteristics of Zen aesthetics is simplicity: "simplicity as the negation of clutter may be spoken of as being 'boundless'—there is nothing limiting, as in a cloudless sky."[38]

Let us complete this section on Hisamatsu by summarizing what is probably his most systematic piece, the topic of which he calls "Oriental Nothingness."[39] He begins by offering a negative delineation. First, nonbeing or nothingness is not the negation of a being or of all beings, as when we say, "there is no desk" or "there is nothing at all." Second, it is not a predicative negation, as, for example, "a desk is not a chair." Third, it is not an abstract concept, as when we say, "nothingness." Fourth, it is not a conjecture, as in the case of imagining oneself dead.

And fifth, it is not an absence of consciousness, such as unconsciousness, deep sleep, fainting, or death (66–75).

The author then proceeds to a positive delineation. Among his very helpful clarifications, let us pay attention to the following ones. Being nothing means that "there is nothing whatsoever in Myself." We must not look to the Self inside, since this "Myself" goes beyond internal and external (in contradistinction to each other). Accordingly he writes that "I, Myself, am this nothing whatever wherever" (76). And consequently "the 'I' which does not have an object, the 'I' which does not have a single thing, is the 'I' which is no longer dependent upon or attached to anything" (77). Or put another way, "I am not delimited or captured by any-thing; I am absolutely free and unbounded." He also uses the words of Plotinus: "since this 'I' is beyond internal and external, it is One-alone—or 'Only-One'" (78).

In his next section, Hisamatsu talks about the "empty-space" which I mentioned in the context of Japanese paintings. Empty-space has ten meanings: no-obstruction, omnipresence, impartiality, broad and great, formless, purity, stability, voiding-being, voiding-voidness, and without obtaining (80–85).

In another section, we are told that Oriental Nothingness "possesses self-consciousness," in the sense that "it has all of the aspects and qualities of mind." Furthermore, "this Mind is Mind possessing all of the characteristics of empty-space" (86).

Next, the author highlights the "Self" nature of Oriental Nothingness. It is "the Mind which sees," the "active seeing" (88). Moreover, he stresses the "Freedom" nature of Oriental Nothingness: whereas reason is never free from dualistic polarities, religion consists in the liberation from such discriminations (91–94). Finally, he mentions the "creative nature" of Oriental Nothingness (94–95), which has been illustrated earlier when we looked at passages concerning history.

Hisamatsu ends up with two illuminating metaphors. First, "that which is reflected in the mirror is not something which comes from outside the mirror, but is something which is produced from within the mirror." Second, according to the analogy of water and waves, "waves are produced by the water but are never separated from the water" (96).

CONCLUDING REMARKS

In this chapter we have seen how traditional Zen wisdom and modern experience continually intersect in the thinking of two brilliant Japanese scholars. Rooted in their Asian tradition and in constant dialogue with Western philosophy, their existential approach to philosophy is marked by both Zen and twentieth-century European thought. Nishitani stresses the total loss of meaning whereas Hisamatsu insists on the antinomy of life. Basically, they offer the same solution to the problem of the human predicament: the emptiness or nothingness of *sunyata*. Far from being a mere psychological concentration that would exclude all forms of consciousness-of, this void integrates all components of our finitude. It embraces history as well as the cosmos. It is the Self that takes up all that is valid in the self, purifies it, and energizes it. Despite differences owing to cultural diversity, that absolute reality consists in the mystical consciousness that parts 1 and 2 of this book have characterized. More will be said on this equivalence in my Conclusion.

Conclusion

In the course of this study, we have repeatedly distinguished three kinds of consciousness. First, consciousness C, which was also called consciousness-of, positional consciousness, or awareness. Second, consciousness B, also called consciousness-in, or nonpositional consciousness, which pervades all our states and activities. Third, consciousness A, or mystical consciousness, called consciousness beyond consciousness in chapter 4, which might also be dubbed metaconsciousness, or "super-consciousness," as Thomas Merton puts it,[1] if we prefer to take consciousness as always meaning consciousness-of. With this latter meaning in mind (consciousness-of), about half of the thinkers we have studied restrict "consciousness" to an individual's consciousness, confined to the subject/object duality. In particular, when Suzuki, as well as Nishitani and Hisamatsu (albeit in different words) insist that Zen is not an experience separate from ordinary experience, what they rule out, as the readers may remember, is a mental concentration on something, a state of mind (whether subjective or objective), or a psychological experience which has to do with *specific* affects or impressions.

Most authors who write on Western meditation or on Zen differentiate only the first (C) and the third (A), offer a poor account of the first (C), and ignore the second (B), which I have situated halfway between objectified awareness (C) and mystical consciousness (A). Nishitani does not know the second, while Suzuki alludes to it without distinguishing it from the *sunyata* experience, and while Schleiermacher has a sense of it but only rarely mentions it. This remark about Schleiermacher can also be said of Eckhart, who notices all forms of consciousness but concentrates on the third. Interestingly Forman points out:

> Actually there are sometimes three "men" in Eckhart: the outer man, by whose means we know the external world; the inner

man, by whose means we feel, think, and know ourselves; and the "innermost" man.[2]

Brentano clearly identifies the mental act that is "the secondary object" of consciousness. Sartre talks very well about our inner, non-positional consciousness, although he does not think we can objectify it adequately, whereas Lonergan thematizes and differentiates it superbly. Thanks to his efforts, we have come to realize that our conscious intentionality (consciousness-of, also called consciousness C) is able to develop an account of ordinary consciousness (consciousness B) and to employ this account analogically so as to make true judgments about mystical consciousness (consciousness A), without presuming that the latter can be fully comprehended.

Consciousness B is not some thing, not even something. It is a conscious doing, bodily and mentally. In consciousness B, since there is no distinction between subject, verb, and object, I can verily say that I am sheer action, pure act.[3] I am not yet, or I am no longer, an ego, an objectified self.

In consciousness A, two situations can obtain, which are noted by Forman, Eckhart, and the Japanese thinkers with whom we have been dialoguing. In both situations, an absolute conviction (we may say, a "reality," provided we do not think of it as the "substance" of the modern West) forces itself upon us and commands attention.

In the first situation, the person awakens to a mystical consciousness which no concept can capture. In utter emptiness, any trace of consciousness-of, including self-awareness, is erased. As one is entirely absorbed into a larger Self, this suspension of the sense of individuality corresponds to Eckhart's Mary, the pure contemplative.

In the second situation, to be equated with Eckhart's Martha, the contemplative in action, consciousness A smoothly coexists with consciousness C. The advanced meditator then partakes of the consciousness that permeates all beings, with no definition added to their suchness. Everything is de-reified, de-substantialized, de-dualized, including "I," "God," "world," "Being," "Nihility." Thus, for example, Plotinus speaks of the all-encompassing Intellect which reconciles all opposites; Eckhart, of the Godhead whose pure indistinctness embraces all distinctions; Heidegger, of a ground-abyss or Being-Nothing which shines through all beings; the Kyoto scholars, of an absolute emptiness-fullness which overcomes both relative negation and relative affirmation.

Those authors are agreed that far from being an identical, static sameness, consciousness A dynamically includes all particulars. Like Eckhart, the Zen philosophers privilege what they call an "awareness" (the sense of which differs from my usage), which does not exclude but pervades all forms of consciousness-of. Because it is not static or reified, such inclusive awareness is not contradicted by a profound experience of communion among persons (beautifully expressed by Nishitani, for example). So the Self, instead of abolishing the selves, thoroughly refashions them.

Insofar as epistemological validity is concerned, I maintain that with the help of a sound representation of consciousness B and C, this book has said something intelligible and true about consciousness A. In other words, mystical consciousness, what the Zen-Buddhist Japanese call awareness or awakening, has been meaningfully situated from the perspective of our limited worldview, as lying beyond its grasp.

Needless to say, interpretations of mystical consciousness are diverse. We have come across a good variety of them in the course of this research. For instance, Plotinus's One, or Heidegger's Being, resides, so to speak, behind the world, whereas for Eckhart and the Zen philosophers the noumenal pervades the phenomenal. Or, we have heard Hisamatsu affirm that nonduality is not a participation; obviously this assertion contradicts Plotinus's, Eckhart's, and Tillich's acceptance of Platonic participation. I have used the notion of participation a few times, since it harmonizes with the reality of a self that partakes of the Self. However, apart from scattered critical remarks, I have decided not to establish a full-fledged dialectic of opposed theses. My aim has been, not to go deep into the metaphysical issues (legitimate, though, such a discussion can be), but to show the similarities, indeed the convergence between several Western and Japanese intimations of what escapes the purview of ordinary consciousness. Put otherwise, my enterprise has been about mystical theory, not about philosophical or doctrinal theology.

This book has reported that many authors highlight the affective side of mystical consciousness. The time has now come to say whether or not love is the kernel of mysticism. Some of our contemporaries answer too quickly in the affirmative, not taking account of the fact that most of the time, Zen Buddhists refrain from talking about love because it is generally viewed as the locus of desire, attachment, pursuit of gratification.[4] In this respect, Suzuki, Nishitani, and Hisamatsu are exceptions; yet, even when they mention love in its positive sense, they qualify it.

Nonetheless, all the thinkers we have presented would undoubtedly concur that mystical consciousness is the most important ingredient of a personal transformation which roots out obstacles to genuine loving. In other words, mystical enlightenment creates an ambience of equanimity (Strasser's and Morelli's state-like basic affect or disposition, spoken of in chapter 2; Suligoj's positive general mood, without specific emotions or contents, spoken of in chapter 3), thanks to which authentic love, compassion, and patience, which allow a person to transcend oneself towards other people, become natural (albeit not easy) and work themselves out in act-like affects and in deeds. According to these distinctions, I would contend that mystical consciousness is a state-like pervasive condition, while its fruit is a matter of act-like affects and deeds.

More precisely, our long inquiry entitles us to affirm that mysticism consists in a consciousness that goes beyond consciousness-of and even beyond ordinary consciousness-in; in a knowing that transcends thinking; and in a lovingness that surpasses acts of wanting this or that, or emotions associated with objects (even with God represented as Object). Human intentionality is fulfilled by rising above its various levels, each of which relates to finite objects (be they impersonal or personal). In other words, mysticism amounts to a unique state in which consciousness equates unrestricted knowing and loving. Mystics have an inkling that they are immersed in a mystery where there is no distinction between consciously knowing, loving, being known, and being loved. In Price's words (see chapter 3; and see also Eckhart, in chapter 5), "mystical consciousness" rules out distinctions whereas "religious consciousness" utilizes them. Only the latter has to do with specific ideas and emotions.

We must acknowledge, however, that the human ego may distort mystical consciousness by putting it at the service of one's own placidity, which turns out to be false peace.[5] People can become attached to a method of meditation, to contemplation, silence, emptiness, even to detachment itself.[6] Or they can complacently enjoy their spiritual performance and thus never truly transcend themselves.[7] Accordingly, this book should not be construed as extolling mystical consciousness as if it were always utterly authentic. For no authenticity is obtained without a strong commitment to the fundamental aim of mysticism: an enlightenment manifesting itself in love and compassion.

As Henri Bergson states, the complete mystic is the person whose "contemplation is engulfed in action." He explains that at the stage of pure contemplation a human potentiality still remains to be actualized, namely, the will, which yearns to become "one with the divine will."[8] And this perfect union is realized in human action. In their insistence on action, Bergson, Eckhart, and the Japanese Zen practitioners remarkably converge.

In this respect, harking back to what I wrote at the end of my Introduction, I would stress the complementarity of the mystical and the prophetic for religious life. This study has highlighted the former. Still, the latter plays an indispensable role, that is, of pointing to the ultimate goal of mystical consciousness. Most of the thinkers discussed here have been fascinated by the *source* rather than by the *goal* of mysticism. In his perceptive comments on Nishitani, Thomas Kasulis contrasts a regressive and a progressive dialectic.[9] (Obviously a regressive dialectic has nothing to do with the psychological concept of regression.) More typical of the East, and, I would add, of thinkers such as Plotinus, Eckhart, and Schleiermacher, the regressive kind of thinking moves back to the origin of all things; more typical of the West, the progressive kind of thinking, rooted in the Bible, moves forward to the universe's final destiny. Because of its interest in the "whence," the former is more concerned with archeology (in its philosophical sense); because of its interest in the "whither," the latter is more concerned with teleology.

Masao Abe disagrees with Kasulis, but his argument is weakened by his own admission that Nishitani's view of history is "an absolutely realized eschatology."[10] Surely, realized eschatology is actual, since the future is already present. Yet can we verily speak of an *absolutely* realized eschatology? In other words, a mysticism that overemphasizes eternity leaves something to be desired insofar as it ignores or diminishes the importance of history as ushering in the future.[11] What propels history is intelligent, active loving—which is part and parcel of consciousness C. With Kasulis and Van Bragt,[12] I would maintain that Nishitani's brave effort to make sense of history in the light of *sunyata*, in the final two chapters of *Religion and Nothingness*, is not totally satisfactory.

Nevertheless, the fact that he and Hisamatsu uncover the nonmundane underpinning of history has a far-reaching import. Furthermore, their idea that historical creativity experienced in a context of nihility and infinity possesses a higher quality than merely secular creativity is a precious insight. I must add that their elucidation of formlessness helps us avoid reifying both our mysterious source and our final goal.[13] In the twenty-first-century scientific culture, expositors of religion can no longer afford to indulge in reified images or concepts.

Finally, by plumbing the depths of both consciousness B and consciousness A with the help of many profound writers, I hope I have demonstrated that, contrary to what is commonly believed, numerous thinkers in the West have delved into the riches of those human discoveries. I am convinced that in a great measure, the new language employed in interfaith dialogue will become more and more, indeed has already become, the language of consciousness. In this study, my objective has been to make a contribution in that direction.

Notes

PREFACE

1. Paul Ricoeur, *The Conflict of Interpretations: Essays in Hermeneutics* (Evanston, IL: Northwestern University Press, 1974), 148–151.
2. Nishida Kitaro, "On the Doubt in Our Heart," *The Eastern Buddhist* 17/2 (Autumn 1984): 7–11, at 10. I introduce Japanese names the way these authors or their editors choose, that is, usually family name first.
3. See T. P. Kasulis, *Zen Action, Zen Person* (Honolulu: University of Hawaii Press, 1981), chap. 8.
4. Graham Parkes, "Practising Philosophy as a Matter of Life and Death," *Zen Buddhism Today* 15 (1998): 139–153.
5. Paul J. Griffiths, *On Being Mindless: Buddhist Meditation and the Mind-Body Problem* (La Salle, IL: Open Court, 1986), xiii; see xiii–xiv.
6. Pierre Hadot, *Philosophy as a Way of Life: Spiritual Exercises from Socrates to Foucault* (Oxford: Oxford University Press, 1995). For a description of such a case, see Louis Roy, "Medieval Latin Scholasticism: Some Comparative Features," in *Scholasticism: Cross-Cultural and Comparative Perspectives*, ed. José Ignacio Cabezón (Albany: SUNY Press, 1998), 19–34.
7. See, for instance, H. M. Enomiya-Lasalle, *Zen—Way to Enlightenment* (New York: Taplinger, 1968).
8. However, I take account of their contribution in my article, "Some Japanese Interpretations of Meister Eckhart," *Studies in Interreligious Dialogue* 11 (2001): 182–198.

INTRODUCTION

1. In the years 1995–1997, the *Journal of Consciousness Studies* published several articles on the interface of brain and consciousness. They have been reprinted, along with other contributions, in *Explaining Consciousness—The 'Hard Problem'*, ed. Jonathan Shear (Cambridge, MA: The MIT Press, 1997). My views are close to those presented in the part entitled "First-Person Perspectives."
2. Charles T. Tart, *States of Consciousness* (New York: Dutton, 1975), 28.
3. For further data on this correspondence between the brain and the mind, see William Johnston, *Silent Music: The Science of Meditation* (New York: Harper & Row, 1974), chaps. 2 and 3; and Eugene G. d'Aquili and Andrew B. Newberg, *The Mystical Mind: Probing the Biology of Religious Experience* (Minneapolis: Fortress Press, 1999).
4. Joseph Maréchal, "Vraie et fausse mystique," *Nouvelle Revue Théologique* 67 (1945): 275–295, at 287 (my translation).
5. "The Spiritual Canticle," in *The Collected Works of St. John of the Cross*, trans. Kieran Kavanaugh and Otilio Rodriguez (Washington, DC: ICS Publications, 1991), stanza 14, §§1–6; stanza 19, §1.
6. Johnson, *Silent Music*, 72, in reference to Joseph de Guibert, *The Theology of the Spiritual Life* (New York: Sheed & Ward, 1953), part 7, chap. 2.
7. Johnston, *Silent Music*, 73.
8. Similarly, basing himself on Alfred North Whitehead, John B. Bennett distinguishes between "awareness of" and "awareness with," in "A Suggestion on 'Consciousness' in *Process and Reality*," *Process Studies* 3 (1973): 41–42.
9. Dom Aelred Graham, *Zen Catholicism* (New York: Crossroad, 1994), 130.
10. Tart, *Psi: Scientific Studies in the Psychic Realm* (New York: Dutton, 1977), 208.
11. Thomas Aquinas, *Summa Theologiae*, I–II, 111, 1, and II–II, 171–175.
12. Friedrich Heiler, *Prayer: A Study in the History and Psychology of Religion*, trans. Samuel McComb with J. Edgar Park (London: Oxford University Press, 1932), chap. 6: "General Characteristics of Mysticism and Prophetic Religion," esp. 135–146.
13. "The Book of Her Life, in *The Collected Works of St. Teresa of Avila*, trans. Kieran Kavanaugh and Otilio Rodriguez (Washington, DC: ICS Publications, 1987), vol. 1, chap. 20.

14. "The Mystical Theology," in Pseudo-Dionysius, *The Complete Works*, trans. Colm Luibheid (New York: Paulist Press, 1987).
15. Robert K. C. Forman, *The Problem of Pure Consciousness* (New York: Oxford University Press, 1990), 5–7. He refers to *Complete Works of St. Teresa*, vol. 1, trans. E. Allison Peers (London: Sheed & Ward, 1957), 119, and to Roland Fisher, "A Cartography of the Ecstatic and Meditative States," in *Understanding Mysticism*, ed. Richard Woods (Garden City: Doubleday, Image Books, 1980), 270–285.
16. Likewise D'Aquili and Newberg, in *The Mystical Mind*, 25–26, distinguish a hyperarousal and a hyperquiescent state.
17. In *Christian Mysticism* (London: Methuen, 1899), appendix A, William Ralph Inge discusses twenty-six definitions of mysticism and mystical theology!
18. Louis Roy, *Transcendent Experiences: Phenomenology and Critique* (Toronto: University of Toronto Press, 2001).
19. Another instance of this broad sense of "experience" is the intelligent and well-documented study by Jonathan Shear, *The Inner Dimension: Philosophy and the Experience of Consciousness* (New York: Peter Lang, 1990).

CHAPTER 1. MAJOR CONTRIBUTIONS

1. Martin Heidegger, *History of the Concept of Time: Prolegomena*, trans. Theodore Kisiel (Bloomington: Indiana University Press, 1992), 13–15, 19–23, 27–29, 46.
2. Franz Brentano, *Psychology from an Empirical Standpoint*, ed. Linda L. McAlister (New York: Humanities Press, 1973), 78–80. Further references to this work will be given in parentheses within the text. The same will be done for other writings drawn upon throughout this book.
3. Dan Zahavi, *Self-awareness and Alterity: A Phenomenological Investigation* (Evanston, IL: Northwestern University Press, 1999), 31. The author pursues the ambitious project of relating self-awareness with "temporality, intentionality, reflexivity, corporeality, and intersubjectivity" (198). Although I shall occasionally quote from this excellent book, I will not lay out its intricate arguments, because they cover a field that is too broad for my purposes here in this inquiry. Note also his equally remarkable piece, "The Fracture in Self-awareness," *Self-awareness, Temporality, and Alterity:*

Central Topics in Phenomenology, ed. Dan Zahavi (Dortrecht: Kluwer, 1998): 21–40, esp. 21–23, and 36, n. 1 and n. 6.
4. David Bell, *Husserl* (London: Routledge, 1995), 11.
5. William James, *The Principles of Psychology* (Cambridge, MA: Harvard University Press, 1981), 234, n. 11. See Brentano, *Psychology from an Empirical Standpoint*, book 2, chap. 4.
6. Edmund Husserl, *Logical Investigations*, trans. J. N. Findlay (London: Routledge & Kegan Paul, 1970), Investigation V, chap. 1, §1, 535.
7. Husserl, *Ideas Pertaining to a Pure Phenomenology and to a Phenomenological Philosophy*, First Book: *General Introduction to a Pure Phenomenology*, trans. F. Kersten (The Hague: Nijhoff, 1982), 68.
8. Husserl, *The Paris Lectures*, trans. Peter Koestenbaum (The Hague: Nijhoff, 1970), 12–13.
9. Husserl, *Phenomenological Psychology*, trans. John Scanlon (The Hague: Nijhoff, 1977), 22.
10. Ibid., 25.
11. Ibid., 27.
12. Elisabeth Ströker, *Husserl's Transcendental Phenomenology* (Stanford: Stanford University Press, 1993), 119.
13. Ibid., 124.
14. Husserl, *Cartesian Meditations: An Introduction to Phenomenology*, trans. Dorion Cairns (The Hague: Nijhoff, 1960), 33, 34.
15. Robert Sokolowski, *The Formation of Husserl's Concept of Constitution* (The Hague: Nijhoff, 1964), 89.
16. Even more radical than Husserl is Heidegger, by whom "the *Dasein* has from the start been deprived of the dimension of consciousness," according to Jean-Paul Sartre's judgment, in *Being and Nothingness*, 73.
17. In *Consciousness and Freedom: Three Views* (London: Methuen, 1971), Pratima Bowes discusses several views on consciousness, among which those of Husserl and Sartre. Unfortunately "consciousness" is equated with "self-consciousness" and said to be "reflective."
18. E.T.: *Time and Free Will: An Essay on the Immediate Data of Consciousness*, trans. F. L. Pogson (New York: Humanities Press, 1971).
19. In *Topics in Education*, Collected Works of Bernard Lonergan, vol. 10, ed. Robert M. Doran and Frederick E. Crowe (Toronto: University of Toronto Press, 1993), Lonergan characterizes Bergson's negative view of thought as follows: "According to Bergson, reality is the

élan vital; it is dynamic, a flow; and any intellectual activity involves a falsification of the flow, an imposition of abstract, rigid categories upon the flow" (186; see 208, 227). Or more critically, in *Verbum: Word and idea in Aquinas*, Collected Works of Bernard Lonergan, vol. 2, ed. Frederick E. Crowe and Robert M. Doran (Toronto: University of Toronto Press, 1997): "Because Bergson conceives the real as the empirically experienced, he concludes that the categories of thought fall short of the reality of movement" (113, n. 33).

20. Jean-Paul Sartre, *The Psychology of Imagination* (New York: Citadel Press, 1991), 15.
21. Sartre, *The Transcendence of the Ego*, trans. Forrest Williams and Robert Kirkpatrick (New York: Farrar, Straus and Giroux, 1972).
22. Sartre, *Being and Nothingness: An Essay on Phenomenological Ontology*, trans. Hazel E. Barnes (New York: Philosophical Library, 1956).
23. Sartre, "Consciousness of Self and Knowledge of Self," in *Readings in Existential Phenomenology*, ed. Nathaniel Lawrence and Daniel O'Connor (Englewood Cliffs, NJ: Prentice-Hall, 1967), 113–142, at 114, 122, 123; see 125, 137.
24. Phyllis Sutton Morris, "Sartre on the Transcendence of the Ego," *Philosophy and Phenomenological Research* 46 (1985): 170–198, at 181. We find the same distinctions in her short piece, "Further Reflections on Reflection," *Philosophical Books* 19 (1978): 56–58.
25. "Sartre on the Self-deceiver's Translucent Consciousness," *Journal of the British Society for Phenomenology* 23 (1992): 103–119, at 107.
26. Ibid., 108.
27. Sartre, *The Emotions: Outline of a Theory*, trans. Bernard Frechtman (New York: Philosophical Library, 1948).
28. Sartre, "Consciousness of Self and Knowledge of Self," 114.
29. Sartre himself speaks of a "duality" and of "separation" in "Consciousness of Self and Knowledge of Self," 126–127.
30. Elizabeth Murray Morelli, "The Duality in Sartre's Account of Reflective Consciousness," in *French Existentialism: Consciousness, Ethics and Relations with Others*, ed. James Giles (Amsterdam/Atlanta: Rodopi, 1999), 19–32, at 26–27.
31. He approvingly quotes Georges Van Riet, who summarizes Sartre's view of consciousness, in "Christ as Subject: A Reply," in *Collection*, Collected Works of Bernard Lonergan, vol. 4, ed. Frederick E. Crowe and Robert M. Doran (Toronto: University of Toronto Press, 1988), 172–173.
32. Husserl, *The Paris Lectures*, 19.

33. Bernard J.F. Lonergan, "Christology Today: Methodological Reflections," in *A Third Collection* (New York: Paulist Press, 1985), 91–92.
34. Lonergan, *Insight: A Study of Human Understanding*, Collected Works of Bernard Lonergan, vol. 3, ed. Frederick E. Crowe and Robert M. Doran (Toronto: University of Toronto Press, 1992), chap. 11 and chap. 18, § 2.5. See also *Method in Theology* (Toronto: University of Toronto Press, 1992), chaps. 1 and 2.
35. Lonergan, *Insight*, 345.
36. Lonergan, *Method in Theology*, 6.
37. Ibid., 30–34, including notes 5 and 6.
38. Lonergan, "*Insight* Revisited," in *A Second Collection* (Toronto: University of Toronto Press, 1996), 273. Note that in this phrase the four levels are mentioned, beginning, this time, with the fourth.
39. Lonergan, "Cognitional Structure," *Collection*, 210.
40. It is this caricature of the inner data of consciousness as private or occult entities that both Wittgenstein and Skinner reject. See Joseph Fitzpatrick, "Lonergan and the Later Wittgenstein," *Method: Journal of Lonergan Studies* 10 (1992): 27–50; Larry Cooley, "A Lonerganian Critique of B. F. Skinner's Radical Behaviorist Theory of the Cognitive Dimension of Consciousness," *Method* 6 (1988): 107–137, and "Hayes' Radical Behaviorist Explanation of the Cognitive Dimension of Consciousness: A Lonerganian Critique," *Method* 7 (1989): 18–30.
41. Lonergan, *Insight*, 350.
42. The assumption that subjectivity can never be correctly objectified in right judgments mars Eugene Webb's interpretation of the otherwise interesting wealth of information he offers in *Philosophers of Consciousness: Polanyi, Lonergan, Voegelin, Ricoeur, Girard, Kierkegaard* (Seattle: University of Washington Press, 1988). On the same oversight in Voegelin, see John Ranieri, "Question and Imagination: Eric Voegelin's Approach," *Lonergan Workshop*, ed. Fred Lawrence, vol. 11 (Boston College, 1995), 105–143, esp. 132–134.
43. Lonergan, "Prolegomena to the Study of the Emerging Religious Consciousness of Our Time," in *A Third Collection*, 58; see "Religious Experience," ibid., 116–117, and "Religious Knowledge," ibid., 143.
44. "Prolegomena," ibid., 57. On this distinction consciousness/knowledge, or registering/being aware, Lonergan quotes Karen Horney: "I shall use the term 'register' when I mean that we know what is going on within us without our being aware of it." See "Prolegomena, ibid., 59, and "Religious Experience," ibid., 117–118.

CHAPTER 2. COMPLEMENTARY CONTRIBUTIONS

1. John R. Searle, *Intentionality* (New York: Cambridge University Press, 1983).
2. Searle, *The Discovery of the Mind* (Cambridge, MA: The MIT Press, 1992), 132.
3. John F. Crosby, *The Selfhood of the Human Person* (Washington, DC: Catholic University of America Press, 1996), 84.
4. Daniel A. Helminiak, *The Human Core of Spirituality: Mind as Psyche and Spirit* (Albany: SUNY Press, 1996), chaps. 3–6.
5. Zahavi, *Self-awareness and Alterity*, 228, n. 57, and 197; see 33.
6. For example, *Understanding and Being*, Collected Works of Bernard Lonergan, vol. 5, ed. Elizabeth A. Morelli and Mark D. Morelli, rev. and augmented by Frederick E. Crowe (Toronto: University of Toronto Press, 1990), 15.
7. Patrick H. Byrne, "Consciousness: Levels, Sublations, and the Subject as Subject," *Method: Journal of Lonergan Studies* 13 (1995): 131–150, at 132, n. 8.
8. Helminiak, "Consciousness as a Subject Matter," *Journal for the Theory of Social Behaviour* 14 (1984): 211–230, at 215 and 216–217.
9. In a letter to me, dated April 19, 2001.
10. Elizabeth A. Morelli, *Anxiety: A Study of the Affectivity of Moral Consciousness* (Lanham, MD: University Press of America, 1985), 80, quoting Lonergan, *Method in Theology*, 115.
11. Morelli, "The Appropriation of Existential Consciousness," *Method* 6 (1988): 50–62, at 51.
12. Morelli, "Reflections on the Appropriation of Moral Consciousness," in *Lonergan Workshop*, ed. Fred Lawrence, vol. 13 (Boston College, 1997), 161–188, at 171.
13. Morelli, "The Appropriation," 51.
14. Stephan Strasser, *Phenomenology of Feeling: An Essay on the Phenomena of the Heart*, trans. Robert E. Wood (Pittsburgh: Duquesne University Press, 1977), 182–183; see the whole of chap. 7.
15. Morelli, "Reflections," 171.
16. Andrew Beards, *Objectivity and Historical Understanding* (Brookfield, VT: Ashgate, 1997), 11.
17. D. C. Dennett, *Content and Consciousness* (New York: Humanities Press, 1969), 114–115.
18. Ibid., 115.
19. Hans-Georg Gadamer, *Philosophical Hermeneutics*, trans. David E. Linge (Berkeley: University of California Press, 1976), 123.

20. Jacques Maritain, *Existence and the Existent*, trans. Lewis Galantiere and Gerald B. Phelan (Westport, CT: Greenwood Press, 1975), 69–70.
21. See Louis Roy, "Wainwright, Maritain and Aquinas on Transcendent Experiences," *The Thomist* 54 (1990): 655–672.
22. See Roy, *Transcendent Experiences*, chap. 10, section entitled "Interpretation."
23. Arthur J. Deikman, M. D., *The Observing Self: Mysticism and Psychotherapy* (Boston: Beacon Press, 1982), 11, 95.
24. Pierre Thévenaz, *What is Phenomenology? And Other Essays*, trans. James M. Edie, Charles Courtney and Paul Brockelman (London: Merlin Press, 1963), 106.
25. Illtyd Trethowan, *Mysticism and Theology: An Essay in Christian Metaphysics* (London: Chapman, 1975), 7.

CHAPTER 3. ACCOUNTS OF MYSTICAL CONSCIOUSNESS

1. Robert K. C. Forman, *The Problem of Pure Consciousness: Mysticism and Philosophy*, and *The Innate Capacity: Mysticism, Psychology, and Philosophy* (New York: Oxford University Press, respectively 1990 and 1998); *Mysticism, Mind, Consciousness* (Albany: SUNY Press, 1999).
2. See Roy, *Transcendent Experiences*, chap. 10, section entitled "Interpretation."
3. See Lonergan's distinction between *conscientia-perceptio* and *conscientia-experientia* in *Collection*, 162–166.
4. Lonergan, *Insight*, 523.
5. The Freudian suggestion that the oceanic feeling is *simply* a return to the infant's experience of immediacy is dubbed "the pre/trans fallacy" by Ken Wilber in *Eye to Eye: The Quest for the New Paradigm* (Boston: Shambhala, 3d ed., 1996), chap. 7; see also *The Atman Project: A Transpersonal View of Human Development* (Wheaton, IL: The Theosophical Publishing House, 2d ed., 1996), x–xiii, xvii–xviii, 58, 62. For a critique of Wilber's views, see Daniel A. Helminiak, *Religion and the Human Sciences: An Approach via Spirituality* (Albany: SUNY Press, 1998), chap. 4.
6. Sebastian Moore, "Consciousness," *The Downside Review* 75 (1957): 305–324, at 306 (my emphasis).
7. Moore, *Let This Mind Be in You* (San Francisco: Harper & Row, 1985).

8. James R. Price III, "Typologies and the Cross-Cultural Analysis of Mysticism: A Critique," in *Religion and Culture: Essays in Honor of Bernard Lonergan, S.J.*, ed. Timothy P. Fallon, S.J., and Philip Boo Riley (Albany, SUNY Press, 1987), 181–190.
9. Price, "Transcendence and Images: The Apophatic and Kataphatic Reconsidered," *Studies in Formative Spirituality* 11 (1990): 195–201, at 200.
10. The same terms recur in Price's piece, "Mystical Texts as an Entry into the Cross-cultural Study of Religion," in *Relations Between Cultures*, ed. George F. McLean and John Kromkowski (Washington, DC: The Council for Research in Values and Philosophy, 1991), 291–303, at 300.
11. Price, "Lonergan and the Foundation of a Contemporary Mystical Theology," in *Lonergan Workshop*, vol. 5, ed. Fred Lawrence (Chico: Scholars Press, 1985), 163–195, at 167. In section 2.5 of "Consciousness and Grace," in *Method* 11 (1993): 51–75, Robert M. Doran's distinction between "God's love for us poured forth in our hearts 'from above'" and our "acts of love 'from below'" may have been inspired by Price's article. See also Doran, "Revisiting 'Consciousness and Grace'," *Method* 13 (1995): 151–159. However, such theological correlations lie beyond the scope of this book, which confines itself to philosophy of religion.
12. David Granfield, *Heightened Consciousness: The Mystical Difference* (New York: Paulist Press, 1991), 108.
13. Karl Rahner, *The Dynamic Element in the Church* (New York: Herder, 1964), 139 (see 131–139), approvingly quoted by Lonergan, *Method in Theology*, 106, n. 4. See Louis Roy, "Toward a Psychology of Grace: W. W. Meissner's Contribution," *Theological Studies* 57 (1996): 322–331, at 328–329.
14. Herman F. Suligoj, "An Essay in Speculative Mysticism," *Religious Studies* 14 (1978): 469–484, at 478.
15. See note 13.

CHAPTER 4. PLOTINUS: CONSCIOUSNESS BEYOND CONSCIOUSNESS

1. On Plotinus's influence upon Schelling, see Xavier Tilliette, "Vision plotinienne et intuition schellingienne," *Gregorianum* 60 (1979): 703–724, esp. 703–707.

2. See Ernst Benz, *Les sources mystiques de la philosophie romantique allemande* (Paris: Vrin, 1968), 11–17; on Böhme's influence, which prolongs Eckhart's, see 17–21 (I shall briefly introduce Böhme's views in chapter 9).
3. John Peter Kenney, "Mysticism and Contemplation in the *Enneads*," *American Catholic Philosophical Quarterly* 71 (1997): 315–337, at 328.
4. See René Arnou, *Le désir de Dieu dans la philosophie de Plotin* (Paris: Alcan, no date), 276–278.
5. All quotations are from A. H. Armstrong's translation of Plotinus's *Enneads*, 7 vols. (Cambridge: Harvard University Press, 1966–1988; vol. 1, which includes Porphyry's "Life of Plotinus," was revised in 1989).
6. The world soul and the individual souls participate in the hypostasis Soul. For useful clarifications on Soul, Intellect, unity, and consciousness, see Gary M. Gurtler, *Plotinus: The Experience of Unity* (New York: Peter Lang, 1988).
7. Gerald J. P. O'Daly, *Plotinus' Philosophy of the Self* (Shannon: Irish University Press, 1973), 89–90. To his list of terms, I would add "someone" (*tis*).
8. Instead of rendering *epibolê* by "a direct awareness," as Armstrong does here, I have substituted his own alternative rendering, "a concentration of attention," at VI.7.39. See J. M. Rist's remarks on *epibolê* in *Plotinus: The Road to Reality* (Cambridge: Cambridge University Press, 1967), 49–51.
9. In "Plotinus and the 'Eye' of Intellect," *Dionysius* 14 (1990): 79–103, esp. 88–91 and 99, John F. Phillips makes it clear that Plotinus's Intellect comprises two stages and that the second stage goes beyond thinking.
10. See Introduction to Plotin, *Traité 38: VI, 7* and to *Traité 9: VI, 9* by Pierre Hadot (Paris: Cerf, 1988 and 1994).
11. Andrew Louth, *The Origins of the Christian Mystical Tradition: From Plato to Denys* (Oxford: Clarendon Press, 1981), 43. See also Hadot, "Les niveaux de conscience dans les états mystiques selon Plotin," *Journal de Psychologie Normale et Pathologique* 77 (1980): 243–266.
12. See H.-R. Schwyzer, "'Bewusst' und 'unbewusst' bei Plotin," in *Les sources de Plotin*, by E. R. Dodds and others (Geneva: Fondation Hardt, 1960, 341–378, esp. 364–377, with his reply in "Discussion," 388–390. In addition to *synesis*, *synaisthêsis* and *parakolouthêsis*, Schwyzer lists *syneidêsis* as also meaning "consciousness." But nowhere in his presentation does he cite a text that

would include *syneidêsis*. The term is not found in *Lexicon Plotinianum*, ed. J. H. Sleeman and Gilbert Pollet (Leiden: Brill, 1980).
13. On the ontological difference between the soul and the One, see O'Daly, chaps. 3–4, and Rist, *Plotinus*, chap. 16.
14. Hence Armstrong's remark on this passage: "*hen amphô* is always used by Plotinus of a perfect union in which the two united retain their distinct natures" (vol. 7, 192, n. 1).
15. Vol. 7, 342–343, n. 1.
16. To my knowledge Mircea Eliade is the author who coined the word "enstasis" to mean "final concentration of the spirit and 'escape' from the cosmos." and to distinguish such yogic state from shamanic ecstasy. See Eliade, *Shamanism: Archaic Techniques of Ecstasy*, trans. Willard R. Trask (New York: Penguin, 1989), 417. See also his *Yoga: Immortality and Freedom*, trans. Willard R. Trask (Princeton: Princeton University Press, 2d ed., 1969), Index, "enstasis."
17. In *Method in Theology*, 88 and 341–342. For a discussion of "object" and "objective" see Roy, *Transcendent Experiences*, chap. 9, section "Intentionality and Transcendence."

CHAPTER 5. ECKHART: WHEN HUMAN
CONSCIOUSNESS BECOMES DIVINE

1. See E. Zum Brunn and G. Epiney-Burgard, *Women Mystics of Medieval Europe*, trans. Sheila Hughes (New York: Paragon House, 1989), "Introduction"; Edmund Colledge, "Eckhart's Orthodoxy Reconsidered?" *New Blackfriars* 71 (1990): 176–184; *Meister Eckhart and the Beguine Mystics*, ed. Bernard McGinn (New York: Continuum, 1997).
2. McGinn, "The God beyond God: Theology and Mysticism in the Thought of Meister Eckhart," *The Journal of Religion* 61 (1981): 1–19, at 17; see esp. 15–19, where Eckhart's "mysticism" is described.
3. Master Eckhart, *Parisian Questions and Prologues*, trans. with an Introduction and Notes by Armand A. Maurer (Toronto: Pontifical Institute of Mediaeval Studies, 1974). In addition to Maurer's introduction, I have found insightful the piece by John D. Caputo, "The Nothingness of the Intellect in Meister Eckhart's 'Parisian Questions'," *The Thomist* 39 (1975): 85–115. The issue of being and thinking is treated in depth by Ruedi Imbach, *Deus est intelligere: Das Verhältnis von Sein und Denken in seiner Bedeutung für das*

Gottesverständnis bei Thomas von Aquin und in den Pariser Quaestionen Meister Eckharts (Freiburg, Switzerland: University Press, 1976).
4. Any German sermon will be referred to as Pr. (= *Predigt*), followed by an Arabic number, whereas the number of any Latin sermon will be Roman. All English translations of the German sermons will be taken from Meister Eckhart, *Sermons & Treatises*, trans. M. O'C. Walshe, 3 vols. (Rockport, MA: Element, 1987), at times with alterations. English translations of the treatises will be taken from Meister Eckhart, *The Essential Sermons, Commentaries, Treaties, and Defense*, trans. Edmund Colledge and Bernard McGinn (New York: Paulist Press, 1981) = ES. Since the vernacular used by Eckhart is Middle High German, the readers must expect spelling different from contemporary German. As in Walsche, Pf stands for the German sermons edited by Pfeiffer in 1857, and QT for those considered as authentic and translated by Josef Quint into contemporary German, in *Deutsche Predigten und Traktate* (Munich: Carl Hanser, 1955); although unavailable in the critical edition, they are incorporated by Walshe into his set of sermons. The German or Latin words in bracket are taken from Meister Eckhart, *Die deutschen und lateinischen Werke,* herausgegeben im Auftrage der Deutschen Forschungsgemeinschaft (Stuttgart: Kohlhammer), 11 vols., 1936-. Because of its traditional symbolic value in mysticism, I accept Walshe's use of the feminine when reference is made to the soul (*anima, sêle*, in Eckhart's Latin or Middle High German).
5. Carlo Sini, *Images of Truth: From Sign to Symbol*, trans. Massimo Verdicchio (Atlantic Highlands, NJ: Humanities Press, 1993), 74.
6. On the seven occurrences of the verb *entbilden* in Eckhart's corpus, see Wolfgang Wackernagel, *Ymagine Denudari. Ethique de l'image et métaphysique de l'abstraction chez Maître Eckhart* (Paris: Vrin, 1991), esp. 18–24, 33–34, 110 & 134–139.
7. Commentary on Genesis, §209.
8. "Of the Nobleman," in *ES*, 247. See McGinn, "Ocean and Desert as Symbols of Mystical Absorption in the Christian Tradition," *The Journal of Religion* 74 (1994): 155–181, at 168. See also Pr. 10, where the word play is with *einung*, oneness.
9. See McGinn, *The Mystical Thought of Meister Eckhart: The Man from Whom God Hid Nothing* (New York: Crossroad, 2001), chap. 3: "Eckhart and the Mysticism of the Ground."
10. In this paragraph, where reference is made to a sermon not retained in the critical edition but nonetheless available in Quint's translation, the words in bracket are the contemporary German rendering by Quint, 420–421. See n. 4.

11. Denys Turner, *The Darkness of God: Negativity in Christian Mysticism* (Cambridge: Cambridge University Press, 1995). See Louis Roy, *Le sentiment de transcendance, expérience de Dieu?* (Paris: Cerf, 2000), chap. 7, section "Mal et non-expérience de Dieu." On traces of Eckhart's personal experience in his writings, see Kurt Ruh, *Meister Eckhart, Theologe, Prediger, Mystiker* (Munich: Beck, 1985), chap. 11.
12. McGinn, *The Mystical Thought of Meister Eckhart*, 149.
13. "Of the Nobleman," in *ES*, 245–246; see "On Detachment," in *ES*, 292.
14. Forman, "Eckhart, *Gezücken*, and the Ground of the Soul," in *The Problem of Pure Consciousness*, 98–120, at 106.
15. Wilber, *The Atman Project*, 88.
16. Counsel 1, in *ES*, 248; see counsels 3 and 21.
17. Caputo, "The Poverty of Thought: A Reflection on Heidegger and Eckhart," in *Heidegger the Man and the Thinker*, ed. Thomas Sheehan (Chicago: Precedent Publishing, 1981), 209–216, at 210.
18. Counsel 20, in *ES*, 270.
19. Counsel 10, in *ES*, 258.
20. Commentary on Exodus, §247, in *TP*, 120.
21. Commentary on John, §50, in *ES*, 139.
22. "The Book of Divine Consolation," in *ES*, 228.
23. Commentary on Wisdom, §154, in *Meister Eckhart Teacher and Preacher* (henceforth *TP*), ed. Bernard McGinn (New York: Paulist Press, 1986), 169; see also §144 and §155.
24. "The God beyond God," 7.
25. Commentary on Exodus, §113, in *TP*, 81, with reference to §104.
26. Commentary on John, §106, in *ES*, 162, and §521. In *Théologie négative et connaissance de Dieu chez Maître Eckhart* (Paris: Vrin, 1960), 175–192, Vladimir Lossky demonstrates that Eckhart's theology of grace is none other than Thomas Aquinas's; see also Edouard-Henri Wéber, "La théologie de la grâce chez Maître Eckhart," *Revue des Sciences Religieuses* 70 (1996): 48–72.
27. Commentary on John, §4, in *ES*, 123; see §29; see also Commentary on Wisdom, §99, in *TP*, 157; and Commentary on Genesis, §77–78 and §100, in *Die lateinischen Werke*, herausgegeben im Auftrage der Deutschen Forschungsgemeinschaft (Stuttgart: Kohlhammer, 1936-), vol. I.
28. "Of the Nobleman," in *ES*, 245.
29. "Counsels on Discernment," in *ES*, 276.
30. See Reiner Schürmann's perceptive comments in *Meister Eckhart, Mystic and Philosopher* (Bloomington: University of Indiana Press, 1978), 14–18. He refers to Ennead IV.8.1 and to Predigt 2.

CHAPTER 6. SCHLEIERMACHER: CONSCIOUSNESS AS FEELING

1. References to Schleiermacher's principal works are given in the body of this article as follows. Unless otherwise indicated, numbers in bracket introduced by § refer to the second edition (1830–31) of *Der christliche Glaube* (Berlin: de Gruyter, 1960), also called *Glaubenslehre* by Schleiermacher and his commentators; translated into English as *The Christian Faith*, ed. H. R. Mackintosh and J. S. Stewart (Edinburgh: T. & T. Clark, 1986). 1799 = first edition of *On Religion: Speeches to Its Cultured Despisers*, trans. Richard Crouter (Cambridge: Cambridge University Press, 1988). 1821 = 3d ed. of *On Religion: Speeches to its Cultured Despisers*, trans. John Oman (New York: Harper & Row, 1958; reprint, Louisville, KY: Westminster/Knox Press, 1994).
2. That is, beginning with *On Religion* (1799). For earlier, partly different usages of the word *Gefühl*, see Julia A. Lamm, "Schleiermacher's Post-Kantian Spinozism: The Early Essays on Spinoza, 1793–94," *Journal of Religion* 74 (1994): 476–505, esp. 500–502, and "The Early Philosophical Roots of Schleiermacher's Notion of *Gefühl*, 1788–1794," *Harvard Theological Review* 87 (1994): 67–105. Out of the three senses of *Gefühl* that she details in the latter article, two of them (i.e., the unifying factor that grounds the various faculties and the apprehension of the Infinite) are still very prominent in the *Glaubenslehre*.
3. See Schleiermacher, *On the "Glaubenslehre": Two Letters to Dr. Lücke*, trans. James Duke and Francis Fiorenza (Chico: Scholars Press, 1981), 39.
4. "Die Permanenz des religiöses Gefühls ist die Stimmung," writes Schleiermacher in 1819. See his *Ästhetik*, ed. Rudolf Odebrecht (Berlin: de Gruyter, 1931), 71; or *Ästhetik, und Über den Begriff der Kunst*, ed. Thomas Lehnerer (Hamburg: Meiner, 1984), 22.
5. "Das Gefühl ist durchaus nichts Subjecktives, wie man gewöhnlich annimmt, sondern geht ebensowohl auf das allgemeine, wie auf das individuelle Selbstbewußtsein." *Dialektik* (1822), ed. Rudolf Odebrecht (Leipzig: Hinrichs Verlag, 1942; reprint, Darmstadt: Wissenschaftliche Buchgesellschaft, 1988), §50, 288.
6. According to Richard R. Niebuhr's rendering, which corrects the Edinburgh translation: see his *Schleiermacher on Christ and Religion: A New Introduction* (New York: Scribner's, 1964), 123, n. 91.
7. Rudolf Hermann, "Schleiermacher II. Theologie," in *Die Religion in Geschichte und Gegenwart*, ed. Hans Freiherr von Campenhausen

et al. (Tübingen: Mohr, 3d ed., 1961), vol. 5, 1430. See also Rudolf Otto, *Mysticism East and West: A Comparative Analysis of the Nature of Mysticism*, trans. Bertha L. Bracey and Richenda C. Payne (London: Macmillan, 1932), 240.
8. William A. Christian, Sr., *Meaning and Truth in Religion* (Chicago: University of Chicago Press, 1964), 46.
9. For whom the *differentia* of religion is emotional intensity; see his *Varieties of Religious Experience* (Cambridge, MA: Harvard University Press, 1985), 41–47. In *Easter in Ordinary* (Charlottesville: University Press of Virginia, 1988), 130, Nicholas Lash calls attention to the fact that, in contradistinction with Schleiermacher, the author of *Varieties* belongs to "a later generation—when the language of "feeling" and "experience" had contracted into empirical description of individual psychological states."
10. Published in 1821–22. See *Kritische Gesamtausgabe*, ed. H. J. Birkner et al., 7, 1–2 (Berlin: de Gruyter, 1980). In this article, I shall use an English translation of a few important passages: "Selections from the First Edition of F. D. E. Schleiermacher's *Christian Belief*," in *Hegel, Hinrichs, and Schleiermacher on Feeling and Reason in Religion: The Texts of Their 1821–22 Debate*, ed. Eric von der Luft (Lewiston, NY: Mellen Press, 1987), 214–238.
11. In between the two editions, this change can be documented thanks to a passage of Schleiermacher's 1826–27 lectures on ethics. See *Introduction to Christian Ethics*, trans. John C. Shelley (Nashville: Abingdon Press, 1989), 73–77.
12. Paul Tillich, *Perspectives on Nineteenth and Twentieth Century Protestant Theology* (New York: Harper & Row, 1967), 96; see 96–99.
13. Christian, *Meaning and Truth in Religion*, 46.
14. Friedrich Beisser, *Schleiermachers Lehre von Gott dargestellt nach seinen Reden und seiner Glaubenslehre* (Göttingen: Vanderhoeck & Ruprecht, 1970), 60.
15. John E. Thiel, *God and World in Schleiermacher's* Dialektik *and* Glaubenslehre (Bern, Frankfurt and Las Vegas: Peter Lang, 1981), 107.
16. *Dialektik*, ed. Ludwig Jonas, in *Friedrich Schleiermacher's sämmtliche Werke* (Berlin: Reimer, 1834–1864), III/4/2, 151; or *Dialektic 1814/15*, ed. Andreas Arndt (Hamburg: Meiner, 1988), I, §215.1; quoted by Thiel, 108.
17. *Dialektik*, ed. Odbrecht, §51, 288, note.
18. Marianne Simon, *La philosophie de la religion dans l'oeuvre de Schleiermacher* (Paris: Vrin, 1974), 130–131.

19. Thandeka, "Schleiermacher's *Dialektik*: The Discovery of the Self that Kant Lost," *Harvard Theological Review* 85 (1992): 444.
20. Werner Schultz, "Schleiermachers Theorie des Gefühls und ihre theologische Bedeutung," *Zeitschrift für Theologie und Kirche* 53 (1956): 89.
21. *Dialektik*, ed. Odebrecht, §51, 288, note.
22. *Introduction to Christian Ethics*, 47.
23. See Gerald A. McCool, *Nineteenth-Century Scholasticism: The Search for a Unitary Method* (New York: Fordham University Press, 1989), 95.
24. As suggested by Raymond Hostie, quoted by Lonergan, *A Third Collection*, 58–59 and 117.
25. This passage is more developed than the original version (1799:112).
26. T. H. Jørgensen calls this *die Bewußtseinstätigkeit*, the activity of consciousness, or the conscious activity. See his *Das religionsphilosophische Offenbarungsverständnis des späteren Schleiermacher* (Tübingen: Mohr, 1977), 214.
27. *Dialektik*, ed. Odebrecht, §51, 288, note.
28. Ed. Odebrecht, §51, 288.
29. Ed. Odebrecht, §51, 293.
30. Thiel convincingly argues for maintaining the traditional English rendering of *schlechthinnig* by "absolute" (*God and World*, 138, n. 64). Christian prefers "unmixed" (*Meaning and Truth in Religion*, 45). Claude Welch suggests the adjectives "utter," "simple," and "unqualified," in *Protestant Thought in the Nineteenth Century*, vol. I (New Haven: Yale University Press, 1972), 65. As Thiel remarks in his previously mentioned note 64, the rendering "absolute" is supported by Schleiermacher's marginal explanation, "Schlechthinnig gleich absolut."
31. Or better, "a self-positing"/"a not-having-posited-oneself-thus," as the pair is translated in Martin Redeker, *Schleiermacher: Life and Thought*, trans. John Wallhausser (Philadelphia: Fortress Press, 1973), 113. I find less satisfactory the way Niebuhr renders the second member of the pair, although he usefully indicates that the first corresponds to relative freedom and the second to relative determinedness of the self. See *Schleiermacher on Christ and Religion*, 122.
32. Hence his well-known remark about the dog as being "the best Christian" since he feels dependence most strongly! See his Foreword to Hinrichs' *Religion in its Internal Relationship to Systematic Knowledge*, in von der Luft, *Hegel, Hinrichs, and Schleiermacher*, §26, 260; see the context on feeling, §22–§28, 257–262.

33. A point emphatically made in Gerhard Ebeling, *Wort und Glaube*, (Tübingen: Mohr, 1975), vol. 3, 119.
34. Thiel writes: "Schleiermacher's criticism of traditional Christian doctrine may be traced to his efforts to articulate the content of pious feeling within the bounds of proper thinking established in the *Dialektik*" (*God and World*, 130; see 4 and 228–229). On this relation of the "Glaubenslehre" to the *Dialektik*, apart from Thiel's study, I have also greatly profited from Christian Berner, *La philosophie de Schleiermacher* (Paris: Cerf, 1995) and Thandeka, *The Embodied Self: Friedrich Schleiermacher's Solution to Kant's Problem of the Empirical Self* (Albany: SUNY Press, 1995). However, I have found Thiel's and Berner's reading of Schleiermacher more convincing than Thandeka's.
35. Georg Wobbermin, *The Nature of Religion*, trans. Theophil Menzel and Daniel Sommer Robinson (New York: Crowell, 1933), 51.
36. *Dialektik* (1811), ed. Andreas Arndt (Hamburg: Meiner, 1986), §5.
37. "Die höchste Stufe des Gefühls das religiöse ist," in *Ethik (1812/13) mit späteren Fassungen der Einleitung, Güterlehre, and Pflichtenlehre*, ed. Hans-Joachim Birkner (Hamburg: Meiner, 1981), "Güterlehre," §69, 33.

CHAPTER 7. WESTERN VIEWS OF THE SELF

1. My position in this chapter is in agreement with Jonathan Shear's in his book (referred to in my Introduction) and his piece entitled "On the Existence of a Culture Independent Core Component of Self," in *East-West Encounters in Philosophy and Religion*, ed. Ninian Smart and B. Srinivasa Murthy (Long Beach, CA: Long Beach Publications, 1996), 359–376.
2. David Hume, *A Treatise of Human Nature*, ed. David Fate Norton and Mary J. Norton (Oxford: Oxford University Press, 2000), book 1, part 4, section 6, 164.
3. See book 1, part 1.
4. Book 1, part 4, section 6, 165.
5. Ibid.
6. William James, *The Principles of Psychology*, 267; see 262–379.
7. Ibid., 284–285.
8. James, "The Place of Affectional Facts in a World of Pure Experience," in *Essays in Radical Empiricism*, (Cambridge, MA: Harvard University Press, 1976), 69. In this book, see "Does 'Consciousness' Exist?" (1904), "A World of Pure Experience" (1904) and "La

Notion de Conscience" (1905). See also his final statement in *A Pluralistic Universe* (Cambridge, MA: Harvard University Press, 1977), lecture 7: "The Continuity of Experience."
9. Reprinted in James, *Essays in Philosophy* (Cambridge, MA: Harvard University Press, 1978), 95.
10. Eric Voegelin, *Autobiographical Reflections* (Baton Rouge: Louisiana State University Press, 1989), 73; see 70–74.
11. Plotinus, *Enneads*, III.2.14 and IV.3.8.
12. Mark D. Morelli, "Lonergan's Unified Theory of Consciousness," *Method: Journal of Lonergan Studies* 17 (1999): 171–188, at 177; see esp. 175–178 and 183–184.
13. John Locke, *An Essay concerning Human Understanding*, ed. Peter H. Nidditch (Oxford: Oxford University Press, 1975), book 2, chap. 27, §9, 335.
14. Ibid., §10, 336.
15. Joseph Flanagan, *Quest for Self-Knowledge: An Essay in Lonergan's Philosophy* (Toronto: University of Toronto Press, 1997), 116; see 112–119.
16. Zahavi, *Self-awareness and Alterity*, 32 and 197.
17. Lonergan, "Christ as Subject: A Reply," in *Collection*, 165. See also "Christology Today: Methodological Reflections," §7: "Person Today," in *A Third Collection*.
18. Joann Wolski Conn and Walter E. Conn, "Self," in *The New Dictionary of Catholic Spirituality*, ed. Michael Downey (Collegeville: The Liturgical Press, 1993), 865–875, at 872.
19. Zahavi, 23; see 34.
20. Helminiak, *The Human Core of Spirituality*, 70.
21. Ibid., 71.
22. For a psychological and spiritual approach to the problems of the self, see Roberto Assagioli, *Psychosynthesis: A Manual of Principles and Techniques* (New York: Hobbs, Dorman & Company, 1965), esp. 17–27, and Louis Roy, *Self-Actualization and the Radical Gospel* (Collegeville: The Liturgical Press, 2002).
23. See "The Response of the Jesuit," in *A Second Collection*, 166–173, and *Method in Theology*, 9–10, 14–20, 104–107.
24. Sallie B. King, "Two Epistemological Models for the Interpretation of Mysticism," *Journal of the American Academy of Religion* 56 (1988): 257–279, at 272.
25. King, *Buddha Nature* (Albany: SUNY Press, 1991), 146–148.
26. King, "Concepts, Anti-concepts and Religious Experience," *Religious Studies* 14 (1978): 445–458, at 456.

27. In *The Problem of Self in Buddhism and Christianity* (New York: Harper & Row, 1979), Lynn A. de Silva makes an interesting case for the complementarity between the Theravada Buddhist doctrine of *anatta* (no-soul) and the biblical doctrine of *pneuma* (Spirit). For him, the overcoming of the substantive ego of modern philosophy can be facilitated if situated in the context of a life of Spirit that is both divinely given and relational.
28. Forman, *The Problem of Pure Consciousness*, 27–28.
29. James R. Price III, "Mysticism," in *A New Handbook of Christian Theology*, ed. Donald W. Musser & Joseph L. Price (Nashville: Abingdon Press, 1992), 318–321, at 319.

CHAPTER 8. JAPANESE VIEWS OF THE SELF

1. "The Sense of Zen," in *Zen Buddhism: Selected Writings of D. T. Suzuki*, ed. William Barrett (New York: Doubleday Anchor Books, 1956), 6–7.
2. Suzuki, "Lectures on Zen Buddhism," in Erich Fromm, D. T. Suzuki and Richard de Martino, *Zen Buddhism and Psychoanalysis* (London: George Allen & Unwin, 1960), 25.
3. Ibid., 28.
4. In Thomas Merton, *Zen and the Birds of Appetite* (New York: New Directions Books, 1968), part 2, "A Dialogue: D. T. Suzuki and Thomas Merton," 107, 109.
5. Suzuki, *Mysticism: Christian and Buddhist* (Westport, CT: Greenwood Press, 1975), 129–131.
6. Suzuki, "Àpropos of Shin," in *The Buddha Eye: An Anthology of the Kyoto School*, ed. Frederick Franck (New York: Crossroad, 1991), 211–220, at 215 and 219.
7. Suzuki, *An Introduction to Zen Buddhism* (New York: Grove Press, 1991), 54, 95.
8. Suzuki, *Studies in Zen*, ed. Christmas Humphreys (New York: Dell, A Delta Book, 1955), 85, 121.
9. "Satori, or Enlightenment," in *Zen Buddhism: Selected Writings of D. T. Suzuki*, 84–85.
10. "Existentialism, Pragmatism and Zen," in *Zen Buddhism: Selected Writings of D. T. Suzuki*, 262–263.
11. *Studies in Zen*, 123.
12. "The Sense of Zen," in *Zen Buddhism: Selected Writings of D. T. Suzuki*, 3.

13. D. T. Suzuki and Winston L. King, "Conversations with D. T. Suzuki," part I, *The Eastern Buddhist* 20/2 (Autumn 1987): 77–88, at 81.
14. Suzuki, "Existentialism, Pragmatism and Zen," 263–264.
15. Suzuki, "Self the Unattainable," in *The Buddha Eye*, 15–21.
16. Suzuki, "What Is the 'I'," in *The Buddha Eye*, 31–46, at 37.
17. Suzuki, "The Buddhist Conception of Reality," in *The Buddha Eye*, 89–110, at 103.
18. Suzuki, *An Introduction to Zen Buddhism* (New York: Grove Press, 1991), 68–69; see 71.
19. Suzuki, "On the Hekigan Roku ('Blue Cliff Records') With a Translation of 'Case One'," *The Eastern Buddhist* 1/1 (September 1965): 5–21, at 7.
20. "Conversations with D. T. Suzuki," part I, 79.
21. Ibid., 85.
22. *Zen and the Birds of Appetite*, 114. For further reading: in *Zen and Japanese Culture* (Princeton: Princeton University Press, 1959), Suzuki admirably situates Zen in its cultural context.
23. Suzuki, A review of *A History of Zen Buddhism* by Heinrich Dumoulin, *The Eastern Buddhist* 1/1 (September 1965):123–126, at 124. Ueda Shizuteru concurs with Suzuki. See "Der Zen-Buddhismus als 'Nicht-Mystik'," in *Transparente Welt*, ed. Günter Schulz (Bern: Verlag Hans Huber, 1965), 291–313.
24. Paul Mommaers and Jan Van Bragt, *Mysticism Buddhist and Christian: Encounters with Jan van Ruusbroec* (New York: Crossroad, 1995), 42–43.
25. "Conversations with D. T. Suzuki," part 2, *The Eastern Buddhist* 21/1 (Spring 1988): 96, 98, quoted by Van Bragt, *Mysticism Buddhist and Christian*, 43. We find the same ambiguity in an earlier series of articles by Suzuki, *An Introduction to Zen Buddhism*, 32, 35–36, 45, 97.
26. Suzuki, *An Introduction to Zen Buddhism*, 54.
27. Ibid., 95.
28. Keiji Nishitani, *Religion and Nothingness*, trans. Jan Van Bragt (Berkeley: University of California Press, 1982). Note that Nishitani often italicizes.
29. Nishitani, "The Standpoint of Zen," *The Eastern Buddhist* 17/1 (Spring 1984): 1–26, at 1.
30. Nishitani, "The Problem of *Anjin* in Zen," *The Eastern Buddhist* 29/1 (Spring 1996): 1–32, at 7.
31. Ibid., 13.
32. Ibid., 20.

33. Hand Waldenfels, "The Search for Common Ground: Being, God, and Emptiness," *Japanese Religions* 11 (September 1980): 113–143, at 134–138. See also Jan Van Bragt, "Contributions of Buddhism to Christianity," *Nanzan Bulletin* 23 (1999): 6–17, at 14–15.
34. Wilber, *The Atman Project*, 94.
35. These reflections are inspired by W. Norris Clarke, "The Self in Eastern and Western Thought," *International Philosophical Quarterly* 6 (1966): 101–109.

CHAPTER 9. WESTERN VIEWS OF NOTHINGNESS

1. See Graham Parkes, "Nishitani Keiji," *Routledge Encyclopedia of Philosophy* (New York: Routledge, 1998), 16–17. I will not report, however, the reception of Eckhart by Suzuki in his book, *Mysticism: Christian and Buddhist*, because I believe his comparative attempt is flawed. See Roy, "Some Japanese Interpretations of Meister Eckhart," *Studies in Interreligious Dialogue* 11 (2001): 183.
2. Martin Heidegger, *The Basic Problems of Phenomenology*, trans. Albert Hofstadter (Bloomington: Indiana University Press, rev. ed., 1982), 90–91.
3. Reported by William Barrett, *Zen Buddhism: Selected Writings of D. T. Suzuki*, Introduction, xi.
4. See Philippe Capelle, "Heidegger et Maître Eckhart," *Revue des Sciences Religieuses* 70 (1996): 113–124.
5. Heidegger, *Schelling's Treatise on the Essence of Human Freedom*, trans. Joan Stambaugh (Athens: Ohio University Press, 1985).
6. Jacob Böhme, *Six Theosophic Points and Other Writings*, trans. John Rolleston Earle (New York: Knopf, 1920).
7. F.W.J. Schelling, *Of Human Freedom*, trans. James Gutmann (Chicago: Open Court, 1936), 87.
8. Heidegger, *Being and Time*, trans. John Macquarrie and Edward Robinson (San Francisco: Harper & Row, 1962). References are to page numbers of the German edition, given in the margins of this English translation. In my quotations from Heidegger, italicizing and hyphenating (alternating with no hyphenating) are by the author himself.
9. Heidegger, *History of the Concept of Time: Prolegomena*, trans. Theodore Kisiel (Bloomington: Indiana University Press, 1985), §30.
10. Heidegger, *Pathmarks*, ed. William McNeill (Cambridge: Cambridge University Press, 1998): "What Is Metaphysics," 82–96, "Postscript

to 'What Is Metaphysics?'," 231–238, "Letter on 'Humanism'," 239–276, "Introduction to 'What Is Metaphysics?'," 277–290, "On the Question of Being," 291–322.
11. Heidegger, *Introduction to Metaphysics*, trans. Gregory Fried and Richard Polt (New Haven: Yale University Press, 2000).
12. Heidegger, *Contributions to Philosophy (From Enowning)*, trans. Parvis Emad and Kenneth Maly (Bloomington: Indiana University Press, 1989).
13. See the very helpful Translators' Foreword to *Contributions*, xv–xliv, at xx. Heidegger remarks that by writing being (*Sein*) as being (*Seyn* = the obsolete eighteenth-century orthography) he wants to "indicate that being here is no longer thought metaphysically" (307).
14. William J. Richardson, "Dasein and the Ground of Negativity: A Note on the Fourth Movement in the *Beiträge*-Symphony," *Heidegger Studies* 9 (1993): 35–52, at 43.
15. Heidegger, *Basic Concepts*, trans. Gary E. Aylesworth (Bloomington: Indiana University Press, 1993).
16. Heidegger, *Parmenides*, trans. André Schuwer and Richard Rojcewicz (Bloomington: Indiana University Press, 1992).
17. Heidegger, *The Principle of Reason*, trans. Reginald Lilly (Bloomington: Indiana University Press, 1991).
18. Heidegger, "The Principle of Identity," *Identity and Difference*, trans. Joan Stambaugh (New York: Harper & Row, 1969), 23–41, at 32.
19. Michael Pinholster, *Fault and Light: Negativity in the Work of Martin Heidegger, 1919–1943* (Ann Arbor: UMI Microform 9707857, 1996), Conclusion.
20. See John D. Caputo, *The Mystical Element in Heidegger's Thought* (New York: Fordham University Press, rev. reprint, 1986), 18–30; Sonya Sikka, *Forms of Transcendence: Heidegger and Medieval Mystical Theology* (Albany: SUNY Press, 1997).
21. For a Heideggerian meditation on the religious significance of nothingness, see Bernhard Welte, *Das Licht des nichts. Von der Möglichkeit neuer religiöser Erfahrung* (Düsseldorf: Patmos Verlag, 1980).
22. Nishitani, "Religious-Philosophical Existence in Buddhism," *The Eastern Buddhist* 23/2 (Autumn 1990): 1–17, at 2.
23. See Louis Roy, "Neither Within nor Outside Time: Plotinus' Approach to Eternity," *Science et Esprit* 53 (2001): 419–426.
24. "Das nichterkennende Erkennen" in Quint's additional Predigten, rendered as "Unknowing-knowing" by Walshe (#1), 9. See Meister

Eckehart [sic], *Deutsche Predigten und Traktate*, ed. and trans. Josef Quint, 421.
25. Nishitani, "Religious-Philosophical Existence in Buddhism," 10–12.
26. For a helpful commentary and many references to Eckhart, see Caputo, *The Mystical Element in Heidegger's Thought*, chaps. 3 and 4.
27. Nishitani, "Reflections on Two Addresses by Martin Heidegger," in *Heidegger and Asian Thought*, ed. Graham Parkes (Honolulu: University of Hawaii Press, 1987), 145–154, at 152.
28. Nishitani, "Nothingness and Death in Heidegger and Zen Buddhism," *The Eastern Buddhist* 18/1 (Spring 1985): 90–104, John Steffney misreads Heidegger and wrongly contrasts his thought with the Zen understanding of *sunyata*.
29. Fred Dallmayr, "Nothingness and Sunyata: A Comparison of Heidegger and Nishitani," *Philosophy East and West* 42 (1992): 37–48, esp. 43–46.
30. Nishitani, "Ontology and Utterance," *Philosophy East and West* 31 (1981): 29–43, at 29.
31. Caputo, *The Mystical Element in Heidegger's Thought*, xvii, xxi, 7–9, 31–46.

CHAPTER 10. JAPANESE VIEWS OF NOTHINGNESS

1. Joan Stambaugh introduces both authors' views on nothingness in *The Formless Self* (Albany: SUNY Press, 1999), chaps. 2 and 3.
2. See Jan Van Bragt, "Nishitani on Japanese Religiosity," in *Japanese Religiosity*, ed. Joseph J. Spae (Tokyo: Oriens Institute for Religious Research, 1971), 271–284.
3. Nishitani, "Encounter with Emptiness," in *The Religious Philosophy of Nishitani Keiji: Encounter with Emptiness*, ed. Taitetsu Unno (Berkeley: Asian Humanities Press, 1989), 1–4, at 4.
4. Nishitani, *Nishida Kitaro*, trans. Yamamoto Seisaku and James W. Heisig (Berkeley: University of California Press, 1991) Preface and the first section of chap. 1; "Zen and the Modern World," *Zen Buddhism Today* 1 (1983): 19–25, esp. 24–25.
5. Nishitani, *The Self-Overcoming of Nihilism*, trans. Graham Parkes with Setsuko Aihara (Albany: SUNY Press, 1990).
6. Nishitani, "Three Worlds—No Dharma: Where to Seek the Mind?" *Zen Buddhism Today* 4 (1986): 119–125, at 120–121.
7. All references in parentheses are to *Religion and Nothingness*.

8. *The Self-Overcoming of Nihilism*, xxxiii, 2, 7; see 198, n. 3, 199, n. 2, 200, n. 11. In Japanese, the terms *mu* and *ku* are sometimes almost synonymous and sometimes quite distinct; see T. P. Kasulis, *Zen Action, Zen Person*, 39–40.
9. See *The Self-Overcoming of Nihilism*, chap. 4. Nishitani probably borrowed this life-affirming aspect of Nietzsche's nihilism from Heidegger, "The Word of Nietzsche: 'God Is Dead'," *The Question Concerning Technology and Other Essays*, trans. William Lovitt (New York: Harper & Row, 1977), and *Nietzsche*, trans. David Farrell Krell (San Francisco: Harper, 4 vols., 1979–87).
10. Nishitani, "Science and Zen," in *The Buddha Eye*, 111–137, at 120–126.
11. Nishitani, "The Problem of *Anjin* in Zen," 5.
12. Nishitani, "Encounter With Emptiness," 3–4.
13. Nishitani, "On Modernization and Tradition in Japan," in *Modernization and Tradition in Japan*, ed. Yshushi Kuyama and Nobuo Kobayashi (Nishinomiya: International Institute for Japan Studies, 1969), 69–96, at 89–92.
14. Nishitani, "The Standpoint of Zen," 25.
15. In a piece from which I quoted in chapter 9, "Ontology and Utterance," Nishitani adumbrates "a domain lying beyond the differentiation between 'who' and 'what,' between personal and impersonal" (32). Later in the same article, the author comments on St. Paul's identification with Christ while being truly himself. Of such concomitant identity and duality, he writes, "They are in 'no-otherness.' This no-other-ness is Love, Life, Reality, and Faith, of which Paul says that 'the life I now live in the flesh I live by the *faith in* the Son of God who loved me and gave himself for me'" (37).
16. Nishitani, "Ontology and Utterance," 40.
17. Nishitani, "The Problem of *Anjin* in Zen," 28.
18. Ibid., 29–30.
19. Nishitani, "The I-Thou Relation in Zen Buddhism," in *The Buddha Eye*, 47–60, at 55.
20. Again in "Ontology and Utterance," Nishitani finds this unification of opposites in St. Paul: "We have dealt with Paul's death mainly in its relation to Christ. This relation consists, so we have said, of a mutual giving over, a reciprocal reflection of life and death, or, more concretely, of life-death and death-life. This relation between Paul and Christ is repeated always as one occurrence in which two movements to and fro are intertwined" (39).
21. Nishitani offers a similar analysis in "Science and Zen," 111–137.
22. Jan Van Bragt, "Religion and Science in Nishitani Keiji," *Zen Buddhism Today* 5 (1987): 161–174, at 165.

23. Faced with the challenge of no-religion, religion must undergo a profound transformation, according to Nishitani, "Encountering No-Religion," *Zen Buddhism Today* 3 (1985): 141–144, esp. 143: "A reformation is needed which adapts religion to the contemporary world—we will have to change our attitudes as well as our religious practices and our everyday life."
24. Perhaps this is one of the values he sees in the mythological. See his piece, "The Nation and Religion," in *Sourcebook for Modern Japanese Philosophy*, trans. David A. Dilworth and Valdo H. Viglielmo (Westport, CT: Greenwood Press, 1998), 392–401. He writes, "The revitalization of Japanese mythology in actuality should not be as mythology per se, but rather as in the spirit which appeared in that mythology." He adds, "Only religion provides the strength to enable one to destroy even the very deepest root of the self" (396).
25. Matsumaru Hisao, "Nishitani's *Religionsphilosophie*: Nihilism and the Standpoint of *Sunyata*," *Zen Buddhism Today* 14 (November 1997): 97–113, at 106.
26. Paul Swanson, "Absolute Nothingness and Emptiness in Nishitani Keiji: An Essay from the Perspective of Classical Buddhist Thought," *The Eastern Buddhist* 29/1 (Spring 1996): 99–108, at 106.
27. Nishitani, "Three Worlds—No Dharma," 124. See also "The Significance of Zen in Modern Society," *Japanese Religions* 3 (April 1975): 18–24.
28. In a helpful commentary, "Nishitani's Challenge to Philosophy and Theology," *The Religious Philosophy of Nishitani Keiji: Encounter with Emptiness*, ed. Taitetsu Unno (Berkeley: Asian Humanities Press, 1990), 13–45, Masao Abe explains that "in itself" (*jitai*) signifies "the mode of being of things in the field of *sunyata* which is neither subjective nor substantial" (31); he also states, "for Nishitani, *jitai* or 'in itself' is simply another term for *sunyata*" (33). See also *Religion and Nothingness*, Glossary, "Selfness," 303.
29. John Maraldo, "Practice, Samadhi, Realization: Three Innovative Interpretations by Nishitani Keiji," *The Eastern Buddhist* 25/1 (Spring 1992): 8–20, at 15.
30. Nishitani quotes *The Mirror of Perfection* (London: Everyman's Library, 1950), CXV:291.
31. See Abe Masao, "Hisamatsu's Philosophy of Awakening," *The Eastern Buddhist* 14/1 (Spring 1981): 26–42.
32. Hisamatsu Shin'ichi, "Ultimate Crisis and Resurrection," part 1: "Sin and Death," and part 2: "Redemption," *The Eastern Buddhist* 8/1 (May 1975): 12–29, and 8/2 (October 1975): 37–65. Again, the readers must expect much italicizing on the part of Hisamatsu.

33. Quoted by Abe, "Hisamatsu's Philosophy of Awakening," 36.
34. "Dialogues, East and West: Conversations Between Dr. Paul Tillich and Dr. Hisamatsu Shin'ichi," *The Eastern Buddhist*, part 1, 4/2 (October 1971): 89–107; part 2, 5/2 (October 1972): 107–128; part 3, 6/2 (October 1973): 87–114. See part 2, 108–109.
35. Abe, "Hisamatsu's Philosophy of Awakening," 30, n. 3.
36. Hisamatsu, "Ordinary Mind," *The Eastern Buddhist* 12 (May 1979): 1–29, at 7; see 16–17.
37. Hisamatsu, "Zen: Its Meaning for Modern Civilization," *The Eastern Buddhist* 1/1 (September 1965): 22–47, at 35.
38. Hisamatsu, *Zen and the Fine Arts*, trans. Gishin Tokiwa (Tokyo: Kodansha International, 1971), 19, 31; see 51.
39. Hisamatsu, "The Characteristics of Oriental Nothingness," trans. Richard De Martino in collaboration with Jikai Fujiyoshi and Masao Abe, in *Philosophical Studies of Japan*, compiled by Japanese National Commission for Unesco (Tokyo: Japan Society for the Promotion of Science, vol. 2, 1960), 65–97. There is also a German translation available in book form: *Die Fülle des Nichts*, trans. Takashi Hirata and Johanna Fisher (Pfullingen: Neske, 3d ed., 1984).

CONCLUSION

1. Merton, *Zen and the Birds of Appetite*, 74.
2. Forman, *The Innate Capacity*, 40, n. 95.
3. David Loy's nondual perception, action, and thinking are cases of consciousness B, while constituting the substratum for consciousness A. See David Loy, *Nonduality: A Study in Comparative Philosophy* (New Haven: Yale University Press, 1988).
4. I am indebted to Miyamoto Hisao, O.P., professor of philosophy at Tokyo University, for this remark.
5. See Merton, *New Seeds of Contemplation* (New York: A New Directions Book, 1972), 12–13, 260. I have discussed this problem and similar issues in two of my books: *Le sentiment de transcendance, expérience de Dieu?*, chaps. 6 and 7, and *Self-Actualization and the Radical Gospel*.
6. See Merton, *Mystics and Zen Masters* (New York: The Noonday Press, 1967), 221; *New Seeds of Contemplation* , 205–208.
7. See Merton, *Zen and the Birds of Appetite*, 73, 76–78, 128–129.
8. Bergson, *The Two Sources of Morality and Religion*, trans. R. Ashley Audra and Cloudesley Brereton (Westport, CT: Greenwood Press, 1974), 210; see 90, 216–223.

9. Thomas P. Kasulis, "Whence and Wither: Philosophical Reflections on Nishitani's View of History," in *The Religious Philosophy of Nishitani Keiji*, 259–278, esp. 261–265. Similarly, Armin Münch contrasts Buddhism as moving backward (*Rückwärtsbewegung*) and Christianity as a forward dynamism (*Vorwätsdynamik*), in *Dimensionen der Leere: Gott als Nichts und Nichts als Gott im christlich-buddhistischen Dialog* (Münster: LIT, 1998), 264–275.
10. Masao Abe, "Will, Sunyata, and History," in *The Religious Philosophy of Nishitani Keiji*, 279–304, at 301; see also 288–291.
11. In a book in progress, provisionally entitled *Religious Experience and Revelation*, I tackle this issue.
12. See Translator's Introduction to Nishitani's *Religion and Nothingness*, xxxviii–xxxix.
13. See Nishitani, *Religion and Nothingness*, 244–247, and Hisamatsu, "Ordinary Mind," 20–29.

Glossary

awareness: the beginning of reflexive attentiveness, when a person pays attention to consciousness B or A; see "reflexive"; this narrow definition is different from Nishitani's "awareness" or from Hisamatsu's "Zen awareness," which amounts to a kind of mystical consciousness, or consciousness A

consciousness C: consciousness-of, or positional consciousness; conscious intentionality as attaining objects through acts of perceiving, understanding, or judging

consciousness B: consciousness-in, or nonpositional consciousness; the consciousness that permeates all our ordinary states and activities

consciousness A: mystical consciousness; the same consciousness as consciousness B, but present in objectless states

emptiness: state of being void of specific images, thoughts, or emotions, beyond the subject/object distinction, beyond reality and nothingness; sometimes called absolute nothingness (in contrast to existing beings), wherein all aspects of the universe are reconciled

experience: the perception of the data of sense, or the awareness of the data of consciousness; an event or episode during which one becomes clearly aware of consciousness B or A

intentionality: the conscious dynamism by which the subject intends objects through its attentiveness to data and through its questions and answers

nothingness: the possibility of a total annihilation of meaning or life—a possibility that opens human beings to enlightenment, called either the manifestation of Being or emptiness object: that which is represented by the imagination, or conceptualized by thinking, or affirmed or denied in judgment

ordinary consciousness: consciousness C and B

prophetic consciousness (as distinct from mystical consciousness): religious consciousness, comprising images, thoughts, emotions

reflection: objectification, thematization; the process by which one understands and affirms particular data regarding oneself or others

reflective: having to do with reflection (as distinct from the prereflective and the postreflective)

reflexive: having to do with self-reflection, self-consciousness, or self-knowledge, that is, with the objectification of one's dynamically related acts and states

self: the ego, the individual, as contradistinguished from the boundless Self, which is experienced in Zen

Bibliography

Bergson, Henri. *Time and Free Will: An Essay on the Immediate Data of Consciousness.* Trans. F. L. Pogson. New York: Humanities Press, 1971.

Brentano, Franz. *Psychology From an Empirical Standpoint,* Ed. Linda L. McAlister. New York: Humanities Press, 1973.

Crosby, John F. *The Selfhood of the Human Person.* Washington: Catholic University of America Press, 1996.

Eckhart, Meister. *The Essential Sermons, Commentaries, Treaties, and Defense,* Trans. Edmund Colledge and Bernard McGinn. New York: Paulist Press, 1981.

———. *Meister Eckhart Teacher and Preacher,* Ed. Bernard McGinn. New York: Paulist Press, 1986.

———. *Sermons & Treatises.* 3 vols., Trans. M. O'C. Walshe. Rockport, MA: Element, 1987.

Forman, Robert K. C., ed. *The Innate Capacity: Mysticism, Psychology, and Philosophy.* New York: Oxford University Press, 1998.

———. *Mysticism, Mind, Consciousness.* Albany: SUNY Press, 1999.

———, ed. *The Problem of Pure Consciousness: Mysticism and Philosophy.* New York: Oxford University Press, 1990.

Franck, Frederick, ed. *The Buddha Eye: An Anthology of the Kyoto School.* New York: Crossroad, 1991.

Granfield, David. *Heightened Consciousness: The Mystical Difference.* New York: Paulist Press, 1991.

Heidegger, Martin. *Being and Time,* Trans. John Macquarrie and Edward Robinson. San Francisco: Harper & Row, 1962.

———. *Contributions to Philosophy (From Enowning),* Trans. Parvis Emad and Kenneth Maly. Bloomington: Indiana University Press, 1989.

———. *History of the Concept of Time: Prolegomena,* Trans. Theodore Kisiel. Bloomington: Indiana University Press, 1985.

———. *Introduction to Metaphysics,* Trans. Gregory Fried and Richard Polt. New Haven: Yale University Press, 2000.

———. *Pathmarks,* Ed. William McNeill. Cambridge: Cambridge University Press, 1998.

Helminiak, Daniel A. *The Human Core of Spirituality: Mind as Psyche and Spirit.* Albany: SUNY Press, 1996.

Hisamatsu Shin'ichi. "The Characteristics of Oriental Nothingness." Trans. Richard De Martino. In *Philosophical Studies of Japan.* Tokyo: Japan Society for the Promotion of Science, vol. 2 (1960), 65–97.

———. "The Ultimate Crisis and Resurrection," *The Eastern Buddhist,* 8/1 (May 1975): 12–29, and 8/2 (October 1975): 37–65.

Hume, David. *A Treatise of Human Nature,* Ed. David Fate Norton and Mary J. Norton. Oxford: Oxford University Press, 2000.

Husserl, Edmund. *Logical Investigations,* Trans. J. N. Findlay. London: Routledge & Kegan Paul, 1970.

Johnston, William. *Silent Music: The Science of Meditation.* New York: Harper & Row, 1974.

King, Sallie B. "Two Epistemological Models for the Interpretation of Mysticism," *Journal of the American Academy of Religion* 56 (1988), 257–279, at 272.

Lonergan, Bernard J. F. *Insight: A Study of Human Understanding.* Toronto: University of Toronto Press, 1992.

———. *Method in Theology.* Toronto: University of Toronto Press, 1992.

———. *A Third Collection.* New York: Paulist Press, 1985.

Moore, Sebastian. *Let This Mind Be in You.* San Francisco: Harper & Row, 1985.

Morelli, Elizabeth. *Anxiety: A Study of the Affectivity of Moral Consciousness.* Lanham, MD: University Press of America, 1985.

Nishitani, Keiji. *Religion and Nothingness,* Trans. Jan Van Bragt. Berkeley: University of California Press, 1982.

———. *The Self-Overcoming of Nihilism,* Trans. Graham Parkes with Setsuko Aihara. Albany: SUNY Press, 1990.

Plotinus. *Enneads.* 7 vols., Trans. A. H. Armstrong. Cambridge, MA: Harvard University Press, 1966–1988.

Price, James. "Transcendence and Images: The Apophatic and Kataphatic Reconsidered," *Studies in Formative Spirituality* 11 (1990): 195–201.

Roy, Louis. *Le sentiment de transcendance, expérience de Dieu?* Paris: Cerf, 2000.

———. *Self-Actualization and the Radical Gospel.* Collegeville, MN: The Liturgical Press, 2002.

———. *Transcendent Experiences: Phenomenology and Critique.* Toronto: University of Toronto Press, 2001.

Sartre, Jean-Paul. *Being and Nothingness: An Essay on Phenomenological Ontology*, Trans. Hazel E. Barnes. New York: Philosophical Library, 1956.

———. "Consciousness of Self and Knowledge of Self." In *Readings in Existential Phenomenology*, Ed. Nathaniel Lawrence and Daniel O'Connor. Englewood Cliffs, NJ: Prentice-Hall, 1967.

———. *The Emotions: Outline of a Theory*, Trans. Bernard Frechtman. New York: Philosophical Library, 1948.

———. *The Transcendence of the Ego*, Trans. Forrest Williams and Robert Kirkpatrick. New York: Farrar, Straus and Giroux, 1972.

Schleiermacher, Friedrich. *The Christian Faith*, Ed. H. R. Mackintosh and J. S. Stewart. Edinburgh: T. & T. Clark, 1986.

———. *On Religion: Speeches to Its Cultured Despisers* (= 1st German ed., 1799), Trans. Richard Crouter. Cambridge, England: Cambridge University Press, 1988.

———. *On Religion: Speeches to its Cultured Despisers* (= 3d German ed., 1821), Trans. John Oman. New York: Harper & Row, 1958; reprint, Louisville, KY: Westminster/Knox Press, 1994.

Searle, John R. *The Discovery of the Mind.* Cambridge, MA: MIT Press, 1992.

Shear, Jonathan, ed. *Explaining Consciousness—The 'Hard Problem'.* Cambridge, MA: The MIT Press, 1997.

———. *The Inner Dimension: Philosophy and the Experience of Consciousness.* New York: Peter Lang, 1990.

Suzuki, Daisetz Teitaro. *An Introduction to Zen Buddhism.* New York: Dell, A Delta Book, 1955.

———. *Mysticism: Christian and Buddhist.* Westport, CT: Greenwood Press, 1975.

———. *Zen Buddhism: Selected Writings of D. T. Suzuki*, Ed. William Barrett. New York: Doubleday Anchor Books, 1956.

Tart, Charles T. *States of Consciousness.* New York: Dutton, 1975.

Zahavi, Dan. *Self-Awareness and Alterity: A Phenomenological Investigation.* Evanston, IL: Northwestern University Press, 1999.

Index

*indicates that item is in the Glossary

Abe, Masao, 178, 180, 191
absolute nothingness. *See* nothingness
affective side. *See* consciousness
Angelus Silesius, 156
Armstrong, A. H., 62, 202 n.5
Arnou, René, 202 n.4
Assagioli, Roberto, 210 n.22
*awareness, xviii–xix, 10–11, 20, 32–33, 44–46

Barrett, William, 213 n.3
Beards, Andrew, 32
Beisser, Friedrich, 97
Bell, David, 6
Bergson, Henri, 10
Berner, Christian, 209 n.34
Böhme, Jacob, 147–148
Bowes, Pratima, 196 n.17
Brentano, Franz, 4–7, 40
Byrne, Patrick, 27

Capelle, Philippe, 213 n.4
Caputo, John, 82, 163
Christian, William A., 207 n.8
Clarke, W. Norris, 213 n.35
Conn, Joann and Walter, 123
*consciousness A, B, and C, xv, 61–63, 69–70, 78–79, 106–109, 131–132, 187–189
   and *intentionality, 4–5, 8–10, 16–18, 21–22, 32–33

affective side, 30–32, 43, 45–46, 49, 51, 59, 95–98, 101, 125–126, 189–190
bare consciousness, 47–49
divine consciousness, 49–50
*ordinary consciousness, *see* consciousness B and C
positional/nonpositional consciousness, xviii, 13–15
*prophetic consciousness, xix–xx, 190–191
pure consciousness event, 37–41
self, 115–128; and the Self, 129–130, 135, 139–143, 178, 180–182, 188
self-consciousness, 10–11, 77–79, 170–174, 178, 180–182, 185
unity of consciousness, 6–7, 122–123
Cooley, Larry, 198 n.40
Crosby, John, 24–26

Dallmayr, Fred, 163
de Silva, Lynn A., 211 n.27
Deikman, Arthur, 34
Dennett, D. C., 32–33
Doran, Robert M., 201 n.11

Ebeling, Gerhard, 209 n.33
Eckhart, Meister, 71–94, 145–146, 159–162
ecstasy, xvii–xviii, 67–69
Eliade, Mircea, 203 n.16
emotion. *See* consciousness, affective side

*emptiness, 73–79, 125–128, 134–136, 153–154, 170–172, 174–176
Epiney-Burgard, G., 203 n.1
*experience, xxi, 38, 137, 187

feeling. See consciousness, affective side
Fisher, Roland, xx
Fitzpatrick, Joseph, 198 n.40
Flanagan, Joseph, 210 n.15
Forman, Robert K. C., 37–41, 128
Francis of Assisi, 176–177

Gadamer, Hans-Georg, 33
Graham, Dom Aelred, 194 n.9
Granfield, David, 49–50
Gregory of Nyssa, 49
Griffiths, Paul J., 193 n.5
ground and unground, 147–148, 152–155
Günter, Anton, 98
Gurtler, Gary M., 202 n.6

Hadot, Pierre, x, 202 n.10 and n.11
Hegel, G. W. F., 182
Heidegger, Martin, 146–158, 162–163
Heiler, Friedrich, xix
Helminiak, Daniel, 26–30, 123–124
Hermann, Rudolf, 206 n.7
Hisamatsu, Shin'ichi, 177–185
Horney, Karen, 198 n.44
Hostie, Raymond, 208 n.24
Hume, David, 116–117
Husserl, Edmund, 7–10, 40

Imbach, Ruedi, 203 n.3
immediacy and mediation, xxi, 41–43, 78
Inge, William Ralph, 195 n.17
*intentionality. See consciousness
interiority, 42–43

James, William, 6–7, 39, 117–119
John of the Cross, xvii
Johnston, William, xvii
Jørgensen, T. H., 208 n.26
Jung, Carl G., 98, 139

Kasulis, T. P., 191, 193 n.3
Kenney, John Peter, 202 n.3
King, Sally, 125–127, 141

King, Winston, L., 138
knowledge by identity, 39

Lamm, Julia A., 206 n.2
Lash, Nicholas, 207 n.9
Locke, John, 119–120
Lonergan, Bernard, 16–20, 40–43, 119–125
Lossky, Vladimir, 205 n.26
Louth, Andrew, 61
Loy, David, 218 n.3

Maraldo, John, 176
Maréchal, Joseph, 194 n.4
Maritain, Jacques, 33–34
Matsamuru, Hisao, 217 n.25
McCool, Gerald A., 208 n.23
McGinn, Bernard, 203 n.2, 204 n.9, 205 n.12
mediation. See immediacy
Merton, Thomas, 130, 218 n.5
Miyamoto, Hisao, 218 n.4
Mommaers, Paul, 212 n.24
Moore, Sebastian, 44–46
Morelli, Elizabeth, 16, 30–32
Morelli, Mark D., 119
Münch, Armin, 219 n.9
mysticism, ix–xi, xix–xxi, 187–191

Needleman, Jacob, 46
neoplatonism, 55, 71, 72, 93–94, 145–146
Niebuhr, Richard R., 206 n.6
Nishida, Kitaro, 165, 178
Nishitani, Keiji, 139–142, 158–163, 165–177
*nothingness, 15–16, 79–81, 146–158, 165–186

*object and objectlessness, xv–xvi, xviii–xix, 4–5, 21, 50–51, 66, 106–107, 109–111, 188
O'Daly, Gerald J. P., 202 n.7
Otto, Rudolf, 207 n.7

Parkes, Graham, 193 n.4
Phillips, John F., 202 n.9
Pinholster, Michael, 214 n.19

Plotinus, 55–70, 145–146, 158–159
Price, James, 46–49

Rahner, Karl, 50–51
Ranieri, John, 198 n.42
Redeker, Martin, 208 n.31
*reflection, reflective, reflexive, 10–14, 28–30, 33, 39, 98–99, 108
Richardson, William, 154
Ricoeur, Paul, 193 n.1
Rist, J. M., 202 n.8
Roy, Louis, xx–xxi, 193 n.6, 200 n.21, n.22, and n.2, 201 n.13, 203 n.17, 205 n.11, 214 n.23, 218 n.5
Ruh, Kurt, 205 n.11

Sartre, Jean-Paul, 10–16, 140
satori, or enlightenment, 131, 133–134
*self, and the Self. *See* consciousness
Schelling, Friedrich, 147–148
Schleiermacher, Friedrich, 95–111
Schultz, Werner, 208 n.20
Schürmann, Reiner, 205 n.30
Schwyzer, H. R., 202 n.12
Searle, John, 21–24
Shear, Jonathan, 195 n.19, 209 n.1
Sikka, Sonya, 214 n.20
Simon, Marianne, 97
Sini, Carlo, 204 n.5
Sokolowski, Robert, 196 n.15
Stambaugh, Joan, 215 n.1
Steffney, John, 215 n.28
Strasser, Stephan, 31

Stroker, Elisabeth, 196 n.12
Suligoj, Herman S., 51
sunyata. *See* emptiness
Sutton Morris, Phyllis, 13–15
Suzuki, Daisetz Teitaro, 129–139
Swanson, Paul, 174

Tart, Charles, xvi, xviii–xix
Thandeka, 208 n.19, 209 n.34
Thévenaz, Pierre, 35
Thiel, John, 97
Thomas Aquinas, xix
Tillich, Paul, 97, 178, 180, 183–184
Tilliette, Xavier, 201 n.1
Trethowan, Illtyd, 35
Turner, Denys, 205 n.11

Ueda, Shizuteru, 212 n.23

Van Bragt, Jan, 137–138, 173, 215 n.2, 216 n.22
Voegelin, Eric, 46, 118

Wackernagel, Wolfgang, 204 n.6
Waldenfels, Hans, 142
Webb, Eugene, 198 n.42
Wéber, Edouard-Henri, 205 n.26
Welte, Bernhard, 214 n.21
Wilber, Ken, 79, 142–143
Wobbermin, Georg, 109

Zahavi, Dan, 5, 27, 123
Zum Brunn, E., 203 n.1